CYCLE C

LECTIONARY PREACHING WORKBOOK

Lent and Easter Seasons Edition

For All Users
Of The Revised Common,
The Roman Catholic, and
The Episcopal Lectionaries

Mark Ellingsen

CSS Publishing Company, Inc.
Lima, Ohio

LECTIONARY PREACHING WORKBOOK
LENT/EASTER EDITION, CYCLE C

For my academic mentors:

Ken Henry
Edward Wimberly
Anne Wimberly
James Costen
Per Lønning

Friends who have taught me in word and deed how
the academy serves the pulpit

FIRST EDITION
Copyright © 2013
by CSS Publishing Co., Inc.

All rights reserved. No part of this publication may be reproduced in any manner whatsoever without the prior permission of the publisher, except in the case of brief quotations embodied in critical articles and reviews. Inquiries should be addressed to: CSS Publishing Company, Inc., Permissions Department, 5450 N. Dixie Highway, Lima, Ohio 45807.

Scripture quotations are from the Revised Standard Version of the Bible, copyrighted 1946, 1952 ©, 1971, 1973, by the Division of Christian Education of the National Council of the Churches of Christ in the USA. Used by permission.

For more information about CSS Publishing Company resources, visit our website at www.csspub.com, email us at csr@csspub.com, or call (800) 241-4056.

ISBN-13: 978-0-7880-2716-1
ISBN-10: 0-7880-2716-6

PRINTED IN USA

Table of Contents

Sermon Planner / Builder 4
The Church Year Calendar 5
Acknowledgments 7
Introduction 8
Lectionary Preaching 8
Approaches to Preaching 8
Outline of the Workbook 9
Introduction to Selected Books of the Bible 12
Charts of the Major Theological Options 27

The Lenten Season
Ash Wednesday 32
Lent 1 40
Lent 2 46
Lent 3 54
Lent 4 60
Lent 5 67
Passion / Palm Sunday (Lent 6) 73
Maundy Thursday / Holy Thursday 81
Good Friday 87

The Easter Season
Easter Sunday 95
Easter 2 102
Easter 3 109
Easter 4 115
Easter 5 120
Easter 6 126
Ascension of Our Lord 133
Easter 7 140

Sermon Planner / Builder

Date: _____ Cycle / Season: _____ Sunday: _____

Cycle / Season / Sunday Theological Clue: _____
_____

Psalm: Central Thought: _____
_____

Collect / Prayer Concern / Focus: _____
_____

Sermon Text(s): _____

Summary of Sermon Text(s): _____
_____
_____
_____
_____
_____

Theological Aim: _____
_____
_____
_____

Pastoral Perspective (what you want to accomplished in people's lives): _____
_____
_____

Type of Sermon: _____
_____

Illustrations / Stories: _____
_____
_____
_____

Sermon Plan / Sketch: _____
_____
_____
_____
_____

The Church Year Calendar

The Christmas Cycle

Advent   Color
Advent 1   purple or blue
Advent 2   purple or blue
Advent 3   purple or blue
Advent 4   purple or blue

Christmas
Christmas Eve / Christmas Day   white
Christmas 1   white

Epiphany
The Epiphany of Our Lord   white
The Baptism of Our Lord (First Sunday after the Epiphany) / Ordinary Time 1   white
Epiphany 2 / Ordinary Time 2   green
Epiphany 3 / Ordinary Time 3   green
Epiphany 4 / Ordinary Time 4   green
Epiphany 5 / Ordinary Time 5   green
Epiphany 6 / Ordinary Time 6   green
Epiphany 7 / Ordinary Time 7   green
Epiphany 8 / Ordinary Time 8   green
The Transfiguration of Our Lord (Last Sunday after the Epiphany)   white

The Easter Cycle

Lent
Ash Wednesday   black or purple
Lent 1   purple
Lent 2   purple
Lent 3   purple
Lent 4   purple
Lent 5   purple
Passion / Palm Sunday   scarlet or purple
Maundy Thursday / Holy Thursday   scarlet or white
Good Friday   black or no paraments

Easter
Easter Sunday   white or gold
Easter 2   white
Easter 3   white
Easter 4   white
Easter 5   white
Easter 6   white
The Ascension of Our Lord   white
Easter 7   white

The Pentecost Cycle

The Season After Pentecost

Revised Common / Episcopal	Lutheran (Other than ELCA)	Roman Catholic	Color
Pentecost Sunday	Pentecost Sunday	Pentecost Sunday	red
Trinity Sunday	Trinity Sunday	Trinity Sunday	white
		Corpus Christi	green
Proper 4	Pentecost 2	Ordinary Time 9	green
Proper 5	Pentecost 3	Ordinary Time 10	green
Proper 6	Pentecost 4	Ordinary Time 11	green
Proper 7	Pentecost 5	Ordinary Time 12	green
Proper 8	Pentecost 6	Ordinary Time 13	green
Proper 9	Pentecost 7	Ordinary Time 14	green
Proper 10	Pentecost 8	Ordinary Time 15	green
Proper 11	Pentecost 9	Ordinary Time 16	green
Proper 12	Pentecost 10	Ordinary Time 17	green
Proper 13	Pentecost 11	Ordinary Time 18	green
Proper 14	Pentecost 12	Ordinary Time 19	green
Proper 15	Pentecost 13	Ordinary Time 20	green
Proper 16	Pentecost 14	Ordinary Time 21	green
Proper 17	Pentecost 15	Ordinary Time 22	green
Proper 18	Pentecost 16	Ordinary Time 23	green
Proper 19	Pentecost 17	Ordinary Time 24	green
Proper 20	Pentecost 18	Ordinary Time 25	green
Proper 21	Pentecost 19	Ordinary Time 26	green
Proper 22	Pentecost 20	Ordinary Time 27	green
Proper 23	Pentecost 21	Ordinary Time 28	green
Proper 24	Pentecost 22	Ordinary Time 29	green
Proper 25	Pentecost 23	Ordinary Time 30	green
Proper 26	Pentecost 24	Ordinary Time 31	green
Proper 27	Pentecost 25	Ordinary Time 32	green
Proper 28	Pentecost 26	Ordinary Time 33	green
	Pentecost 27		green
	Reformation		red
All Saints	All Saints	All Saints	white
Thanksgiving Day (USA)			white
Christ the King	Christ the King	Christ the King	white

Acknowledgments

When you've been ordained over 35 years like I will have been when this book sees the light of day, you travel to the distant past to remember your mentoring. But the names on the dedication page (though two are deceased) have never been far away from me, as their lessons (most of them delivered informally and by example) have been conversation partners with me throughout most of my ministry (even if only through memories). Though different by denominational and ethnic background, these academic mentors share a lot in common. Besides the friendship all have shared with me, the fact that unlike most in the academy who have reputations akin to that of these friends, those I seek to honor in this book have been remarkably free of the need to practice self-promotion. They are all first-rate scholars or academic administrators who love the church. In the academic environment, where being too religiously or ecclesiastically oriented is not much help to your career, where preaching is seen as a "practical" discipline far removed from the academy, none of these friends have displayed such hang-ups. With some friends in the academy I would be nervous dedicating something like this book to them. No such concern with the folks named below on this page. All would agree that our academic work is designed precisely to serve the preaching moment that this workbook is all about.

I will work backward in making my introductions. The longest friendship of the eminent group to whom this book is dedicated is my *landsmann* (fellow Norwegian), Per Lønning. We met in 1982, serving on the staff of the Centre D'Etudes Oecumeniques, an international theological research agency based in Strasbourg, France. In my early thirties when we met, I effectively served as the research assistant for this internationally renowned bishop, professor, politician, acclaimed hymn writer, and theologian. (Of course he never made me feel like I was his assistant but more like his peer [even though I knew better]). What a storybook opportunity for this American reared in a Norwegian immigrant home to work with and become friends with one of Norway's greatest scholars (and preachers)! What a wonderful advisor and inspiration he has been over the years, along with the friendship his wonderful wife Ingunn has offered my wife Betsey and me.

Everyone else to whom this book is dedicated is or has served in my most recent academic home: the Interdenominational Theological Center in Atlanta (but we all go back nearly twenty years in our relationships). All four are African-American Brothers and a Sister, hardly surprising given the fact that the center is the largest accredited historic African-American seminary in existence.

When you are a Norwegian serving in an African-American setting you need a lot of teachers in order to avoid dumb mistakes. These friends have certainly played that role for me, though like Per, none ever did it in a way as to make me feel somehow "less" their partner. Jim Costen is one of the two best seminary presidents I have ever known. Not caught up on his authority, very pastoral, but willing to support faculty who upheld standards, he is the one who brought me to the Center, in many ways both teaching and supporting me. Though deceased for a number of years, his legacy continues to challenge the present administration to get around to doing the right things in the seminary he served, and his legacy is also vibrantly alive on another seminary campus in Kenya led my many of his former students.

Ed Wimberly was the best provost I have ever experienced, but I liked him and his wife Anne even when they were just peers at the seminary we serve. Both are accomplished, widely published scholars. They are the best theologians I have ever encountered among colleagues in more practical departments. They are wise and caring (great advisors I can testify to first hand) and lovers of the church.

Last but not least is my deceased friend Ken Henry. As my closest colleague at the Interdenominational Theological Center (we were *the* Church History Department), he was the colleague who has taught me most of what I know about the black church and its ethos, a tradition that he so clearly loved. We just clicked from the first time we met. Our friendship reflected so clearly that whenever we would walk the campus together there would be students (over 90% African American on the campus) who would run up to us with big smiles on their faces saying "it's the church historians, you're always together," in effect celebrating with us how this white guy and his eminent black friend and advisor made such an obviously close team. Part of the chemistry was that we always wanted to relate history to the pulpit and the pew. What a great teacher and model he was (still is) for me (and I'm glad his wife Pearl is still able to see me put in writing about Ken what she and the Henry family already knew concerning how I felt about him).

Of course as in the case of the last workbook, my wife Betsey deserves a lot of thanks and the biggest hugs for her contribution to this book, doing the first editing along with good conversation and support during the writing process, as she has for my previous sixteen books. But we both wanted the first books in this series to be dedicated to my mentors. Nothing has changed since the Cycle B book I wrote in this series. Any time I get it right in ministry or in life, Betsey deserves my loving gratitude. Then I am also indebted on that score to all the friends to whom this book is dedicated.

Introduction

Like the other volumes in this series, I envision this book and my role in pulpits of readers as that of conversation partner, providing a few new ideas in the midst of a busy, often hectic ministry. Although I've got some very definite convictions when it comes to preaching, I've aimed to structure this book in such a way that readers can use it on their own terms. Let's review its structure.

Lectionary Preaching

Obviously the books in this series are organized on the principle that users function as lectionary preachers. Once again the publisher has directed me to offer sermon resources assigned by the Revised Common Lectionary its semi-continuous readings. However, in this volume as well as the others this does not negate the value of the book for Episcopalian and Catholic priests who employ their own lectionaries or even for Lutherans and others who employ the Revised Common Lectionary complementary readings (prioritizing after Pentecost 2 the first lessons that thematically identify with the gospel). In these cases I have provided a brief summary of these first lessons and pointed to pages in the book that resource the development of a sermon on these alternate lessons. Many Sundays in the Catholic and Episcopal lectionaries and the Common Lectionary share common texts. When they do not, it frequently happens that the assigned texts in the Roman Catholic and Episcopal lectionaries appear on another Sunday in the Common Lectionary, so that sermon helps pertaining to the Catholic and Episcopal texts appearing on these other Sundays can be employed (with some modification) for the Sunday Episcopal and Catholic preachers need them.

Using the lectionary, no matter which one, also entails observing the church year calendar, since the lectionary follows this liturgical calendar. Advantages of this approach to preaching deserve our renewed attention.

Preaching on the lectionary ensures that we don't let our preaching be driven by our own agendas. The lectionary will not let us get away with that. It forces us to take up biblical themes that sometimes we would just as soon forget.

Likewise the church year lifts us away from the rhythms of daily, mundane life and puts us on holy ground. While the world busily goes about the late November-early December accumulation of goods (Christmas shopping) in church the new year and dreams of the end of time are celebrated. When the world is done with Christmas by December 27 or 28, liturgical churches continue the celebration until January 6. Easter lasts a lot longer in liturgical churches too. It is a little easier or one is more likely to experience awe and holiness in worship when it is removed from the rhythms of daily life.

Commemoration of the church year entails that all that happens in worship (altar paraments, the music, the tone of the service, even the sermon) is to give testimony to the Theme of the Day on the calendar. This is another salubrious consequence for preaching. Observing the church calendar takes the pressure off preachers. Even if it has not been a good day for preaching, the flock will still be fed with the day's message from the Theme of the Day reflected in the worship as a whole. Preachers celebrating the church year make preaching a less frightening task, something to be enjoyed. (It is for this reason that I also love the historic liturgy. Because ancient liturgies put us in touch with the way all Christians who use them are worshiping just now as well as all those through the ages who have worshiped in this format, their use assures us that we are truly participating in the community of faith, and so that the word of God is being proclaimed, even if my preaching that Sunday stinks.) Use this workbook consistently and it will make you a lectionary preacher.

Approaches to Preaching

In order to ensure that this book functions merely as a tool and does not mandate adoption of my own preaching style, it is wise to review the different approaches to preaching. Of course there is a rich variety of styles, but if I characterize three major options it will help you begin to understand what you are presently doing and also aid you in determining what and how you can use this workbook on your own terms. Do any of these approaches fit your style?

1. *Narrative Preaching*: Tell the story (not your own, but the biblical text's story). Tell it in such a way that your congregation identifies with the biblical characters gathered around Jesus or following Him and God. Introduce them personally to

Jesus and God as you encounter Him in the text. If the pericope is from the epistles, the Psalms, the prophets, or Revelation, try getting your worshipers to identify with the biblical author and his circumstances or with those of his hearers. Since this is my favorite approach (it was the model of many of the early Protestant Reformers and is still the dominant model in African-American Christianity), the Gimmick, many of the ideas in the Sermon Moves section, as well as the Wrap-Up for each suggested sermon will reflect this sermon strategy. But this handbook will work for readers even if they prefer other styles (as I myself use from time to time).

2. *Expository Preaching* (the three-point or five-point sermon): Explain the text and the main point (the Theological Aim) to the congregation. Some do this with straight explanation; others rely on illustrations and stories. Users of this style, you will find the handbook's identification of the Theological Aim for each sermon as well as the categories titled Exegesis; Theological Insights; Socio-Economic, Political, Psychological, and Scientific Insights; Stories/Examples provided in the Sermon Moves, and even sometimes the Gimmick and Wrap-Up helpful in sermon planning.

3. *Storytelling or Sharing Sermons*: This often conversational style may be the most popular approach to preaching today. This model involves trying to find links between the preacher's own life stories or the congregational and social context and the biblical witness, either by interpreting the text in light of what is going on in life and your stories or by using your stories as a parallel for the biblical text. Because I don't know the life history of readers, I can't help much with these stories. But those using this approach need to be clear on their context as well as about Exegesis and even some of the Theological Insights I provide about the text to be sure the "contextualizing" done is responsible. Other categories I provide that might be of use to proponents of this approach: The book (especially the analysis of the Socio-Economic, Political, Psychological, and Scientific Insights I provide) can be useful in helping readers understand their context. And the Gimmicks and Wrap-Ups for each sermon may also been of use.

Outline of the Workbook

It is wise to review each of the book's sections. Two tools aimed to help you in your preaching follow immediately:

1. *Introductions to Selected Books of the Bible*
These introductions are provided for books that are repeatedly assigned in the lectionary for the year (esp. Luke, John, Psalms, Isaiah, Jeremiah, Acts, 1 Corinthians, 2 Corinthians, Galatians, Timothy, Ephesians, Hebrews, and Revelation). You will receive brief summaries regarding their Historical Background, Main Sections, Central Themes, and Distinct Emphases. There may be some good Bible study material here. For books of the Bible only used a few times during the year, I will provide this data in the weekly Exegesis (see below).

2. *Charts of the Major Theological Options*
My commitment to preparing a workbook just for *you* reflects in this tool. No effective sermon can fail to have a theological purpose, to aim to communicate a conviction of the church. What I can provide for everyone is to identify what the assigned lectionary texts are about theologically, but what you do with this insight is closely related to your own denominational affiliation and faith commitment. I am an unashamedly Confessional Lutheran, but you need the tools to help you adjust my suggestions for you. The charts will allow you to do that. Most of the sermon suggestions that follow identify which doctrines (God, Trinity, Christology, Creation and Providence, Human Nature, Sin, Atonement, Justification, Sanctification [Christian Life], Predestination/Election/Free Will, Church, Ministry, Sacraments, Eschatology, and Social Ethics) are at stake. But if you don't like the way I am taking you in the sermon suggestions because we don't share common theological convictions, you will have a chart on the doctrine(s) at stake that Sunday to help you identify what it is you do believe about that teaching of the church, so you can tweak my suggestions in ways compatible with your own convictions. These charts might also serve you in Bible studies and other educational events in the life of your parish as well.

After these two tools, you will be able to find in the appropriate order Introductions to Each Season or Major Festival [beginning immediately with Advent, and later on for Christmas, Epiphany, Transfiguration, Lent, Easter, and Pentecost/Trinity]. For each Sunday or festival you can expect the following:

Theme of the Day
I'll identify what the texts have in common and how they relate to the Sunday of the church year.

Collect of the Day
Again an analysis of the historic prayer assigned in the Lutheran lectionary along with the lectionary texts. This will relate to the Theme of the Day. As in other workbooks, users from other traditions might still find the analysis of these prayers helpful in suggesting their own prayers which fit the Theme of the Day.

Psalm of the Day
An exegesis of the assigned Psalm to help you guide your flock in seeing connections between it, the Theme of the Day, and the assigned texts. Some Sundays these insights may launch your preaching. When using this section, consult the Introduction to Selected Books of the Bible (where there is a section on Psalms).

Sermon Texts and Title
I'll provide a sketch of three possible sermons (one on each text or a combination of the texts) for each Sunday. This provides you with a wealth of ideas, allowing you to draw on the one that might best fit your context and needs. For each sermon you will see a section with insights on the following sermon components:

1. *Theological Aim of the Sermon and Strategy*
Identifying relevant doctrinal themes, often directing the reader to the Chart of Major Theological Options, so users of this workbook can conveniently identify what they believe in order to understand precisely what witness to make.

My colleague Mark Lomax insists that students in our seminary state a theological proposition for every sermon they prepare, on grounds that "no proposition, no sermon." He's right in that expectation, isn't he? If you can't summarize what you are trying to do with the gospel on a given Sunday, are you saying anything? With this insight in mind, you are ready to strategize about how to get this message across. Consider the type of sermon you will use and also the pastoral perspective you want to take, what your Theological Aim seeks to accomplish in the lives of the people you address.

2. *Exegesis*
(Often relying on the analysis of the book of the Bible in which the text appears as provided in the previously mentioned Introductions to Selected Books of the Bible. When this is not offered in the previously mentioned tool, I provide the background on the particular book in this section.)

I need to emphasize that what you will receive in this workbook is but a brief summary of the biblical texts' richness. In formulating my exegetical observations, there are seven steps I have taken, and I encourage you to take them in order to gain your own insights into the text on which you preach. You should:

1) Determine the text's boundaries:
• Establish the text's literary context, its relation to other pericopes and to the dominant themes in the book in which it occurs. In a preliminary reading, identify the text's overarching themes.
2) Establish the text:
• Identify the most authentic manuscript and provide an accurate translation.
3) Employ form criticism:
• Identify the grammatical features and syntactical structures of the passage. Determine its genre. Then employ the technique appropriate to the kind of literary genre with which you are working.
4) Do comparative philology:
• Study a text with a similar literary genre from the same historical period in order to determine the possible range of meanings of the pericope in question.
5) Compare parallel texts (source and redaction criticism):
• Use *gospel parallels* if the text is from the Synoptics.
• Identify how the cited passage has been used in your text if the text cites another pericope.
• Question whether the text's use of a concept or term differs from that of analogous biblical texts. Determine what this reveals about how tradition material is functioning in the text.
6) Investigate key words:
• In light of the preceding step, identify terms in the text that may be especially significant for its meaning.

- Use a concordance to identify how the term was used by other biblical authors in comparison to your text. Use the comparison to find clues to the term's meaning in the text.

7) Consolidate the findings:
- On the basis of the research undertaken, identify again the text's literary context in order to determine the issues in the life of the Christian community to which the text credibly applies.
- Summarize how the text deals with this issue.

3. *Theological Insights*

I'll not only elaborate on the major theological/doctrinal themes of the text, but also in many cases provide the ideas (even quotations) of the some of the major theologians of the church pertaining to the texts or the theological issues they address. Consult the Charts of the Major Theological Options to determine whether I am taking you in a direction your own faith commitments want you to go. These charts should also help you identify your alternative to the theological visions I am sketching.

I must add a word about my presuppositions at this point. My Lutheran commitments lead me almost instinctively to think about the Bible and theology in terms of the distinction between law and gospel. This distinction operates with the conviction that all scripture and other Christian discourse is either in the form of a demand by God (law) or unconditionally (gospel). The gospel should always have the final word. But the two must be kept distinct at all costs, Luther argues, lest the unconditional affirmation of the gospel be transformed into one with conditions (*Luther's Works*, Vol. 26, pp. 270, 330, 115). I have not systematically pointed out my use of this supposition in each sermon, lest I seem to impose such Lutheran conviction on readers of other traditions. Yet you should be cognizant of my reliance on this principle, and I would urge you to consider it in your preaching (identifying which verses of the Bible lessons are law and which ones are gospel, making sure God's unconditional love is not made conditional and always has the final say).

4. *Socio-Economic, Political, Psychological, and Scientific Insights* (where they exist)

Besides providing you with insights into your own context, sometimes I will provide ideas for preaching sermons on political issues. This workbook appears too soon before these sermons are to be preached to provide you with the sort of up-to-date polling and political commentary which usually permeate my sermons. Be sure to subscribe to *Emphasis* (CSS Publishing online subscription) that carries my column, "The Political Pulpit." It will furnish you with the most recent of this sort of up-to-date data just in time for your sermon.

5. *Gimmick*

Every good sermon needs to grab the congregation's attention. I'll give you an idea how to do that for each sermon suggestion I offer.

6. *Possible Sermon Moves and/or Stories/Examples*

The emphasis here is on "Possible" Sermon Moves. I almost decided not to provide this section for fear that I would inadvertently be imposing my ideas for sermons on you. But as in the previous workbook, I included it only to provide an example of how to execute the Theological Aim and Strategy of each sermon, and of how to get from the Gimmick to the Wrap-Up. Thus you might find it helpful to ignore this section in your in your sermon preparation (except for attending to the bullet points providing quotes, stories, and examples). As I have already noted, I want this book to aid you in preaching *your* sermon.

7. *Wrap-Up*

A good sermon needs to end well (and that can't be postponed too long in most American churches). Martin Luther once claimed that the mark of good preachers is that they know "when to stop" (*What Luther Says*, p. 1109).

I'll try to help you know when and how to stop.

I need to reiterate one other and perhaps the most important step in preparing for a sermon. *Practice the delivery.* Without a dynamic or at least a smooth delivery of the sermon, all the work done in the study and all the ideas in this workbook won't have much impact on the flock. Finding the time to practice comes a little easier when we appreciate the awesomeness of the moment involved in preaching. For the sermon is not just discourse about God and talking about Him. No, as Martin Luther reminded us: "For the preaching of the gospel is nothing else than Christ coming to you, or you are brought to Him" (*Luther's Works*, Vol. 35, p. 121).

How amazing to think that our words in the pulpit could, by God's grace, be the means by which Christ could visit our flock and could bring hearer's into His presence. That awareness will keep us busy in our studies and get us to make time to rehearse the delivery. Cherish and be bold in your awesome task.

Introduction to Selected Books of the Bible

Genesis

1. Historical Background
• Like all five of the books of the Pentateuch, Genesis is probably the product of several distinct literary traditions. This book is just comprised of three: (1) J, a ninth/tenth century BC source, so named for its use of the name *Jahweh* or *Yahweh* (translated "Lord"); (2) E, an eighth century BC source named for its use of the divine name *Elohim* (translated "God"); and (3) P, or Priestly source, dated from the sixth century BC.
• Attributing this and other books of the Pentateuch by the tradition to Moses was a way of establishing the continuity of the faith of successive generations that gave rise to these books.

2. Main Sections
• Primordial history (chs. 1-11)
• Abrahamic cycle (12:1—25:18)
• Jacob cycle (25:19—36:43)
• The saga of Joseph and his brothers (chs. 37-50). These sections seem structured by means of repeated genealogical formulas (2:4; 5:1; 6:9; 11:10-32; 25:1-19; 36:1; 37:2).

3. Central Themes
• The relation of the creation to the world history that follows.
• Both are to be understood in light of the divine will for the chosen people.
• Promises made to the patriarchs are interpreted as eschatological prophecies of the coming Exodus.
• Fertility, space, and time are determined by God, overriding all conflict. Human events are viewed pessimistically, but never in such a way as to connote that God would abandon us.

4. Distinct Emphases
• Promises made to the patriarchs entails that the individual stories of the Fathers are eschatologically framed (become stories pointing to the future). This safeguards ever reducing the narrative to ontology, or to rendering the stories to mere illustrations of the way things are in the world.
• The book is structured as a whole by means of repeated genealogies (2:4; 4-5; 6:9-10; 10; 11:10-32; 25; 36:1-4, 9-42; 37:2). This is what connects the creation of the world to what happens next. Typical of their function in the ancient Near East these genealogies serve to legitimate existing social realities. But in the context of the structure of the book as a whole they also trace the line of God's chosen.

Deuteronomy

1. Historical Background
• This book is primarily the work of D, a version of Israel's history related to, if not rooted in the sweeping religion's reforms under King Josiah in the early seventh century BC. This literary strand also influenced the histories of the books of Joshua, Judges, 1 and 2 Samuel, as well as 1 and 2 Kings.
• The book's basic theme is evidenced by the meaning of its title ("Second Law"). Portrayed in the form of Moses' farewell address, it is the reaffirmation of the covenant between God and Israel. The legal tradition of the book of Exodus is reinterpreted in contemporary terms of Josiah's 621 BC religious reforms (2 Kings 22-23).
• It has been contended that Deuteronomy may be the book of the law prompting Josiah's reform (2 Kings 22:11).

2. Main Sections
• The address of Moses in three parts:
    - Moses' memories of Israel's journey (1:6—4:40);
    - Elaboration of the Horeb (Sinai) Covenant, promulgation of statutes, covenantal ratification rites, and sanctions (chs. 5-28);
    - A covenant renewal that refers to what lies ahead in the future (chs. 29-30).
• The remaining chapters pick up the story from Numbers, reporting the concluding events of Moses' life.

3. Central Themes
• Centralizing/unifying the revelation of Yahweh, especially the centralizing of worship in the Jerusalem Temple, for God is one.
• Rejection of self-glorification, since Israel's existence owes solely to Yahweh.
• Testimony to the fact that God does not forget promises made to the Fathers, though His covenant is still offered to all people.
• A witness that everything follows from the basic commandment of loving Yahweh with the whole of one's soul and might (6:4).

4. Distinct Emphases
• The only book of the Bible to identify itself repeatedly as a record of the Mosaic Torah (divinely sanctioned instruction) (1:5; 4:8, 44; 17:18-19; 27:3, 8, 26; 28:58, 61).
• In relativizing the importance of chronological time, each new generation becomes fully involved in the events of the Exodus. There is thus an eschatological, "between the times" sense for readers of the book. It is also a commentary on how future generations should regard the law.
• Centralization of worship in one place is also a distinct emphasis of D (ch. 12).
• The book is also characterized by the typical Jewish tension between Yahweh's mercy or election and a conditional view of salvation dependent on what Israel does.

1 Kings

1. Historical Background
• 1 and 2 Kings were originally one book, providing an account of Israel's history from the death of David through Jehoiachin's release from a Babylonian prison. There is some speculation that these texts are the product of the Deuteronomistic reform of Josiah, but later revised after the Exile in 587 BC.
• The book recounts the history of Israel from the death of David through the history of the divided kingdoms and the death of the Israelite king Ahab.

2. Main Sections
• Death and Solomon's reign (chs. 1-11)
• History of the divided kingdom through Jehoshaphat (in Judah) and Ahaziah (in Israel).
• Different prophets are featured in this book, not just Elijah, but also Nathan, Ahijah, and Micaiah (chs. 12-22).

3. Central Themes
• Largely follows Deuteronomist themes, especially evident in the evaluations made of each king and in comments made on other historical events. These comments include:
  - The Lord is Israel's only God and so the worship of other gods is forbidden.
  - All the kings of the Northern Kingdom followed the evil example of their predecessor Jeroboam who set up rival sanctuaries outside Jerusalem, even worshiping other gods. The people are also condemned.
  - Such crimes led to the north's conquest.
  - In Judah, Solomon's willingness to allow worship of other gods was punished by Northern secession.
  - Although until Hezekiah, these kings allowed irregular worship in sanctuaries outside Jerusalem, and Judah still followed the north's evil ways and was conquered, yet God's promise that David (the one wholly true to God [1 Kings 9:4; 11:4-6]) would have an eternal dynasty remained secure, for He is a long-suffering merciful God, restricted in His presence to just the temple and the nation of Israel.
  - Throughout the book Elijah is portrayed as proclaiming God's will.

4. Distinct Emphases
• Each king is evaluated by how well he upheld the primacy of God and the temple in Jerusalem, finding most to have departed from the ways of David.
• David is portrayed as the ideal king (9:4; 11:33, 38).
• The promise to David of an eternal dynasty and his portrayal as the ideal king seem to suggest messianic implications.

2 Kings

1. Historical Background
- See first bullet point in this section for 1 Kings.
- This book recounts the history from the reign of Ahaziah (850-849 BC) to the Assyrian destruction of Samaria (721 BC) as well as the story of Judah through the Babylonian Exile (586 BC).

2. Main Sections
- Description of the reign of Ahaziah of Israel and Jehoshaphat in Judah until the fall of Samaria (chs. 1-17).
- The story of Judah from the fall of Israel through the destruction of Jerusalem, ending with the elevation of King Jehoiachim in exile (chs. 18-25).

3. Central Themes
- See this section for 1 Kings.
- Throughout the book, prophets (esp. Elijah, Elisha, and Isaiah) rise up to proclaim God's will.

4. Distinct Emphases
- See this section for 1 Kings.

Psalms

1. Historical Background
- Book of Hebraic hymns of praise, most of which were composed to accompany worship in the temple.
- Ascription of nearly half the Psalms to David does not historically substantiate his authorship; it is indicative of the great esteem in which David as a great singer was held. The tradition that David wrote all the Psalms developed much later than the book itself.
- Some Psalms were probably composed early in Israel's history and others after the Babylonian Captivity.
- Rhyme is not systematically used in ancient Hebrew poetry, as in English poems. Rather, parallelism characterizes most of the Psalms and other Hebraic hymns as are found in the prophets from time to time. This means that one line of the Hebrew poem is followed by a line that says the same things in different words and in so doing enriches the meaning of the previous verse. (See Psalm 1:1-2; 2:1-2.) This is an important point to keep in mind when interpreting Psalms and other Old Testament poetry.
- Another stylistic format is the use of the *acrostic* principle. Every second verse begins with the next successive letter of the Hebrew alphabet (Psalms 9-10).
- Types of Psalms:
    - Personal laments (3-7, 10, 12, 13, 17, 22, 25, 26, 28, 31, 32, 34, 35, 37-39, 41, 43, 49, 51, 61-64, 69, 73, 77, 86, 88, 102, 130, 139, 143)

    These may also take the form of Psalms of confidence, penitential Psalms, or Psalms of vexation.
    - National laments (44, 60, 74, 80, 83, 85, 89, 90, 123, 125, 126)

    May take the form of God's judgment of the people (50) or national Psalms of confidence (123, 125)
    - Personal Psalms of praise (9, 18, 30, 31:19ff, 32, 34, 40, 66, 86, 92, 116, 138)
    - National hymns of praise (114, 124, 129)
    - Descriptive hymns of praise (8, 19, 23, 29, 33, 47, 55:7-11, 65, 66, 81, 93, 96, 98, 100, 103-107, 111, 113, 115, 116-118, 133, 135-136, 145-150)
    - Psalms of pilgrimage and hymns of Zion (46, 76, 84, 87, 122)
    - Psalms of benediction (91 [esp. vv. 14-16], 115:9-15, 118:25ff, 122)
    - Royal Psalms (2, 18, 20, 21, 45, 72, 89, 101, 110, 132)
    - Wisdom Psalms (1, 19:7ff, 37, 91, 107, 112, 119, 127, 128, 133)

2. Main Sections
- Book 1 (1-41)
    - Psalms of David (3-41)
- Book 2 (42-72)
    - Elohistic Psalms, *Elohim* rather than *Yahweh* used to refer to God

- Korah Psalms (42-49)

    Once independent collection of Psalms, probably by a professional Levitical musician (or his heirs) of that name (see 1 Chronicles 15:16-22; Nehemiah 12:41-46). These Psalms may rather be attributed to one of Israel's chief groups of singers (see 2 Chronicles 20:19).
- Asaph Psalm (50)

    An additional Psalm by another Levitical musical tradition; see 2 Chronicles 29:30, for Asaph.
- Elohistic Psalms of David (51-72)
- Book 3 (73-89)
    - Elohistic Psalms (73-83)

        Asaph Psalms (73-83); see above for explanation
    - Korah Psalms (84-85, 87-88)

        Another family of Psalms indebted to a different Levitical musical tradition.
    - Royal Psalm of Ethan (89)
- Book 4 (90-106)
    - Yahweh is king Psalms (93-99)
    - Psalms of praise (103-106)
- Book 5 (107-150)
    - Psalms of praise (107, 111-118, 135-136, 146-150)

        Psalm 113-118 are the Egyptian Hallel Psalms used in connection with great festivals.
    - Tribute to the law (119)
    - Songs of ascent (or Pilgrim Psalms) (120-134)

        A family of Psalms that may be pilgrim songs by those returning to Jerusalem from Exile.
    - Psalms of David (140-143)

        Psalm 138-139, 144-145 are regarded as having been appended to this original collection.

3. Central Themes
- The collection is placed in the context of the first Psalm's message that it is through the ancient means of praise that we can learn the way of righteousness (cf. also 19; 119).
- Eschatological themes (69:34-35; 98; 102:15-16; 126:4ff; 130:5-6). When combined with royal Psalms (2; 72; 132) could in this context be interpreted as messianic prophecies.
- Complaints/laments and prayers for deliverance, often related to the themes of death and rebirth (3-7; 9-10; 17; 22; 26-28; 31-35; 44; 51; 54; 59-61; 63-64; 69-70; 74; 77; 79-80; 85-86; 90; 94; 102; 120; 123-126; 129; 130; 139-144).
- Praise and thanksgiving, often for God's mighty deeds or His creation (8; 21; 33; 48; 66; 67; 75; 93; 96-99; 104-106; 111; 113-114; 146).

4. Distinct Emphases
- The richness of the hymns in speaking various forms of human suffering the Psalms provide an invaluable resource for the care of souls (*Calvin's Commentaries*, Vol. IV/2, pp. xxxvi-xxxvii).

Isaiah

1. Historical Background
- Two or three books in one.
- Prophet Isaiah proclaimed his message to Jerusalem and Southern Kingdom from 742 BC to 701 BC, a period during which the Northern Kingdom had been annexed by Assyrian Empire.
- Second section of the book originated immediately before the fall of Babylon (in 539 BC).

2. Main Sections
- Chapters 1-39 can be assigned to Isaiah.

But even it has been redacted, as we find oracles of unknown prophets after the Babylonian Exile (587 BC-538 BC) against the nations which were not international forces in the historical Isaiah's lifetime.
- Chapters 40-66 emerged in the later period; the hypothesized third section (56-66) of the book, perhaps written by Second Isaiah or by one of his disciples in view of the close stylistic similarities, begins at the conclusion of the Babylonian Captivity and is likely written after the restoration of exiled in Judah, expressing some disappointment about what has transpired since the Exiles' return.

- The relation between the book and the Deuteronomistic reform demonstrates that there is no conflict between the law and the prophets.

Luke

1. Historical Background
- A story of Jesus originally combined with Acts as its companion volume. As one of the three Synoptic Gospels, along with Matthew, it is thought to be dependent on Mark.
- Usually attributed to Luke, a physician and associate of Paul (Colossians 4:14; 2 Timothy 4:11; Philemon 24), whom tradition claims to have been Gentile.
- Addressed to Theophilus (1:1). Not clear if this means the work was written for a recent convert or a Roman official from whom the church sought tolerance. But since Theophilus means "lover of God," it is also possible that the author addressed all the faithful.

2. Main Sections
- Births of John and Jesus (ch. 1-2)
- Activity of John and Jesus' baptism (3:1-22)
- Genealogy of Jesus (3:23-28)
- Temptation of Jesus (4:1-13)
- His activity in Galilee (4:14—9:50)
- Events and teachings on the way to Jerusalem (9:51—19:27)
- The last week in Jerusalem (19:28—23:56)
- Resurrection (24)

3. Central Themes
- The universal mission of Jesus and His followers (2:32; 3:23-38; 7:1-10; 10:8)
- The Spirit empowers Jesus' ministry (4:1-8; 2:27, 40; 4:1, 14; 11:13).
- The success of His ministry is closely linked to miracles (Hans Conzelman, *The Theology of St. Luke*, pp. 137-138).
- The focus on the church's worldwide mission bespeaks a waning of the immanent expectation of Christ's return among early Christians. References to judgment day as a future reality (9:27; 21:5-36). This is also a distinct emphasis.

4. Distinct Emphases
- Jesus' preoccupation with the poor (a concern reflected much more frequently in Luke than in the other gospels) (6:20; 14:12-14; 16:19-31; 14:12-14).
- Not much about Justification by Grace, but more stress on what we must do (5:30-32; 15:7).
- Engages in political apologetics to make Christianity less offensive to Rome. John the Baptist's imprisonment and Jesus' ministry are not related to Roman politics (3:19; 4:18ff; 12:11; 20:26; 23:22).

John

1. Historical Background
- Long recognized to be the last of the gospels written, probably not until 80s or 90s AD. Very different in style than the other three (Synoptic) Gospels. Probably based on Synoptic accounts of Jesus.
- Identification of the author with John the Son of Zebedee, the disciple whom Jesus loved is ancient, dating back to Irenaeus in the second century (*Ante-Nicene Fathers*, 1:414). May well have been a disciple of John who wrote it. The first post-biblical church historian, Eusebius of Caesarea claimed that John had perceived the external facts made plain in the gospel and had been inspired by friends and by the Spirit to compose a spiritual gospel (*Nicene and Post-Nicene Fathers*, 2/1:261).
- Probably written for a Jewish Christian community in conflict with the synagogue, one in which Christians had been expelled from Jewish society. Its aim was to encourage its readers to believe that Jesus is the Messiah, the Son of God (20:31).

2. Main Sections
- Prologue (1:1-18)
- Book of signs (1:19-12)

- Jesus Christ the object of faith (1:19—4:54)
  - Christ's conflict with unbelievers (5-12)
- His fellowship with believers (13-17)
  - Farewell discourse (14-17)
- His death and resurrection (18-20)
- Appendix (21)

3. Central Themes
- God's incarnation in Jesus (1:1, 14; 5:18; 20:31)
- Interweaves Spirit and church (16:1-8)
- Faith leads to life (3:36; 5:24; 6:40, 47; 20:31)
- Clear distinction between light and darkness, Spirit and flesh (1:5; 3:6, 19-21; 6:63; 8:12, 44f; 9:39-41). Images of light, life, and bread associated with God and the deity of Christ (*logos*) make (eternal) life possible.
- Realized Eschatology; judgment takes place in Christ's coming (3:19; 5:24; 11:25f; 17:3)

4. Distinct Emphases
- Strong stress on incarnation (the deity of the Man Jesus Christ)
- Jesus regularly identifies Himself with "I am" sayings (8:12; 12:46; 14:6; 15:1, 5); may be a way of identifying with Yahweh (which literally means "I am that I am")
- Events described characteristically evolve into speeches.
- Readers given glimpses into significance of events and speeches of Jesus that His followers in the text do not have.
- Of all the gospels, displays the best Greek and the most reliance on concepts of Greek philosophy.
- The verb "belief" occurs more times in the gospel than in any other New Testament author
- There is a mutually abiding of believers in Christ (6:56; 14:18-23; 15:4-7).
- Critical references to "Jews" probably only refers only to synagogue authorities of the era and not to the Jewish people as a whole.
- Portrays the Passion of Christ and omits details emphasizing horror of crucifixion in order to allow Jesus' glory to shine through His humiliation.
- Concedes that the church's ideas about Jesus changed after His lifetime as a result of the work of the Holy Spirit.

Acts

1. Historical Background
- Continuation of the narrative of the gospel of Luke (1:1), tracing the story of the Christian movement from the resurrection of Jesus to the time Paul came to preach in Rome. This is the first book of church history.
- Usually attributed to Luke. See Historical Background of Luke. References in the first person plural (16:10-17; 20:5-15; 21:1-18; 27:1—28:16) could suggest that the accounts from a travel diary that Luke, as Paul's companion had drawn up. There is dispute about the date. Some argue it must have been published prior to Paul's martyrdom under Nero in 65-67 AD. But there are indications that the work may have been composed much later, possibly after the destruction of the Jerusalem Temple in 70 AD.
- The author shares the gospel of Luke's concern about the universal mission of the church (1:8). This fits the concern to demonstrate the validity of Paul's ministry. He is treated as a representative of a valid ministry. He must be defended as a unique bridge between the old covenant and the Gentile ministry.

2. Main Sections
- Church in Jerusalem (1-7)
    - Jesus' ascension
    - Pentecost
    - Ministries of Peter and John
    - Sharing of goods
    - Choice of the seven and Stephen's martyrdom
- Church growth in Samaria and seacoast (8)
    - Conversion of the Ethiopian eunuch (8:27-40)
- Paul's conversion (9:1-31)

- Peter's ministry to Joppa and the Gentiles (9:32—11:18)
- Paul's missions to Cyprus, Asia Minor, and Iconium (13-14)
- Jerusalem Council (15:1-35)
- Paul's second mission (15:36—18:21)
- Paul third missionary journey (18:22—20:6)
- Paul's return to Palestine, arrest, and ministry in Rome (20:7—28)

3. Central Themes
- The universal mission of the church (1:8)
- The validity of Paul's ministry
- Spirit empowers the church (2:13) and guides its witness (15:28; 16:6-7)

4. Distinct Emphases
- The focus on the church's worldwide mission bespeaks a waning of the immanent expectation of Christ's return among early Christians. References to judgment day as a future reality (10:42; 17:31; 24:25); when Paul's mission to Thessalonica described, no reference made to the eschaton, though he himself made much of it.
- Typically accuses Jews, rather than Roman authorities, as the persecutors of Christians (13:50; 17:5-7, 13; 21:27). Could illustrate either the author's Gentile heritage or concern to gain Roman good will toward the church.
- Paralleling the gospel of Luke, Roman officials state principles of noninterference in purely religious matters (18:15; 25:20, 26-27). Kind of separation of church and state posited.

Romans

1. Historical Background
- Written by Paul between 54 AD and 58 AD to introduce himself to the church in Rome (which may have been comprised largely of Jewish Christians).

2. Main Sections
- Salutation and thanksgiving (1:1-15)
- Theme of the letter: The gospel as God's power of salvation for everyone who has faith (1:16-17)
- The world's need of redemption (1:18—3:20)
- God's saving act in Christ (3:21—4:25)
- Life in Christ: The struggle with sin; living one's baptism (5-8)
- Role of the Jewish nation in God's plan (9-11)
- Ethics and personal remarks (12-16)

3. Central Themes
- Righteousness of God and justification are linked together, since the Greek word in each case is closely linked. Both transpire by faith (1:17; 3:21-26).
- Inclusion of Gentile Christians in the church does not compromise God's promises to the Jews. Some scholars have interpreted references to the righteousness of God in this light, as an affirmation that God keeps His promises.
- Christology and Christ's role in justification (1:1-6; 3:17, 22, 24)
- Christian life as struggle with sin (7:14-25)
- Baptism as paradigm for Christian living (6:1-14)
- Original sin (5:12-14; 7:14-23)

4. Distinct Emphases
- Justification by grace through faith (3:21-26; 8:31-39)
- Freedom from the law (4:13-15; 7:1-12; 8:3-4; 10:4)
- Christian life as a struggle with sin and life of sacrifice (6:15-23; 7:14-23; 8:5-11; 12:1-2)
- Love fulfills law (13:8-10)
- Predestination/election and the status of the Jews (9-11)
- Obedience is owed governing authorities (13:1-7)
- Imminent second coming (13:11-14)

1 Corinthians

1. Historical Background
- One of Paul's authentic letters, written from Ephesus prior to his Epistle to the Romans, to a church he had established (Acts 18:1-11). Relations had become strained with the church. This letter aims to address doctrinal and ethical problems disturbing the Corinthian church.

2. Main Sections
- Epistolary address (1:1-9)
- Divisions in Corinth (1:10-17)
- Christ crucified (1:18—2:5)
- Addressing disorders and divisions in Corinth (2:6—6:20)
- Marriage (7)
- Christian life in a pagan environment (8—11:1)
    - Also defends his apostolic rights
- Propriety in communal life (11:2-14)
    - Deals with Lord's Supper
    - Spiritual gifts
    - What to make of tongues
- Resurrection (15)
- Specific plans on what lies ahead (16)

3. Central Themes
- Christ crucified (1:18—2:5)
- Christian freedom (10:23ff)
- Priesthood of all believers (12)
- Gifts of the Spirit (12-14)
- Christian love (13)
- Resurrection (15)

4. Distinct Emphases
- Freedom from the law for service (6:12-13; 10:23ff)
- Justification as conformity to Christ (6:16-17; 13:5)
- Rejects Christian involvement in lawsuits (6:1-8)
- Marriage as mutual submission (7:1-7); against divorce and remarriage (7:10-15)
- Those who proclaim the gospel should get paid (9:14)
- On receiving Christ worthily in the Lord's Supper (11:17-34)
- Gifts of the Spirit (12-14)
- Nature of the church (12:14-26)
- Subordinates *glossolalia* to other gifts (14)
- Eschatology (1:7; 2:6ff; 4:5, 9; 7:29ff; 10:11, 23, 15)

2 Corinthians

1. Historical Background
- Written by Paul to address relations with the Corinthian church, which had further deteriorated during the period after 1 Corinthians had been written.
- Chapters 10-13 are so different in style and tone from the first chapters as to lead many scholars to conclude that it is the "severe letter" mentioned in 2:4.

2. Main Sections
- Introduction (1:1-11)
- Controversies between Paul and the church (1:12—7:16, though some scholars regard these chapters as a letter of reconciliation)

- Collection for the church in Jerusalem (8-9)
- Defense of Paul and his work (10-13)

3. Central Themes
- Reconciliation and the office of an apostle (ministry) belong together constitutively (2:10ff)
- Christological grounding of the eschatological hope (5:8, 10)
- Christian life as lived between old and new ages (4:7-12)
- Collection for the relief of the Jerusalem church (8-9)

4. Distinct Emphases
- Distinction of letter and spirit (3:6)
- Hiddenness of the gospel and of Christian life (1:18—2:2; 4:3; 6:8-10; 7:29-32)
- Walk by faith, not by sight (5:7)
- Christ dwells in the faithful (13:5)
- Nature of the Christian life prepares Christians for death (5:1-10)

Galatians

1. Historical Background
- Polemical letter written by Paul to a church he had founded in order to affirm that Gentiles do not need to become Jews in order to become Christian.

2. Main Sections
- A defense of Paul's apostolic authority and of the validity of his teaching (chs. 1-2)
- An exposition of the doctrine of justification by faith (chs. 3-4)
- Practical and moral applications of his teaching (chs. 5-6)

3. Central Themes
- Justification by faith
- Freedom from the law
- Sanctification

4. Distinct Emphases
- The stress on freedom and grace is perhaps nowhere clearer than in this book.

Ephesians

1. Historical Background
- A circular letter, either written by Paul from prison late in his career or by a follower of Paul who had had a hand in assembling the collection of his epistles. These conclusions follow from the fact that the letter includes vocabulary and stylistic characteristics different from the Pauline corpus.
- Likely addressing a younger, later generation of Christians (1:15).

2. Main Sections
- Salutation and thanksgiving: God's cosmic plan (1)
- Christ's benefits: Our inclusion in the cosmic plan (2)
- Role and mission of church and life in relation to the cosmic plan of God (3:1—5:20)
- Relationships within a Christian household (5:21—6:9)
- Christian life as struggle, as warfare with God's armor (6:10-20)

3. Central Themes
- Justification by faith (2:4-5, 9-10, 15-16)
- The church is a cosmic reality, with Christ as its head (1:22-23; 3:10; 4:11-16)
    - Concept of a universal/catholic church developing (2:20)

4. Distinct Emphases
- The delay in Christ's return leads to a lessening of the Pauline emphasis on what will happen in time (Romans 13:11-12), in favor of describing the end more in terms of indicating Christ's heavenly glorification (1:20; 2:6)
- Single predestination (1:4-5)
- Sin as passions of the flesh (2:1-3)
- Justification as intimate union with Christ (3:16-17)
- Third use of the law (4:17—6:20)

Philippians

1. Historical Background
- A letter written by Paul while a prisoner to Christians in a province of Macedonia. There is some debate about whether the epistle in its present form might be a combination of three separate letters (as early theologian Polycarp, *Philippians*, 2.3, spoke of Paul's letters to this church). Its immediate occasion was to thank the Philippians for their gifts, by way of the return of Epaphroditus to Philippi (2:25-30) who had brought these gifts to Paul.
- Paul's main purpose is to urge persistence in faith in face of opposition, using himself as an example. Following the mind of Christ gets one less concerned with one's fate and more focused on proclaiming Christ along with the joy that goes with it.

2. Main Sections
- Salutation (1:1-2)
- Thanksgiving (1:3-11)
- Paul's present circumstances (1:12-30)
- Humility and Christ (2:1-8)
- On plans for Timothy and Epaphroditus (2:19-30)
- A warning (3:1-11)
- Confession and exhortation (3:12-21)
- Final appeals (ch. 4)

3. Central Themes
- Christology
- Justification
- Sanctification, including perseverance and celebration
- Eschatology

4. Distinct Emphases
- The letter in its final canonical form serves as Paul's last will and testament, offering the church a witness on how to respond faithfully even when he is no longer present.

Colossians

1. Historical Background
- A circular letter that was either written by Paul from prison (4:3, 10, 18) late in his career or by a follower of Paul who had had a hand in assembling the collection of his epistles. Again these conclusions follow from the fact that the letter includes vocabulary and stylistic characteristics different from the Pauline corpus.
- The letter addresses Christians in a town in Asia Minor near Ephesus, which though not likely founded by Paul was basically in line with his teachings though threatened by ascetic teachings (2:21, 23), ritual practices rooted in the Jewish traditions (2:16), and philosophical speculation (2:8, 20), all of which were related to visionary insights.

2. Main Sections
- Salutation and thanksgiving (1:1-14)
- Celebration of the cosmic Christ, including a Christ hymn and warnings against false teachings (1:15—2:23)
- Discussion of the Christian Life (3:1—4:6)
- Epilogue (4:7-18)

3. Central Themes
• The lordship of Christ over the whole cosmos and all its dimensions, including the church (1:15-23)
• Grace and election (2:6-7, 12-14; 3:12, 13b)
• The nature of the Christian life (3:1—4:6)

4. Distinct Emphases
• Christ's cosmic lordship
• More emphasis on how faith has transformed the present, not just a partly fulfilled Eschatological fulfillment (1:13; 2:10, 12). (Yet this Realized Eschatology remains in some tension with Future Eschatology [3:24].)
• Employs the terminology of wisdom (1:9-10, 28; 2:2-23; 3:10, 16; 4:5)

1 Thessalonians

1. Historical Background
• An authentic letter by Paul to a church of mostly Gentiles in a Greek city threatened by social pressures and some persecution to return to the values of secular culture.
• The letter may be the earliest piece of New Testament literature, written in the early 50s. It may contain fragments of several letters.

2. Main Sections
• Salutation and thanksgiving (ch.1)
• Recounting of Paul's ministry in Thessalonica (2:1-6)
• An expression of his affection for the church (2:17—3:13)
• Exhortation to purity (4:1-12)
• Questions concerning the second coming (4:13—5:11)
• Concluding exhortations (5:12-28)

3. Central Themes
• Paul's expressed appreciation for the steadfastness of the Thessalonian faithful (1:6; 3:6-10).
• The recognition that Christians can expect opposition (3:3).
• Emphasis on holiness (Sanctification) (4:1-12)
• A warning of the need for readiness regarding Christ's second coming (Eschatology) (5:6-12).

4. Distinct Emphases
• Because the Thessalonians addressed were not Jewish, Paul does not refer explicitly to Judaism (except in 2:14-16). The Old Testament is also not quoted.
• Paul makes clear that there is no advantage to be living when Christ returns, for all believers will be with the Lord forever (4:13-18).

2 Thessalonians

1. Historical Background
• Though closely resembling 1 Thessalonians, the authorship of the letter is often questioned. Some see forgery evident in 2:2 and 3:17.
• This has led some scholars to regard this book as either written so soon after 1 Thessalonians that Paul still recalled his earlier wording or else it was written by a later writer using the first Thessalonians' letter as a model.
• While 1 Thessalonians assumes the end is near, this letter contends that if we cannot know the exact time we can know that it will not come at once, a struggle with evil must take place first, and it will be delayed. As such, this book prepares the church for a period of continued life in the world, and so the faithful should continue the pursuits of daily life.

2. Main Sections
• Salutation and thanksgiving (1:1-4)
• The judgment of God (1:5-12)
• The day of the Lord (2:1-2)

- Thanksgiving and exhortations (2:13-17)
- Closing appeals, rebukes, and prayers (ch. 3)

3. Central Themes
- Comfort in the midst of persecution
- The wrath of God
- Christian life (Sanctification)
- Future Eschatology

4. Distinct Emphases
- The waning of eschatological urgency. As such the book functions as a commentary on the earlier Pauline Eschatology (what it all means for the later generations of Christians).

1 Timothy

1. Historical Background
- One of the pastoral epistles (along with 2 Timothy and Titus), so named because of their concern with pastoral leadership.
- None are probably written by Paul, despite their claim to be Pauline works due to how widely they differ from the authentic Pauline letters in vocabulary and style. They also reflect a concern with godliness, good works, and church order not apparent in the Pauline corpus. Some estimate they are products of the early second century.
- The author seems to have known at least some of the authentic Pauline Epistles and Acts. The ostensible addressee was Timothy, one of Paul's closest coworkers (Acts 16-19; 1 Corinthians 4:17; Philippians 2:19-24). In this letter, Timothy's presence in Ephesus is assumed, and he is presented as the ideal church leader. So the letter is less to Timothy, but is a general teaching to the congregation (probably in Ephesus) with Timothy as a cipher for the ideal church leader.
- The letter has two purposes: (1) To provide guidance in the problems of church administration; and (2) To oppose false teaching of a speculative, moralistic, Gnostic type.

2. Main Sections
- Salutation and warning against false teachers (ch. 1)
- Regulations for worship (ch. 2)
- Qualifications of bishops and deacons (ch. 3)
- Instructions regarding false teachings of Gnostic-influenced ascetics (4:1-5)
- Advice to church leaders (4:6—6:2)
- Final directions (6:2-21)

3. Central Themes
- Provide guidance in church administration (ministry)
- The goodness of the physical creation affirmed
- Christ as living Lord who is active (1:15; 2:4; 5:21; 6:13-14)
- Expectations on the faithful in view of the gift of grace

4. Distinct Emphases
- Church order

2 Timothy

1. Historical Background
- See the first three bullet points in this section for 1 Timothy.
- This is the most personal of all the Pastoral Epistles. Most of it is directed specially to Timothy, and as such may have the best claim to being authentically Pauline.
- It should be noted, however, that in the first centuries the form of a personal letter was used pseudonymously to give teaching that could be applied beyond the situation of a particular recipient.

2. Main Sections
- Salutation, thanksgiving, and exhortation (1:1-7)
- An appeal to show courage (1:8—2:13)
- The pastor and the flock (2:14—4:5)
- Concluding reflections (4:6-22)

3. Central Themes
- Advice on what makes a church leader, stressing endurance
- Sanctification receives special attention.

4. Distinct Emphases
- Good works a sign of faith (3:17)
- Less attention to church order than the other pastoral epistles.
- Paul's farewell. His role is to be held by his writings (3:15ff).

Hebrews

1. Historical Background
- An anonymous treatise which, given its argument for the superiority of Christ's sacrifice to those of the Levitical priests, was likely written prior to the destruction of the Jerusalem Temple in 70 AD. Remarks in 2:3-4 suggest it was written by a member of a generation of Christians after the apostles.
- In ancient times, Eusebius of Caesarea opened this discussion contending that the epistle was a work of Paul, but that Luke translated it for the Greeks. (*Nicene and Post-Nicene Fathers*, 2/1:261). He cited Origen's opinion that the book was written by a follower of Paul based on the apostle's teachings (*Ibid.*, p. 273).
- Not in the format of a traditional Hellenistic epistle. Modern scholars more inclined to regard it as a sermon, possibly modified after it was delivered to include travel plans, greetings, and closing (13:20-25)
- Christians addressed are thought to have been in danger of falling away from their confession (3:1; 4:14; 10:23); they had endured persecution (10:32-36)

2. Main Sections
Consists of doctrinal strands mixed with an exhortation or ethical strand
- Prologue (1:1-4)
- Christ's superiority to the angels and the prophets (1:5—4:13)
    - Exhortation (2:1-4; 3:1—4:13)
- Christ the high priest, superior to Levitical priesthood (4:14—10:18)
    - Exhortation (4:14-16; 6:1-12)
    - The heavenly sanctuary and the New Covenant (8:1-13)
- Exhortations and warnings (10:19—13:19)
- Greetings and closing (13:20-25)

3. Central Themes
- Superiority of Christ to the prophets and the angels (1:5—4:13)
- Christ the high priest (2:17; 4:14—5:14; 9:11-14)
- Relation of life under the old covenant to life in the new covenant (10:1, 19-23)
- Faith the substance of things not seen (11:1)

4. Distinct Emphases
- Satisfaction theory of atonement (2:17; 4:14—5:14; 9:11-14; 10:12-15)
- Teaches grace; Jesus the author and finisher of faith (12:1-2)
- New covenant involves a spontaneous desire to do good, for the law is written on our hearts (8:10-11; 10:19-23)
- Teaches striving for perfection and the laying on of hands (6:1-2)

3. Central Themes
- God as Holy One (6:1-4)
- Confronted by God we learn we are sinners (6:4-7)
- Judgment of Judah, its sacrificial cult, its practice of oppression of the poor and ill-considered foreign alliances (1; 3; 5:8-30; 9-10; 28; 29:9-24; 30; 33; 56:9—59)
- Oracles against other nations (10; 13-23; 30:27—31:9; 34; 40:15-17; 41)
- Comfort that the time of captivity is coming to an end (40:1-2; 43:1) or words of general comfort (61:1).
- Eschatological prophecies include the uplift of the poor (2; 4-5:7; 14:1-2, 24-27; 29:1-8; 32; 35; 40—56:8; 60-66)
  - Messianic prophecies of a royal eschatological figure (9; 11)
  - Suffering Servant who seems identified with Israel (42:1-4; 49:1-6; 50:4-11; 52:13—53:12)

4. Distinct Emphases
- The addition of post-Babylonian Exile prophecies to the original utterances of the historical Isaiah need not necessarily be seen as a corruption of the message of the original prophet, but as a liberation of his word from its original historical circumstances to be viable for addressing the future.
- Messianic Prophecies, especially the Suffering Servant Songs.
- References made to God's Holy Spirit (67:10-11).
- The eschatology of the final chapters attributed to Third Isaiah is more transcendent, less tied to historical circumstances than even Second Isaiah. The final chapters are more concerned with cultic matters and the realities of life in the restored community. Messianic prophecies are not clearly found in these chapters.

Jeremiah

1. Historical Background
- A book of prophecies of a late seventh to early sixth century BC prophet of Judah, dictated to his aide Baruch, from the reigns of Josiah, Jehoiakim, and Zedekiah through the era of the Babylonian Captivity.
- Some of the prophet's criticism of the house of David and the temple, giving more attention to the Sinai Covenant, may relate to his being an ancestor of one of David's high priests, Abiathar, who lost control of the temple and was finally banished.
- Three sources of the book have been identified:
  1) An authentic poetic strand;
  2) Biographic pose; and
  3) Deuteronomic redaction. The interplay of these strands suggests that the final editors saw Jeremiah's past prophecies as relevant in the new context.

2. Main Sections
- Introduction and oracles of judgment against Judah from the time of Josiah and Jehoiakim (1:1—20:18, of which chs. 11-20 are laments).
- Oracles from the time of Zedekiah (21:1—25:14).
- Oracles against the nations (25:15-38; chs. 46-51).
- Baruch memoirs (chs. 26-45, which include promises concerning salvation, chs. 30-33)
- Historical appendix (ch. 52).

3. Central Themes
- In a manner reminiscent of the Deuteronomistic source, there is a preoccupation with God rewarding and punishing those who fail to keep the Mosaic Law (esp. criticizing Judah's worship of other gods and attendant evils in cult and daily life).
- Laments (both personal and for the nation [esp. 11:18—20:18]).
- God's covenant people must repent and return.
- Eschatology — promises of hope regarding God's faithfulness to His promises in the future (30-32).

4. Distinct Emphases
- The personal laments (11:18—12:6; 15:10-21; 17:14-18; 18:18-23; 20:7-18) are unique, for in no other book do we find a comparable reflection of the spiritual struggle with God.
- There is also a wealth of detail about the various trials the prophet endures during his career (chs. 26, 44).

Revelation

1. Historical Background
• An Apochryphal book of the late first century expressing hope for salvation after a world-ending new creation. Although parts of the book may predate the fall of Jerusalem, it is likely that it achieved present form during the reign of Emperor Domitian between 81 and 96 AD. Christians were being persecuted for refusing to address him as lord and god.
• Written by John (1:1, 4, 9; 22:8), whose identity is not clear despite the tradition's identification of him with the disciple. The book's Semitic Greek style suggests that its author was Jewish. It is the report of seven (the mystical Hebrew number for fullness) dreams. It relies heavily on eschatological images of the book of Daniel and other Old Testament texts (see 1:7 [cf. Daniel 7:3]; 1:12-16 [cf. Daniel 10:5-9]; 3:10 [cf. Daniel 12:1]; 10:5-7 [Daniel 12:6-7]).

2. Main Sections
• Prologue (1:1-8)
• Preparatory vision and letters to the seven churches (1:9—3:22)
• Vision of the glory of God and of the lamb and the opening of six seals (3:23—7:17)
• The seventh seal, demonic plagues, and the measuring of the temple (8:1—11:19)
• Vision of the woman, the child, the dragon, and the two beasts (12:1—14:20)
• The seven bowls of the wrath of God (15:1—16:21)
• The fall of Babylon (representing a prophecy of Rome's fall), dirges, and praise, and Christ's victory (17:1—19:21)
• The binding and loosing of Satan, final conflict and judgment, and vision of the New Jerusalem (20:1—22:5)
• Epilogue (22:6-21)

3. Central Themes
• Visions receive divinely authorized interpretation (1:1; 17:1-8; 21:9ff)
• Recurring themes of seven revelations
• Conflicts between a righteous minority (followers of Christ) and a wicked majority are understood in an ontologically dualistic manner, as a clash between God and Satan.
• After a period of intense conflict, God prevails and creates a new reality to reward the faithful. The book testifies to God's final victory.
• Human time is transcended, for God already rules, the judgment has transpired, and His kingdom has come (1:8; 4:8; 14:7; 15:4; 164ff).
• The faithful are called to endure (Sanctification) (13:10; 14:12).

4. Distinct Emphases
• One of two apocalypses in the Bible (Daniel being the other). Such a revelation is a first-person narrative of an ancient biblical figure relating visions about the future.
• Eschatology is understood Christologically (20:17ff).

Charts of the Major Theological Options

God

Relation to the World
- *Transcendent*: God not of the world, existing in a dimension beyond space and time
- *Immanent*: God resides in the world
    - Pantheism: God identified with world
- *Panentheism*: God both transcends the world, but is also in it. God a vast ocean and the universe but a sponge dropped into it.

Nature of God
- *Just*: God will condemn and strike down the sinner; His justice must be placated if we are to be forgiven.
- *Love*: God's actions characterized by forgiving love; even wrath serves love.
    - Wrath a misperception of God's love

Trinity
- Like a three-link chain, each link distinct but indivisible.
- Like different forms of water (a river, its source, its ocean outlet).
- Father and Son relate to each other like the sun to its rays.
- Like fire passed among three torches.
- Resembles the threefold structure of the human mind — the mind, begetting self-knowledge, from which self-love proceeds.
- The Father is God's Polentiality, the Son is God's Action, and the Spirit brings God's potential to love and the divine life of action together.
- Father loves the Son and Holy Spirit the love who makes them one.
- Because God is what He does, His three works (Creation, Redemption, and Sanctification) make Him three, but because these three works are in harmony, in executing these works in harmony God constitutes Himself as one.

Christology
- *Alexandrian*: Whatever is said of one of Jesus' natures can be attributed to the other. As Jesus suffers, so does God.
- *Antiochene*: Each attribute of Jesus belongs either to His divine nature or to His humanity. God did not suffer when Jesus did.

Creation and Providence
- *Creation in seven days*: Total denial of evolution
- *Creation an ongoing process*: Interpret evolution as driven by God; creation still continuing in the daily events of life.

Providence: God's Involvement in Everyday Events
- *Deism*: Free will affirmed; God said to be not involved directly in any daily events.
- *Sovereign God*: All events of life determined by God.
    - God compels us to do His bidding
    - God works through our wills
- *God as Band Leader*: Like a band leader and movie producer, God determines the plot and lures us to a behavior, but sometimes mistakes (and evil) mar the way to the outcome.

Sin
- *Totally sinful in everything we do, feel, or say*: Sin is usually depicted as a condition of selfishness or concupiscence. We are in bondage to sin; all sins are equally heinous.
- *We are inclined to sin*: We are disposed to sin in all we do. But sometimes it can be avoided as we make progress in the Christian life.
    - Sin can only be avoided with the help of grace
    - We can choose to avoid sin
    - Some sins are not as bad as others

- Temptations are not sin
- Not every deed is a sin
• Sin is a choice.

Atonement
• *Classic view*: Jesus defeats evil, death, the devil, and sin in the passion event.
• *Moral influence theory*: Jesus' life is an example that saves by providing a model to emulate.
• *Satisfaction theory*: Jesus dies to take away the punishment for sin, which we deserve.
• *Governmental theory*: Jesus' passion restores the created order that sin had disrupted; it is not God who demands punishment of the sinner, but the created order making this demand, contrary to God's will.

What Christ's Saving Work Accomplishes
• *Possibility for salvation*: Christ's work makes it *possible* to be saved, if we accept the offer of salvation.
• *Actuality of salvation*: Christ's work puts us in a new situation in which our salvation is assured.

Justification / Salvation

How It Happens
• *By grace*: Salvation is entirely God's work; even faith is a work of God
• *By faith*: You must believe to be saved. (If the Holy Spirit is never given credit as the source of faith, Pelagianism is implied as faith is turned into a work.)
• *By grace and works*: God does His part; you do yours. Or if you do your part (if you tithe, repent, etc.), God will bless you. (If the human response is portrayed as something we do without God's aid, Pelagianism is again implied.)

• *By works and faith*: Faith saves you, but you must do something with it to be saved.
• *Pelagianism*: We can only be saved if we live righteously/morally, etc.

What Happens
(What It Means To Be Born Again)
• *Forensic justification (declared righteous)*: God doesn't regard us as sinners anymore (even though we still are).
• *Made righteous (given new qualities of holiness)*: We are not the same since being redeemed/justified, we are no longer sinners.
• *Deification*: We have been made God-like; references made to the God in you.
• *Intimate union (conformity to Christ)*: We are now part of Christ, like the spouse of a beloved husband. We share Jesus' legacy like happily married couples share community property.

Sanctification / Christian Life
• *Good works spontaneous*: Sanctification begins in justification; good works transpire freely without exhortation and is usually combined with a situational ethic.
  - *Simultaneously saint and sinner*: Since we remain in sin in all we do, even our good deeds (for which the Holy Spirit gets all the credit), there is no growth in the Christian life.
• *Good works must be exhorted*: We must be taught what good works to do (or be exhorted to do them) usually with instruction from the Ten Commandments or other biblical laws.
  - *Growth in grace*: Though we are sinners, we can advance in the Christian life by enhanced obedience to the commandments.
  - *Perfection*: We may grow in grace to the point of being gifted with perfection (no longer wanting to sin). For some, such perfection is a process. For others, it is an event that follows salvation/justification and holiness/sanctification.

Predestination / Election / Free Will
• *Pelagianism*: Free will to choose to believe
• *Possibility of salvation*: God offers salvation to all. In believing we are aided by the Holy Spirit.
• *Arminianism*: God elects people to salvation or damnation based on divine foreknowledge or whether they will come to believe or not.
• *Double predestination*: God unconditionally gives faith to some but not to all. This gift is given by the Holy Spirit either in violation of the human will or through the structures of the will.

- *Single predestination*: All are elect but some throw away the gift of faith and salvation (which is already in the hands of each).
- *Universal salvation*: All are (not just will be) saved.

Grace and the Human Will
- *Heteronomy*: Grace dominates the will, forcing the will to do what it must do.
- *Autonomy*: The human will is totally free to do what it wishes with grace.
- *Theonomy*: Grace prevails over human autonomy but works though the dynamics of the human will.

Church
- *God's work, created through word and sacrament*: Church's holiness not dependent on the holiness of its members.
    - Built on the foundations of an apostolically ordained ministry: Church's holiness not dependent on the holiness of its members.
- *Mother of all Christians*: Entails no one is a Christian apart from the church.
- *Hospital for sinners*: Entails the church is only for sinners.
- *Community of the faithful*: A fellowship of the born again, administered with discipline exercised on the members in order to keep them active and holy.

Ministry
Why Pastors/Priests Set Apart for Leadership
- Set apart in the line of the apostles
- Set apart to do a special job (preaching God's word or administering the sacraments)
- Set apart to lead or facilitate the flock
    - Priesthood of all believers
- Set apart as an example of Christian living
- Set apart to lead by exercising authority over laity

Sacraments

Baptism
- *Born again in baptism*
- *Symbol*: The born-again experience transpires prior to and independent of baptism, which merely symbolizes this experience.
- *Seal of election*: Baptism like a government seal making a document/declaration official. God's eternal electing love for the baptized made public and official in baptism.

The Lord's Supper
- *Symbol*: Christ spiritually present but not in the elements.
- *Seal*: Christ not the elements, but really bodily present. Recipient is brought by the Holy Spirit to Christ in heaven.
- *Real Presence*: Christ *in* the bread and wine though the elements remain bread and wine.
- *Transubstantiation*: Christ in the bread and wine, but after consecration they are no longer bread and wine (as their substance has been changed).

Eschatology
- *Future Eschatology*: Interpret references to kingdom of God as a reality to come.
    - *Apocalyptic*: Talk about Christ's return as a cataclysmic event.
    - *Rapture*: Believe the faithful will be returned to heaven without tasting death as a prelude to the Christ's second coming.
    - *Millennial speculation*
    - *Premillennialism*: Christ will return prior to a 1,000-year period of blessedness during which God will reign on earth.
    - *Postmillennialism*: Christ will return after God establishes His 1,000 year reign of blessedness prior to the end of time.
    - *Amillennialism*: Rejection of the teaching of a millennium.

- The dead are judged (rewarded) based on works done with grace.
- Those with faith are saved.
- Some openness to salvation of all.

• *Realized Eschatology*: Interpret kingdom of God as reality at least to some extent present, so that we are already in the end times. (An urgency about the present and decisions to be made in the present, an appreciation that we are no longer bound by our pasts, characterize this commitment.)

Social Ethics
Church-State Relations

• *Absolute separation of church and state*: The church and Christians need to stay out of politics.

• *Church and state in paradoxical tension*: We need to get common values (right and wrong) reflected in the laws of the land, not to legislate distinct Christian principles.
- Appeal to natural law to make political judgments

• *Christianizing society*: This is a Christian nation, and we need to get Christian values legislated.

Christianity and Economics

• *Preferential option for the poor*: God favors the poor. Critical of the free market, tends to favor managed economies.

• *Prosperity gospel*: God blesses the faithful with prosperity. A close link between faith and capitalism (the free market) is posited.

The Lenten Season

The Meaning of the Season
• Forty days of repentance and preparation for the Easter festival. The name of the season derives from the Anglo-Saxon word meaning "spring."
• The forty days of the season were originally intended to commemorate the forty hours during which Jesus lay in the tomb. Later the forty days came to symbolize Christ's temptation of forty days in the wilderness.
• The forty days are counted by not including Sundays, because that day, unlike other weekdays during Lent, were not days of fasting. Sundays are also not part of the calculation of the days of Lent because they commemorate Easter.
• The season begins with Ash Wednesday, during which ashes of the palms of the previous Palm Sunday are administered to the foreheads of the faithful (applied in the emblem of a cross) to remind them of their finiteness and the death they deserve due to their sins. As such, it is a day of mourning and repentance.

The Origins of the Season
• The season has its origins in the early church practice of baptisms on Easter. Since most baptisms prior to the fifth century were of believers, a six-week period of Catechetical instruction was standard.
• When Christianity was established in the Roman Empire in the fourth century, Lent became a period of preparation for everyone.
• Meanwhile, by the fourth century, the practice of observing six days prior to Easter (Holy Week) was developing in Jerusalem. They were designated days of fasting.
• The six days of these Holy Week commemorations grew to 36 days (a length chosen to symbolize the 365 days of a year) and were in turn lengthened to the present forty.
• By the time of Charlemagne in 730 AD, the forty days of Lent were established. In the Middle Ages it became a period of penitence with fasting and solemnity, as an attempt to identify with Jesus' suffering and to appease God. Protestant adaptations are to interpret the season penitentially and as providing opportunities to contemplate Christ's passion.
• In the modern period, fasting was relaxed in order to allow for lunches. Since Leo I in the fifth century, fasting has been interpreted as creating opportunity to give what we forego to the poor.

The Mood of the Season
• Expressed by the seasonal color, purple — a season of solemnity and sobriety for our sin.
• The mood of Good Friday is expressed by the use of black on that day — a time of mourning (for Jesus and our sin).

Preaching Strategies
• To call the faithful to an awareness of and repentance for their own and American social sins that have mandated Christ's atoning death.
• To present Jesus' and the biblical authors' interpretation of Christ's atoning work.
• To accompany Jesus and His followers on the way to the Cross (recognizing our complicity in it and vicariously to experience His suffering) in order to experience God's forgiving love for us. This may take the form of sermons helping us understand the doctrines of sin (and our own sinfulness) and Justification by Grace (its significance in our everyday lives).
• Teaching sermons about the faith and its doctrines (to commemorate the origins of Lent in the Catechetical period prior to Easter baptisms). This is an especially useful strategy for the mid-week services held by many traditions during Lent.

Ash Wednesday
February 13, 2013

Revised Common	Joel 2:1-2, 12-17 or Isaiah 58:1-12	2 Corinthians 5:20b—6:10	Matthew 6:1-6, 16-21
Roman Catholic	Joel 2:12-18	2 Corinthians 5:20—6:2	Matthew 6:1-6, 16-18
Episcopal	Joel 2:1-2, 12-17	2 Corinthians 5:20b—6:10	Matthew 6:1-6, 16-21

Theme of the Day   Sorrow for sin and the way out.

Collect of the Day   Two options are provided. The first is a prayer of repentance. After praising God for His love, we pray for new and honest hearts in our penitence. At least this is an affirmation of the role of grace in causing us to repent, but forgiveness seems contingent on the repentance. The second prayer is more devoted to petitions regarding Social Ethics and Sanctification. God's love is said to have created us to be people who serve our neighbors. Petitions are offered to God to call forth prayers and acts of kindness as well as to strengthen us when facing death.

Psalm of the Day   *Psalm 51:1-17*
• A lament Psalm for healing and moral renewal, traditionally ascribed to David after being condemned by Nathan for transgressions with Bathsheba.
• Urges God to have mercy and cleanse our sin (vv. 1-4, 7, 9). God has no interest in sacrifice (vv. 16-17).
• Sin is only sin if committed against God (v. 4). Ordinary guilt is not sin.
• Reference to something like original sin (v. 5) and the Holy Spirit (v. 11).
• Justification leads to Sanctification. A prayer by the forgiven sinner is that we be given a new heart, a new and right and willing spirit (vv. 10-11). This transformation will lead to evangelism (v. 13) and praise of God (vv. 15, 17).

Sermon Text and Title
"Get Moving!"
Joel 2:1-2, 12-17

1. Theological Aim of the Sermon and Strategy
An opportunity to deal with sin and the urgency of repentance (Realized Eschatology) and opening our eyes to the gift of God's forgiving love (Justification by Grace and Sanctification along with repentance as necessary fruits).

2. Exegesis
• A cultic prophet, exercising his ministry in the temple (probably during the period of Persian domination of Israel [539 BC -331 BC]). The book's historical theme is the plague of locusts that have destructively descended on Israel (1:4).
• The book is also characterized by apocalyptic/eschatological elements — references to day of the Lord (2:1-11, 28-32; 3:1-3, 9ff). There is an evolution in this concept from being a day of judgment, not one of salvation, to the suggestion that it is a theme of hope and salvation (4:1ff).
• Main Sections: (1) Prophetic liturgy of national lament (1:1—2:27); and (2) A series of proclamations (2:28—3:21). Some have speculated that the second section is the later work of an editor of the period of the Maccabees in the second century BC.
• Central Themes: (1) God judges and punishes sin; (2) Call for repentance; (3) God is declared to be gracious and merciful; this assures Israel of its future safety from trials of judgment; and (4) Eschatology/Apocalypse: The Holy Spirit poured on all as a sign of the end (2:28-29).
• A cry of alarm for the cataclysmic day of the Lord is said to be coming (2:1-2). See above on day of the Lord. The great and powerful army is probably the plague of locusts ravaging the land (though they might just symbolize the cataclysm).
• A call to repentance by which the calamity might be averted (vv. 12-17). Fasting, weeping, mourning, and offerings in the temple are commended, but above all a repentance of the heart is exhorted (vv. 12-13, 15). An assembly to sanctify the people is called (vv. 15-16). There and the remaining verse of the lesson take the form of a traditional liturgy. Priests (also called "ministers of the Lord") are called on to weep for the people in the temple and urge God to spare the people, that the truth of their commitment to Yahweh no longer be questioned by Gentiles (v. 17).

- God is said to be gracious and merciful, slow to anger, and abounding in steadfast love (v. 13). After the lesson ends, God graciously promises to end the plague and care for the people (vv. 18-27).

3. Theological Insights (see Charts of the Major Theological Options)
- The focus of the text is on sin as sloth as well as on Justification by Grace with attention to the spontaneity of Sanctification and good works as well as repentance. The reference to the theme of the imminent day of the Lord (vv. 1-12) indicates that the text testifies to Realized Eschatology. See pertinent observations on that theme in Theological Insights for the Gospel, Epiphany 3 and Advent 1. It is noted that we need this emphasis because sin tends to make us unrepentant.
- Martin Luther commented on God's way of dealing with His people, illustrated in this text:

> *This, however, is the custom of God almighty, that He takes His faithful to hell before He brings them back. Finally, however, after condemning and terrifying them, He brings them back and comforts them.* (*Luther's Works*, Vol. 18, p. 98)

- For John Calvin the lesson is a message of urgency and mercy: "The object of the narrative then, is to make the people sensible, that it was now no time for taking rest…" (*Calvin's Commentaries*, Vol. XIV/1, p. 44).
- We need this warning, Calvin claims, because we tend "to delay the time, as the profane and scorners are wont to do, who trifle with God from day to day…" (*Ibid.*, p. 56).
- Yet God has a way of hastening our response, he adds: "Hence the prophet now [in v. 13] represents God as propitious and merciful, that He might thus kindly allure the people to repentance" (*Ibid.*, p. 55).
- God needs to operate this way on account of our sin, Calvin also notes. "We are at first torpid when God invites us, except He applies His many goads…" (*Ibid.*, p. 62).
- Procrastination may be termed sloth, sinful behavior deeply rooted in our sense of unworthiness. About this malady Karl Barth claims that it is a function of imprisonment by anxiety and care about the hopelessness of the future (*Church Dogmatics*, Vol. VI/2, pp. 471-472).
- Sin is a state from which there is no escape. Martin Luther claimed that that is because we are turned in on ourselves and can never stop being selfish:

> *The reason is that our nature has been so deeply curved in upon itself because of the viciousness of original sin that it not only turns the finest gifts of God in upon itself and enjoys them (as is evident in the case of legalists and hypocrites), and indeed it even uses God Himself to achieve these aims, but it also seems to be ignorant of the very fact that in acting so iniquitously, so perversely, and in such a depraved way, it is even seeking God for its own sake.* (*Luther's Works*, Vol. 25, p. 291)

Augustine's idea of sin as concupiscence (self-seeking desire or lust) also fits this conception (*Nicene and Post-Nicene Fathers*, First Series, Vol. 5, pp. 273-274).

4. Socio-Economic, Political, Psychological, and Scientific Insights
- It is interesting to note the love and spirituality flood the brain in high quantities with the same neurochemical, dopamine (a brain chemical with properties of amphetamines) (Helen Fisher, *The Anatomy of Love: A Natural History of Mating, Marriage, and Why Stray*; Dean Hamer, *The God Gene*, pp. 72ff). In both cases, then, love and spirituality are addictive.
- For data implying the American public's neglect of the doctrine of sin, see the fifth bullet point of this section for the First Lesson, Transfiguration.

5. Gimmick
Ask the congregation if they agree that it has not been a very good year since last Lent, if they agree that we have not served the Lord, not lived lives worthy of our calling, as we should.

6. Possible Sermon Moves and/or Stories/Examples
- Our lives have been marred by greed, selfishness, unkind thoughts, fickleness, apathy, and envy. All of us have sinned and fallen short of God's glory since last Ash Wednesday.
- It is for us that Christ went to the Cross. We were the people yelling to Pilate to crucify Him; we put Him on that Cross.
- We need to repent! Not just for the outward sins, but for the hidden ones — for the hatred or lust we have felt. There is not a person in the building (or the pulpit) who does not deserve the death that awaits us. That is what the ashes of Ash Wednesday do. They remind us of who we are (sinners), and where we are headed (back into the ground because of sin).
- Note how such rhetoric goes against the grain the way most Americans think. See leads for data in the last bullet point of Socio-Economic, Political, Psychological, and Scientific Insights. We like to talk about having free will and about being basically good people. But it's a lie!

- It is a lie because there is no escape from our sinful condition apart from the grace of God. Martin Luther makes that clear. Use the last bullet point of Theological Insights and Romans 7:14-23 to clarify how our selfishness in everything we do is a condition from which we cannot extricate ourselves.
- Selfishness, the high provided by the brain chemical, is even involved in human love. See Socio-Economic, Political, Psychological, and Scientific Insights. The dopamine released in human love is not just pleasurable. It is addictive. This explains how our selfish sin traps us.
- Another way of expressing how we are trapped by this condition of selfishness was effectively offered by Martin Luther in an interesting image to express why we can never really rid ourselves of sin and why we always need repentance. Original sin, he claims, is like a man's beard:

> *The original sin in a man is like his beard, which though shaved off today so that a man is very smooth around his mouth, yet grows again by tomorrow morning. As long as a man is alive, such growth of the hair and the beard does not stop. But when the shovel beats the ground on his grave it stops. Just so original sin remains in us and bestirs itself as long as we live.*
> (*Tischreden*, No. 138)

- So Joel calls us to repentance (v. 12). He says there is time to waste, for the end times are coming (v. 1). Cite John Calvin in the third bullet point of Theological Insights.
- We do not want to hear that message. It really is like the old German proverb that Martin Luther once quoted in a biblical commentary: "All men are pleased with what they do. A world of fools I'm telling you" (*Weimar Ausgabe*, Vol. 48, p. 10).
- We are procrastinators, almost as inclined in this direction as we are in our selfishness. Cite next-to-last bullet point of Theological Insights. Our hopelessness about things ever getting better traps us.
- Yet Joel proclaims, "Get moving; repent." Not that we can do it ourselves. This wonderful God of Joel's and ours gets us moving. This is a God "gracious and merciful, slower to anger, and abounding in steadfast love." (v. 13). Such a God goads us out of our sloth; use the fifth and sixth bullet points of Theological Insights.

7. Wrap-Up
No, we are inclined to put things off, especially when it comes to our sin. But God says don't put it off, to get moving. Repent. But He does not leave us alone. He comes to us with an overwhelming, abounding love. He comes as a "pure and fiery flame," Martin Luther says (*Complete Sermons*, Vol. 4/2, p. 331). And that love sets us on fire too, John Calvin says (*Calvin's Commentaries*, Vol. V/1, p. 302). Ash Wednesday is all about God getting us off the dime, pushing us to shave the sinful "beards" of ours, and getting us moving. The ashes we are about to receive can be vehicles of God's flame, a fire that can change our lives.

Sermon Text and Title
"The Hiddenness of Life's Truths"
2 Corinthians 5:20b—6:10

1. Theological Aim of the Sermon and Strategy
To proclaim the hiddenness of the gospel and of Christian living (Justification by Grace and Sanctification) and the reasons (the ongoing struggle with sin in the Christian life).

2. Exegesis (see Introduction to Selected Books of the Bible)
- Paul is either responding to critics of his ministry or writing part of a letter of reconciliation.
- He urges the Corinthians for Christ's sake to be reconciled to God (5:20b); Christ became sin so we might become the righteousness of God (5:21). Justification and righteousness of God are here woven together.
- Paul proceeds to urge that we not accept God's grace in vain (6:1).
- Citing Isaiah 49:8 about God listening at an acceptable time, helping the faithful on the day of salvation, Paul notes that now is the moment to act (the end is near) (6:2).
- No obstacle will be put in the way of any believer, and so no one can rightly criticize his ministry (6:3).
- He accounts the suffering and persecution he has experienced in ministry (6:4-7). In antiquity, hardship and virtue were closely linked. These hardships magnify Paul's virtue.
- Concludes with seven antithetic clauses, illustrating the hiddenness of the gospel — under dishonor, death, suffering, sorrow, poverty (vv. 8-10).

3. Theological Insights (see Charts of the Major Theological Options)
- The text pertains to Christology, Atonement, Realized Eschatology (in the sense of the urgency of accepting the work),

Justification by Grace (as Intimate Union), and even Sanctification (esp. the hiddenness of the Christian life).
• Regarding verse 21 Martin Luther claims that in bearing our sin, Christ became the greatest of all sinners:

> *And all the proponents saw this, that Christ was to become the greatest thief, murderer, adulterer, robber, desecrator, blasphemer, etc. there has ever been anywhere in the world.* (*Luther's Works*, Vol. 26, p. 277)

• Regarding the focus on Justification by Grace Through Faith, John Calvin nicely explained the doctrine while expositing this text.

> *It is in the same manner, assuredly, that we are now righteous in Him — not in respect our rendering satisfaction to the justice of God by our own works, but because we are judged of in connection with Christ's righteousness, which we have put on by faith, that it might become ours.* (*Calvin's Commentaries*, Vol. XX/2, p. 242)

• John Wesley noted that the lesson teaches that "all things are ours if we are Christ's" (*Commentary on the Bible*, p. 526).
• In a similar vein, commenting on "now" being the moment to act (6:2), Martin Luther proclaimed:

> *All our sins are forgotten; He takes no note of the sins of the past nor of those of the present. In short, we are in a realm of mercy, where are only forgiveness and reconciliation. The heavens are now open.* (*Complete Sermons*, Vol. 4/1, p. 136)

• The hiddenness of the gospel described (6:8b-10). This entails that because sin so thoroughly surrounds us even the Christian life is hidden. This is the idea of our being simultaneously saint and sinner, as Martin Luther observes:

> *You see, the whole of Christian life has to be hidden and remain hidden this way. It cannot achieve great fame or put on much of a display or show before the world. So let it go at that. Do not worry about the way it is hidden, covered up, and buried, and the way that no one notices. Be content with the fact that your Father up there in heaven sees it.* (*Luther's Works*, Vol. 21, pp. 163-164)

For more on hiddenness, see Theological Insights for the Gospel, Advent 4 and for the Second Lesson, Palm Sunday. The Reformer relates this hiddenness of the Christian life to the fact that though made righteous in justification, Christians ever remain sinners: "Therefore I am at the same time a sinner and a righteous man, for I do evil and I hate the evil which I do" (*Luther's Works*, Vol. 25, p. 63). "From all this it is evident that sin remains in the baptized and the saints as long as they are flesh and blood and live on earth…" (*Ibid.*, Vol. 32, p. 20). "Every good work of the saints while pilgrims in this world is sin" (*Ibid.*, p. 59).
• For Luther this is a function of the hidden character of the word. As he puts it: "The heritage of Christ is 'splendid' and distinguished inwardly… that is, in mystical and hidden things that were not seen in outward forms…" (*Luther's Works*, Vol. 10, p. 107). As he put it later in his career (but still prior to the Reformation):

> *And universally our every assertion of anything good is hidden under the denial of it, so that faith may have its place in God, who is a negative essence of goodness and wisdom and righteousness, who cannot be possessed or touched except by the negation of all our affirmatives.* (*Ibid.*, Vol. 25, p. 383)

• Even the Christian life is hidden in the Reformer's view: "A Christian is even hidden from himself; he does not see his holiness and virtue, but sees in himself nothing but unholiness and vice" (*Ibid.*, Vol. 31, p. 411).

4. Socio-Economic, Political, Psychological, and Scientific Insights
• For statistics that depict the hardships America faces, the poverty, suffering, obstacles, and dishonor, see statistics in First Lessons, Advent 1, Advent 3, Epiphany.
• Surprising novelty seems to be good for the human brain and is pleasurable. Research conducted by Oscar Arrias-Carrion and Ernst Poppel indicate that the pleasurable, good-feeling brain chemical dopamine is secreted in greater quantities when a reward is greater than expected (*Acta Neurobioliae Experimentalis* [2007], pp. 481-488; cf. Stefan Klein, *The Science of Happiness*, pp. 35-37, 56-58, 107).

5. Gimmick
The ashes of Ash Wednesday are emblems of the hiddenness of God's ways. Ashes derive from life and then in a hidden way lead us back to life.

6. Possible Sermon Moves and/or Stories/Examples
• God works in hidden ways. Read 6:8b-10.
• Ask the congregation why God works in this hidden way. Ask if the members are happy with this. Would it not be better if God willed an end to death, sadness, and suffering?

- Our Second Lesson gives us some answers to come to terms with the paradoxes of life, why everything is not turning out just right for Christians. It has to do with sin, Paul says. In fact, Christ had to *become sin*. That's how we got saved (5:20).
- The nature of the good news of our faith is that God works in hidden ways. Use the next-to-last bullet point of Theological Insights; also see Theological Insights for First Lesson, Epiphany 2.
- Reiterate the point how God had to work through evil in order to overcome it with good. This explains the ashes tonight, how ashes, the symbol of death (ashes were originally living things), get us back to life.
- It also explains why there is still death, sadness, and suffering. In a hidden way God struggles with these realities and uses them to give life, joy, and health.
- This sort of hidden working by God gets us to focus more on Him. Reiterate the quotation by Martin Luther in the next-to-last bullet point of Theological Insights. We have nowhere else to look for good, but in Jesus. Even our Christian beliefs and style of life are hidden under sin. Use the sixth and last bullet points of Theological Insights.
- In all Christians do (even our good deeds) they are marred by sin. Refer to our sinfulness and concupiscence explained in the last bullet point of Theological Insights for the First Lesson in order to help parishioners see how even outwardly good deeds can still be sinful. In a sense, this appreciation of the hidden character of the Christian life links with Martin Luther's call to become a brave sinner. He once wrote:

> *... be not a false but a real [brave] sinner; not only in words but in reality and from the heart acknowledge yourself worthy before God of His wrath and eternal punishment, and bring before Him in truth these words, "me a poor sinner."*
> (*Complete Sermons*, Vol. 2/2, p. 367)

Next time you are uncertain of God's and Christ's presence in your life, be a brave sinner. Acknowledge that you really sin in all you do, even in your seemingly good deeds. Besides reiterating the preceding bullet point, elaborate on the last bullet point of Theological Insights for the First Lesson.
- A radical, courageous affirmation of the hiddenness of the truths of life drives us to the arms of God.
- There is even another, related benefit that comes with appreciating the hidden character of God's ways. It entails that God operates in surprising ways, just like it's a surprise that suffering can lead to joy and that death can lead to life.
- Surprise is what makes life beautiful. It's like Charlton Heston once said: "Life is full of surprises, isn't it?" Early twentieth-century Russian poet Boris Pasternak calls our attention to the joys of surprise: "Surprise is the greatest gift which life can grow." British-American Anthropologist and Humorist Ashley Montagu makes this point in even more depth with regard to the happiness of surprise: "The moments of happiness we enjoy take us by surprise, it is not that we seize them, but that they seize us."
- Note how living with surprises and novelty, like the Christian who appreciates God's hidden ways, leads to happiness and pleasure.

7. Wrap-Up
Invite the congregation the next time they encounter despair or impatience about life, about God's ways, to reflect on the hidden character of the gospel and to confess their sin bravely. Doing that gets us ready to look for the wonderful surprises of life that God has in store for us. The ashes of Ash Wednesday testify to God's wonderful, surprising ways, of bringing life out of death, good out of bad, and hope out of despair. He may have that planned for the members this week, this year!

Sermon Text and Title
"Even Busybody Hypocrites Like Us Can Be Forgiven and Changed"
Matthew 6:1-6, 16-21

1. Theological Aim of the Sermon and Strategy
Helping people to see sin even in their best deeds, how such hidden sin often leads to the pursuit of wealth, in order to prepare the flock for the good news of forgiveness (Justification by Grace) and a Christian life (Sanctification) that blossoms from grace.

2. Exegesis (see Epiphany)
- Part of the Sermon on the Mount; teaching of practical piety. Most of the lesson is peculiar to Matthew's gospel.
- Jesus warns against a hypocritical piety (Matthew usually has in mind with "hypocrisy" the Pharisees) that aims for others to notice one's faith (v. 1). Likewise it is said to be better to give alms (gifts of charity in synagogues) without fanfare but so "the left hand does not know what the right hand is doing" (vv. 2-4). Likewise it is better to pray privately than ostentatiously in public (vv. 5-6).

• After a critique of long public prayers (vv. 7-8), the Lord's Prayer (vv. 9-13), and exhorting forgiveness (vv. 14-15), Jesus urges that fasting not be done ostentatiously so that only the Father knows (vv. 16-18). (In this era, pious Jews fasted twice a week.) Here we observe Matthew's anti-Pharisaism coupled with a moral strategy.
• Jesus critiques trust in worldly goods, which are prone to destruction (vv. 19-20). In ancient times a large part of wealth consisted in costly garments liable to destruction by moths.
• One's treasure is indicative of one's heart (v. 21), i.e. one's moral priorities.

3. Theological Insights (see Charts of the Major Theological Options)
• An explanation of sin and the hopelessness of the human condition (esp. about how it permeates even our best actions and prompts us wantonly to pursue wealth). Along with repentance for such sin, the forgiving word of Justification by Grace is introduced, which in turn helps us understand Christian life (Sanctification) as a gift of grace.
• John Calvin nicely warns us of how insidious our hypocrisy, wanting credit for our goodness is: "But, as hypocrisy is always ambitious, we need not wonder that it is blind" (*Calvin's Commentaries*, Vol. XVI/1, p. 312). "Men are grown mad with an insatiable desire of gain" (*Ibid.*, p. 332).
• Martin Luther echoes these points regarding our false motives for doing good:

> *It is incredible how common this blasphemy and vice is in the world... how few people there are who do good works without seeking the honor or favor of the world this way.* (*Luther's Works*, Vol. 21, p. 132)

• Regarding verse 3 Martin Luther claims that Jesus urges that when giving alms the faithful not inform the left hand what the right hand is doing, lest the left hand will try to take more away than the right hand gave (*Luther's Works*, Vol. 21, p. 135). Another possibility, given the impossibility of the right hand doing anything not under the control of the same central nervous system controlling the left hand, is that if a person's left hand does not know what the right hand does, then that person's heart (which craves a reward) does not know what has been accomplished and is not motivating the good that has been accomplished.
• Augustine powerfully explains the misery of our sinful condition. We are "a people curious to know of other's lives, but slow to correct our own" (*Nicene and Post-Nicene Fathers*, Second Series, Vol. 1, p. 142). Though enjoying to endure, we would rather we had nothing to endure. In adversity we desire prosperity, and in prosperity fear adversity (*Ibid.*, p. 153). We are never satisfied.
• Eighteenth-century French intellectual Blaise Pascal further elaborated on the futility of our sinful condition and its course toward the grave: "*Man's condition*: Inconstancy, boredom, anxiety" (*Pensées*, p. 24). "Man is nothing but a subject full of natural error that cannot be eradicated except through grace" (*Ibid.*, p. 45).
• The reference to the need for grace suggests our dependence on God's forgiving love. Our sinful condition is not irredeemable. Martin Luther makes this point concisely (affirming Justification by Grace): "Therefore sinners are attractive because they are loved; they are not loved because they are attractive" (*Luther's Works*, Vol. 31, p. 57).
• He tells us more about this loving forgiving God in a comment about the Psalm of the Day:

> *This is a description or definition of God that is full of comfort: that in His true form God is a God who loves the afflicted, has mercy upon the humbled, forgives the fallen, and revives the drooping. How can any more pleasant picture be painted of God?* (*Luther's Works*, Vol. 12, p. 406)

• Only in grace (as a Christian), Luther contends, are good works possible:

> *Therefore no one can do a truly good work unless he is a Christian. If he does it as a man, then he is not doing it for the glory of God, but for his own glory and advantage. On the other hand, if he claims that it is for the glory of God, that is a lie that smells to high heaven.* (*Ibid.*, p. 134)

• Luther made a similar point this way:

> *The Spirit came pouring into their hearts, making them different beings, making them creatures who loved and willingly obeyed God... He wrote in those hearts His pure and fiery flame restoring them to life and causing them to respond with fiery tongues and efficient hands. They became new creatures, aware of possessing altogether different minds and different tendencies. Then all was life and light; understanding, will and heart burned and delighted in whatever was acceptable to God.* (*Collected Sermons*, Vol. 4/2, p. 331)

• John Calvin makes a point in the same vein while commenting on the Psalm of the Day, asserting how good works (Sanctification) are inspired by grace:

> *Those who have been mercifully recovered from their falls will feel inflamed by the common law of charity to extend a helping hand to their brethren.* (*Calvin's Commentaries*, Vol. 5/1, p. 302)

For other resources in affirming Justification by Grace and how it leads to Sanctification, see First Lesson, the last two quotes by Calvin in Theological Insights.

4. Socio-Economic, Political, Psychological, and Scientific Insights
• See this section for the First Lesson for data regarding the American neglect of the doctrine of sin.
• Martin Luther well explained our inertia in aiding the poor, which is called for in this text:

> But true almsgiving is a rare thing in this world. Not only is there so much ordinary robbing and stealing going on everywhere in the world that no one does anything good for his neighbor, but goes on scratching on his own manure pile without asking how his neighbor is getting along. But even if they do good works, they are only looking out for their own advantage.
> (*Luther's Works*, Vol. 21, p. 137)

• John Calvin noted the radical socio-economics that ensue from Jesus' reference to our treasures indicating where are hearts are. Interpreting this text he wrote:

> He [Christ] only intended to show that we must not be satisfied with bestowing on the poor what we can easily spare, but that we must not refuse to part with our estates, if their revenue does not supply the wants of the poor.
> (*Calvin's Commentaries*, Vol. XVI/1, p. 333)

• Google "Poverty in America in 2011" for the most statistics on the percentage of poor people in America. For earlier figures, see the first two bullet points in this section for the First Lesson, Advent 1.
• Ours is an ethos of self-promotion and celebrity, not of a work-ethic, on the job and in the village (Christopher Lasch, *The Culture of Narcissism*, pp. 116-117).

5. Gimmick
Begin with a recount of the setting for the lesson, Jesus' Sermon on the Mount. Probably delivered while seated (the common position for Jewish rabbis while teaching in the first century), note that He proclaimed verse 1 of the lesson (read it) pertaining to the dangers of practicing our piety before others. Elaborate on verses 16-18. Then after a pause, ask to whom was He addressing: the Pharisees (note that they were the most devout religious people of Jesus' day [*Luther's Works*, Vol. 21, pp. 132ff]). But then suggest that they were people like you and those in attendance.

6. Possible Sermon Moves and/or Stories/Examples
• Note how we like to think we are religious people. We are, even showing up twice this week for church. The Pharisees Jesus was criticizing at this point in the Sermon on the Mount were religious too.
• Jesus went after folks who were very visible in their piety, who wanted others to know how religious they are (vv. 1, 16-18). This is a very common disease. Cite the quote by Martin Luther in the third bullet point of Theological Insights. We are always looking for recognition, for credit in what we do. Such self-promotion is the way of the world in our new economy (see last bullet point of Socio-Economic, Political, Psychological, and Scientific Insights).
• We have to look busy and successful. Use the second and third bullet points of Theological Insights. Elaborate on how hypocritical and self-seeking we are. The last sentence of the quotation by Martin Luther in the ninth bullet point of Theological Insights especially highlights our lying hypocrisy.
• Continue elaborating on the emptiness of our life of self-seeking. Use quotations by Augustine and Pascal in the fifth and sixth bullet points of Theological Insights. We really are busybodies, unwilling to work on ourselves, never satisfied — simultaneously bored and anxious.
• Blaise Pascal further sums up our misery, our need to keep busy, butting in on matters and projects that really don't matter, ultimately are of no use:

> What people want is not the easy peaceful life that allows us to think of our unhappy condition... but the agitation that takes our mind off it and diverts us.
> (*Pensées*, 136)

> All our life passes in this way: we seek rest by struggling against certain obstacles, and once they are overcome, rest proves intolerable because of the boredom it produces. We must get away from it and crave excitement.
> (*Ibid.*)

We really are very miserable and unhappy in our aimless business.
• Jesus warns us in the sermon we read today against trusting in the pursuit of the things of world (vv. 19-20).
• Our Psalm of the Day points us to a way out. It refers to the hope of God's mercy (vv. 1-2, 11), to the way in which God will create the clean heart (v. 10) that Jesus says in our gospel is the only way out (v. 21).
• Note John Calvin's comments on this Psalm in the last bullet point of Theological Insights. This grace, Calvin contends, gets you on fire.

• Martin Luther's similar point in the next-to-last bullet point of Theological Insights. Even busybody hypocrites like us can be forgiven and changed!

7. Wrap-Up
Lent is a time for coming to terms with our sin. Jesus' Sermon on the Mount helps us do that. Tell the congregation that the next time they feel burdened with their meaningless business (burned out), feel bad about themselves, we have this wonderful God who gives a way out. Use the quote about God by Martin Luther in the eighth bullet point of Theological Insights. Here we find a picture of God full of comfort, a God who will revive us when we feel like we are drooping! There is indeed a way out of our aimless hustling. Note the next-to-last bullet point of Theological Insights again: Wrapped up in the flaming love of God we will start finding delight in the things of God.

Lent 1
February 17, 2013

Revised Common	Deuteronomy 26:1-11	Romans 10:8b-13	Luke 4:1-13
Roman Catholic	Deuteronomy 26:4-10	Romans 10:8-13	Luke 4:1-13
Episcopal	Deuteronomy 26:(1-4) 5-11	Romans 10:(5-8a) 8b-13	Luke 4:1-13

Theme of the Day   Confessing a God who delivers us. This theme is rooted in the tradition of commemorating the First Sunday in Lent in relation to its roots as the beginning of a period of religious instruction preparing those who would be baptized on Easter to confess their faith.

Collect of the Day   The God who led us through the wilderness to the Promised Land is petitioned to guide us, so that following His Son we may walk through the wilderness. Justification by Grace and a concern with the Christian life (Sanctification) are evidenced.

Psalm of the Day   *Psalm 91:1-2, 9-16*
• A wisdom Psalm, meditating on God as protector of the faithful.
• Those abiding in the shelter and shadow of the almighty (Shaddai) will look to Him for refuge and trust Him (vv. 1-2).
• Because the Lord has been made our refuge, no evil will befall us (vv. 9-10). His angels guard us (vv. 11-12).
• In a concluding divine oracle probably uttered by a priest, El Shaddai claims that He will deliver those who love Him, answer those who call, be with them in trouble, and bless them with long life, showing salvation (vv. 14-16).

Sermon Text and Title
"Faith and Gratitude"
Deuteronomy 26:1-11

1. Theological Aim of the Sermon and Strategy
To proclaim how in faith, its confession and ritual promote gratitude and joy.

2. Exegesis (see Introduction to Selected Books of the Bible)
• As part of the final section of Moses' Second Address these verses are a large segment of a liturgy for presentation of the first fruits sacrifice at the central sanctuary.
• This begins with an introduction that what follows is to be undertaken after Yahweh *Elohim* settles Israel in the Promised Land (v. 1).
• The occasion for this offering is a harvest pilgrimage festival, the Feast of Weeks, a thanks to God for the land and for the harvest at which time the offering is to be presented with some of the harvest's first fruits (vv. 2-4; cf. 16:9-12).
• The liturgy is fundamentally a confession and recitation of the early nomadic life of the progeny of Jacob, the time spent in Egypt as slaves, and the liberation leading to the land flowing with milk and honey (vv. 5-9). The participant then indicates he has brought the first fruit of the ground to Yahweh (v. 10).
• Instruction follows mandating that a celebration of the bounty is to be made with Levites and with all who reside in the region (v. 11).

3. Theological Insights (see Charts of the Major Theological Options)
• The text witnesses to the goodness of Creation, Providence (Social Ethics in the sense of Ecology), Justification by Grace, and so Sanctification (our joyful response).
• John Calvin claimed that the object of the celebration of the first fruits festival by the Hebrews was "that they might renew every year the recollection of their adoption…" (*Calvin's Commentaries*, Vol. II/1, p. 494).
• Commenting on the Psalm of the Day, Calvin explains the God who displays this profound love along with His power:

> *If we tremble to think of His majesty He presents Himself to us under the lowly figure of the hen: if we are terrified at the power of our enemies, and the multitude of dangers by which we are beset, He reminds us of His own invincible power, which extinguishes every opposing force.*
> (*Calvin's Commentaries*, Vol. V/2, p. 484)

- John Wesley stressed how it is God's will (v. 11) that we and the Hebrews are to be cheerful in celebrating God's ordinances (and so presumably be cheerful in our giving) (*Commentary on the Bible*, pp. 144-145). Martin Luther made a similar point (*Luther's Works*, Vol. 9, p. 255).
- Reflecting on the nature of the confession of faith in this litany, famed modern theologian Karl Barth reminds us of the undeserved status of being God's people:

  There is a people like this, a people of Jesus Christ, elected and called by God. But there are no men who have any right or claim to be this people. They can be what they are, namely this particular people, only by free grace.

  (*Church Dogmatics*, Vol. IV/3 Second Half, p. 726)

- Process theologians John Cobb and David Griffin have been at the forefront of theological efforts to address the ecological agenda. They propose a "reverence for life" (*Process Theology*, p. 76).

4. Socio-Economic, Political, Psychological, and Scientific Insights

- For an appreciation of how sharing rituals (like common confessions) enhances life, see the last bullet point of this section for the First Lesson, Transfiguration. For more on how common ritual enhances social solidarity, see Nicholas Wade, *The Faith Instinct*, pp. 78-81, 92-96, 197ff.
- In such self-transcendent experiences, the parietal lobe of the human brain (located in its rear) grows dim, the prefrontal cortex is in turn activated, leading to its saturation with dopamine and so results in experiences of happiness (see Socio-Economic, Political, Psychological, and Scientific Insights for the Gospel, Advent 2).
- The text reflects some ecological sensitivity. A 2007 University of Missouri survey revealed that only 7 of 10 Americans want government to do more on behalf of ecology (only 3 in 10 want a lot more involvement). A later 2008 poll conducted by Pew Trust revealed that 2 in 5 American Christians would oppose stricter environmental regulations.
- Google the latest information on nuclear waste global warming and environmental racism (dumping trash in poor neighborhoods in which African-American or Hispanic-American citizens are the majority). Do not overlook the fact that America is responsible for a disproportionate share of the waste.

5. Gimmick

What does a harvest festival in ancient Israel, the Feast of Weeks, have to do with Lent? Quite a bit. Hear the story. Both of these worship events (Feast of Weeks and the First Sunday in Lent) have to do with the kind of training in the faith (Religious Education) that nurtures a living faith that matters in everyday life. Ask the congregation if they want that sort of faith. Then these commemorations are for them.

6. Possible Sermon Moves and/or Stories/Examples

- Essentially our First Lesson is all about the institution of a liturgy for this Festival, the Feast of Weeks. Use especially the first and third bullet points of Exegesis and the Historical Background for the Book. The point of our text is to help the faithful in Judah appreciate the festival they were to celebrate, recognizing its ancient roots and also to get them worshiping the right way (to teach the liturgy). How interesting that the First Sunday in Lent historically had a similar educational role. Use the explanation of the Sunday in Theme of the Day.
- Ever go through worship service and it was just dry ritual? All that happened was your mind wandered? One of the great and typical sins of Christians (even church-goers) — not getting involved in worship, making it their own event of praise. Moses in our lesson, the writers of the book of Deuteronomy, want to give us resources for avoiding blasé, mind-wandering forms of worship. They want to get us more grateful in our faith-walk. They want to teach us a common worship, so we can get focused on worshiping together, get into it because we understand what is happening and have a share in it. That's why this Sunday's stress on Christian Education, on learning the faith and making it your own, can make worship better for us.
- Use the second and fourth bullet points of Theological Insights in order to elaborate further on what the celebration of this Jewish festival of the Feast of Weeks (a harvest festival) has to do with us. The stress of the festival in the views of John Calvin, John Wesley, and Martin Luther was on recollection and celebration. Good idea: Remembering and celebrating are what the high points in life are all about. Think of worship that way and it will be harder to get bored.
- Analyze the liturgy prescribed for the Festival (see next-to-last bullet point of Exegesis). It is the familiar story about the nomadic life of Judah's ancestors, their enslavement, liberation, and finally settlement in the Promised Land.
- Use the next-to-last bullet point of Theological Insights, noting Karl Barth's claim that this liturgy is a celebration of the free grace of God. We need that sort of instruction for today in our context where we frequently speak of a "meritocracy," deluding ourselves with the media's help into thinking that Americans earn everything we have (Robert Reich, *The Work of Nations*; Christopher Lasch, *The Revolt of the Elites*, pp. 39-44). A liturgy like we find in our lesson (it is one we can use)

can help us appreciate that anywhere you get that's good is by the grace of our loving God. In this connection, elaborate on Calvin's comments in the second bullet point of Theological Insights.
• These insights about all the good that we have being a gift of God's grace, realizing from where we have come (bondage), along with this wonderful vision of a God who nurtures us like a hen, while powerful enough to overcome opposing force, can only lead to gratitude.
• Repeat the word "gratitude." Note what a good thing it is. Use the following quotation by late medieval mystic Meister Eckhart: "If the only prayer you said in your whole life was 'thank you,' that would suffice." Gratitude also seems to make you happy, at least according to research by psychologists. People keeping gratitude journals or other expressions of thanksgiving tend to poll happier (Robert Emmons, *Thanks: How Practicing Gratitude Can Make You Happier*).
• Learning the basics of the faith with someone else, worshiping together with a shared liturgy like the people of Judah learned for the Feast of Weeks, can also enhance well being. Alone and isolated like we Americans are (use data in Socio-Economic, Political, Psychological, and Scientific Insights for the Second Lesson) we need an antidote. Many of our present insalubrious business dynamics are results of our isolation and determination to "get" for ourselves, and to heck with everyone else (Jean Twenge and W. Keith Campbell, *The Narcissism Epidemic*).
• It is different, though, when we worship together, confess the faith together, like our lesson taught the Judeans. Then we are together in a common liturgy and confession of faith! Follow the leads in the first bullet point of Socio-Economic, Political, Psychological, and Scientific Insights. This data indicates that in common worship we experience a community with our fellow worshipers that enhances our solidarity, a significant antidote to the individualistic, narcissistic characteristics of contemporary American society noted above.

7. Wrap-Up
Learning the faith together, learning common ways to worship, is what this Bible lesson, this Sunday, is all about. Learning about, believing in the wondrous love of God leads to gratitude, a sense of unity that might help America, a sense of excitement and joy in worship and in life that is hard to beat. (If the congregation uses a creed and a set order of worship remind them of this joy.) A communal approach to worship makes it a better experience, an expression of gratitude, a lot more joyful. As Martin Luther once said: "God wants us to be cheerful and He hates sadness" (*Weimar Ausgabe Tischreden*, Vol. 1, p. 52). Christian education, taking ownership of our faith, makes life a lot happier.

Sermon Text and Title
"A Protestant (and Catholic) Way to Confess"
Romans 10:8b-13

1. Theological Aim of the Sermon and Strategy
To explain and celebrate the nature of confession (in a Protestant sense) and how faith is nurtured by it. Justification by Grace and Sanctification are highlighted.

2. Exegesis (see Introduction to Selected Books of the Bible)
• Continuing discourse on how righteousness comes by faith.
• Refers to the word of faith (v. 8b). Salvation comes as we confess that Jesus is Lord and believe God raised Him from the dead (v. 9).
• One who believes is justified, and one who confesses is saved (v. 10). Citing Isaiah 28:16 Paul notes that no one who believes in Christ will be put to shame (v. 11).
• No distinction between Jew and Gentile. The Lord is lord of all and generous to all (v. 12).
• Citing Joel 2:32 (applying reference to Yahweh to Jesus) Paul states that "everyone who calls on the name of the Lord shall be saved" (v. 13).

3. Theological Insights (see Charts of the Major Theological Options)
• The text addresses Justification by Grace (received through confession of faith) and Sanctification (the life of confession).
• Commenting on the Psalm of the Day John Calvin speaks of "rest[ing] with a sweet confidence in God…" (*Calvin's Commentaries*, Vol. V/2, p. 489).
• Famed theologian of the early church Augustine nicely summarizes what "confession" in Paul's, Moses', and Jesus' sense means:

For when I am wicked, confession to you [O Lord] means being displeased with myself; but when I am good, confession to you means simply not attributing my goodness to myself. (*Nicene and Post-Nicene Fathers*, First Series, Vol. 1, p. 142)

- Martin Luther echoes these sentiments regarding confession and its purpose:

  For confession is the principal work of faith by which as man denies himself and confesses God and thus he both denies and confesses to such an extent that he would deny his own life and all things rather than affirm himself. For in confessing God and denying himself he dies. (*Luther's Works*, Vol. 25, p. 411)

- The text clearly gives witness to Justification by Grace. About that matter Luther wrote:

  It follows, then, that a Christian must not believe that we are justified by an other righteousness. Let all works by which we aim to gain righteousness and all our own merits depart, because we are built upon the foundation not by doing works but by believing. Therefore let every godly man, terrified by sin, run to Christ as the mediator and propitiator, and let him leave all his own works behind. (*Luther's Works*, Vol. 16, pp. 230-231)

- Martin Luther tried to bring clarity to what is the heart of this text:

  Believing in Him [Christ] is the thing. It is useful and gives the power that we have from this: that neither hell not the devil can take us and all others who believe on Him captive nor can they do us harm. (Robert Kolb and James A. Nestingen, *Sources and Contexts of the Book of Concord*, p. 249)

- Elsewhere Luther made the point with reference to how Christ is present whenever He is preached:

  But in addition to the preaching, He himself comes, is spiritually present and speaks and preaches to the hearts of the people, just as the apostles address their words orally and physically to the ears of the people. Then Christ preaches to the spirits who are in captivity in the prison of the devil. Thus the going, like the preaching, should be understood in a spiritual sense. (*Luther's Works*, Vol. 30, p. 114)

4. Socio-Economic, Political, Psychological, and Scientific Insights
- Americans feel abandoned by their leaders, some pundits say. A 2009 Gallup poll testifies to the low level of trust we have toward our politicians (about 10% of the public trust them), lawyers (13%), business executives (12%), and even clergy (just 50%).
- More Americans than ever are living alone. One in four households are made up of just one member, up 7% from 1940.
- From 1985 to 2006 the number of people who said there was no one with whom they discussed important matters tripled, to 25% of the public. Apparently Facebook only broadens your network, not the depth of friendship.
- For other statistics on our social isolation, see the first bullet point in this section for the Second Lesson, Epiphany.

5. Gimmick
Confession: many Protestants are inclined to say that confession is Catholic and stop there. Or we hear it said, "Confession is good for the soul." Even then we are likely to hear it like Roman Catholics, to suppose it means that we are to recount all our sins. We don't need confession in our church! Or do we?

6. Possible Sermon Moves and/or Stories/Examples
- Paul gives us a model for confession of the faith in the book of Romans. Recall this is a letter of introduction to the church in Rome, which he had never visited. How does he make introductions? With a confession of faith!
- Note Paul does not confess his sins in our lesson today. Review the second through fifth bullet points of Exegesis. Confession here is a confession of the core of what he believes. We had other examples of that in the First Lesson (the confession of faith of the Hebrews in Deuteronomy 26:5-9) and the gospel (as Jesus confesses His faith [quotes scripture] in response to the devil's temptations in Luke 4:4, 8, 12).
- Confession in this biblical, catholic sense is about faith, the faith of the church. The apostles and Nicene Creeds are examples of confessions of faith like Paul, the Hebrews, and Jesus. They are summaries of scripture. (If Lutheran or Reformed, note that the denominational founders in the Reformation era also formulated Confessions that govern the teachings of the denomination.)
- Just to recite the creeds (or the denominational Catechisms) is not to be involved in confession. We only really confess when we know what we're saying and believe it. Keep that in mind the next time you recite the Creed, the next time you have a chance to *confess* it!
- Of course confession needs to be in harmony with the whole church. If what you say is just your own private opinion it is not a confession of faith you offer. An authentic confession of faith expresses the church's faith! It's precisely this dimension of an authentic confession of faith that gets us away from the loneliness and self-serving individualism that characterize our

present ethos. (See the leads in Socio-Economic, Political, Psychological, and Scientific Insights and relevant comments in the next-to-last bullet point of this section for the First Lesson.) A communal confession unites us together in a way that can critique all these individualistic trends.

• Elaborate on the first bullet point of in Socio-Economic, Political, Psychological, and Scientific Insights. Emphasize how as we confess the faith together over the years we come to feel that we are kin in hearts and minds. We come to trust each other. (I also forget about myself, as I come to focus more on the confession's content and with whom I share the confession.) This results in social solidarity. The other-directed dimensions of confession promote activity in the front part of the brain (the prefrontal cortex) resulting in the secretion of the amphetamine-like, pleasurable brain chemical dopamine, creating pleasure and joy (see Socio-Economic, Political, Psychological, and Scientific Insights for Second Lesson, Advent 1).

• Confession is good for the church, good for society, and nurtures happy believers. This becomes even clearer when we examine what it is we are to confess, what Paul confessed.

• Paul makes clear that his confession is about Justification by Grace (vv. 10, 13). Develop this point citing the next-to-last and third-to-last bullet points in Theological Insights. Confession leads to confidence. Also consider the quote by John Calvin in the second bullet point of Theological Insights.

• The focus on being saved by grace alone defines what Confession is, at least that is what Saint Augustine thought. Share his definition of Confession (third bullet point of Theological Insights). If time, share Luther's similar view in the fourth bullet point of that section. Confession is about not attributing too much to ourselves, giving all the credit to God!

7. Wrap-Up

To confess the faith in this Protestant/Catholic way gives confidence and joy. Temptation and despair don't have a chance if we have renounced our own goodness. A confessor of the faith doesn't face the problems of life alone, and he or she does not even have to be the one to fight these trials. A confession of faith reminds us that we are totally dependent on God and that He will take care of all our problems. Against that, temptation and despair are bound to wither away!

Sermon Text and Title
"Tempted? Jesus Understands"
Luke 4:1-13

1. Theological Aim of the Sermon and Strategy

To proclaim Jesus' empathy with us when we are tempted (for He Himself was also tempted) and to celebrate the nature of confession (in a Protestant sense) and how faith is nurtured by it. Justification by Grace and Sanctification are highlighted.

2. Exegesis (see Introduction to Selected Books of the Bible)

• An account of the temptation endured by Jesus at the beginning of His ministry. More details are provided here than in the earlier Markan version (1:12-13).

• Full of the Holy Spirit, Jesus is said to have returned from the Jordan and gone into the wilderness (v. 1).

• He was reportedly tempted for forty days when He ate nothing (v. 2). The devil appears, baiting Him that if He were Son of God He could command a stone to be a loaf of bread (v. 3).

• Jesus responds citing Deuteronomy 8:3 that we do not live by bread alone (v. 4).

• The devil next tempts Jesus with all the world's kingdoms if He will worship the devil (vv. 5-7).

• Jesus responds citing Deuteronomy 6:13 that only the Lord God is to be worshiped and served (v. 8).

• The devil offers a third temptation, taking Jesus to the top of the temple in Jerusalem, instructing Him to jump for (quoting Psalms 91:11-12) if He were Son of God the angels would protect Him (vv. 9-11).

• Jesus responds to the temptation demonstrating His power by quoting Deuteronomy 6:16 that we not put the Lord God to a test (v. 12).

• When the devil had finished every test he departed (v. 13).

3. Theological Insights (see Charts of the Major Theological Options)

• The text puts us in touch with the realities of temptation and Jesus' identification with us in these tests (sin) as well as the good news that the confessed faith by grace overcomes (Justification by Grace).

• Commenting on the Psalm of the Day John Calvin notes,

> *Troubles, it is true, of various kinds assail the believer as well as others, but the Psalmist means that God stands between Him and the violence of every assault, so as to preserve him from being overwhelmed.* (Calvin's Commentaries, Vol. V/2, p. 484)

- Martin Luther claimed that Christ is our best intercessor because He Himself was tempted in our flesh (*What Luther Says*, p. 1347).
- See the references to confession of faith in this section for the previous lessons.
- Regarding how ordinary events of life foreshadow the kingdom, Martin Luther writes:

   [The kingdom comes] Whenever our heavenly Father gives us his Holy Spirit, so that by His grace we may believe His Holy word and live godly lives, both here in time and hereafter in eternity.

   (*The Book of Concord* [Kolb and Wengert, eds.], p. 357)

4. Socio-Economic, Political, Psychological, and Scientific Insights
- With reference to the temptation Jesus endured to gain political power (vv. 5-7), it needs to be noted that political power may be the ultimate temptation, insofar as the ruling ideas of every age are always the ideas of the ruling class. Those with political power get us to want/desire what they say is important. It is their values that tempt the working classes (Alain de Botton, *Status Anxiety*, pp. 209-213).

5. Gimmick
"Gee that's tempting!" How often we say these words, not intending much by them. Yet temptation is one of the boundary situations in life — one of those profound moments in which you and I become who we are. Jesus knows about that. He too was tempted.

6. Possible Sermon Moves and/or Stories/Examples
- What a comfort to know that Jesus, and that through Him, God Himself has endured temptation! Use the third bullet point of Theological Insights. (See Christology in Charts of the Major Theological Options. These Sermon Moves presuppose the Alexandrian Model. Proponents of the Antiochene Model should amend this comment and others accordingly.)
- Our story about Jesus' temptations appears in Matthew (4:1-11), Mark (1:12-13), and Luke. The version assigned to us today, Luke, is a little different from the other two — more realistic with more rough edges.
- Review the three temptations Jesus endures in the third through eighth bullet points of Exegesis — temptations of materialism, of political power, and of sensationalism.
- Regarding the devil's role, we have all experienced him, a sense that the temptations we face are bigger than we are. That's the nature of sin and temptation. They feel bigger than we are.
- Review each of the temptations Jesus endured, identifying with how we face the temptations: (1) To place our own physical comforts and well-being before our commitment to Jesus; (2) To let government's agenda or our own desire for power become more important than the church; and (3) To act as though God owes us a bail out, no matter how careful we have been.
- Jesus really is our spiritual brother. But not only do we have the comfort now of knowing and feeling that He and God the Father understand us in our temptations, Jesus also provides us with a way of overcoming temptation. We can do what He did: "Confess the faith!"
- Review the relevant bullet points in Exegesis. In each case, Jesus dealt with the devil's temptations by confessing the faith (esp. by citing scripture in response).
- Confession. Use Gimmick for Second Lesson and then the third, fifth through seventh, and last bullet points of this section for the Second Lesson.
- Review Augustine's point again: When wicked, displeased with ourselves, and when good simply attributing it all to God. Though Himself word of God, Jesus directs us to the word in our struggle with temptations.

7. Wrap-Up
All of us do indeed face temptation from time to time. But it's not so bad with Jesus at your side. When you confess the faith like He did, you get a lot of companions, happiness (form the pleasurable brain dope), and even Jesus' companionship (for He is the word we are confessing). See the last bullet point of Theological Insights for the Second Lesson. Temptation, unhappiness, loneliness, and oppression don't have a chance!

Lent 2
February 24, 2013

Revised Common	**Genesis 15:1-12, 17-18**	**Philippians 3:17—4:1**	**Luke 13:31-35**
Roman Catholic	**Genesis 15:5-12, 17-18**	**Philippians 3:17—4:1**	**Luke 9:28-36**
Episcopal	**Genesis 15:1-12, 17-18**	**Philippians 3:17—4:1**	**Luke 13:(22-30) 31-35**

Theme of the Day   Hanging around the Lord changes you. This theme meshes with the historic purpose of the Second Sunday in Lent, aiming to call candidates for baptism on Easter to practice purity.

Collect of the Day   After remembering the covenant of God, how the mystery promises everlasting life to the world, petitions are offered that all may be gathered into the Lord's arms, be sheltered with mercy, and be led to celebrate the life we share in Christ. Justification by Grace and Sanctification are maintained.

Psalm of the Day   *Psalm 27*
• An act of devotion and prayer for deliverance attributed to David.
• Begins with a song of trust, expressing confidence that because Yahweh is our salvation and stronghold we need fear no one, for adversaries will fall (vv. 1-3). He will hide and shelter us (v. 5). In this context, the Psalmist vows asking the Lord that he can seek to live in Yahweh's house forever and behold His beauty (v. 4). Promise is made to offer sacrifices in the Lord's tent and sing to Him (v. 6).
• A cry for help follows, pleading for graciousness and that we not be forsaken by the Lord (vv. 7-9).
• Confidence is expressed that even if forsaken by parents the Lord will not (v. 10).
• The Lord is asked to teach us His way and lead on a level path and not to be given over to the will of enemies who are breathing violence (vv. 11-12).
• The Psalmist expresses confidence that he will see the Lord's goodness in life and exhorts waiting for Yahweh and remaining strong (vv. 13-14).

Sermon Text and Title
"God's Promise Never Fails!"
Genesis 15:1-12, 17-18

1. Theological Aim of the Sermon and Strategy
To proclaim the good news that God's promises endure, are not dependent on what we do (Justification by Grace Alone). Some attention is given to the joy of this message and its implications for living faithfully (Sanctification).

2. Exegesis (see Introduction to Selected Books of the Bible)
• The story of the everlasting covenant with Abraham and Sarah as related by J (paralleling and earlier than the version of the call and covenant reported by P in 17:1-7).
• Yahweh appears to Abram in a vision, identifying Himself as Abram's shield and indicating that his reward will be great (v. 1).
• Abram laments that a slave born in his house, Eliezer, is to be his heir, since he has no offspring (vv. 3-4). Yahweh reiterates an earlier promise made to Abram (12:1-2), claiming that he will have true heirs, who shall be as numerous as the stars (15:4b-5).
• Abram is said to have believed the Lord, and it was reckoned to him as righteousness (v. 6).
• Yahweh reminds Abram that He is the one who brought him from Ur of the Chaldees to the Promised Land of Palestine, which he and his offspring were promised to possess (v. 7; cf. 11:31; 12:1). Ur is located in the southern part of modern Iraq. But since the Chaldeans did not occupy it in the early second millennium BC (the likely era Abraham lived) the city's biblical moniker (as belonging to the Chaldees) is likely anachronistic, the results of later editing of an oral tradition. (It is interesting that many of the names of the Abrahamic accounts are found in state archives of the royal house of Ebla, which ruled the region of Ur. This includes Abram's ancestor Eber [11:15-17] whose namesake was a great king of the Ebla dynasty.)
• After asking for assurance that the land promised would be his (15:8), Abraham is instructed to offer a sacrifice by cutting

animals in two (vv. 9-10). Abraham is reported as falling into a deep sleep (v. 12). Verses omitted in the lesson (vv. 13-16) report Yahweh's prophecy that Abram's progeny would live as aliens and slaves, though would return to the Promised Land.
• In the dark that Abram experienced, a smoking fire pot and flaming torch (symbolizing God's presence) appeared and God made His covenant with the chosen one, giving his descendants the land of Palestine (vv. 17-18).

3. Theological Insights (see Charts of the Major Theological Options)
• A text witnessing to Justification by Grace through Faith (the Forensic View) and the unconditional love of God.
• John Wesley noted that God is a shield to His people (v. 1) "to secure them from all destructive evils, a shield ready to them, and a shield round about them, should silence all perplexing fears" (*Commentary on the Bible*, p. 37). John Calvin made a similar point regarding God's care:

> *Moreover, by the use of the word "shield," He signifies that Abram would always be safe under His protection... so let us know that the same blessing is promised to us all, in the person of this one man.* (*Calvin's Commentaries*, Vol. I/2, p. 399)

• This God is a friend, according to Martin Luther:

> *For God speaks with Abraham in a manner that is no different from the way a friend speaks with a close acquaintance and another friend. It is God's practice to do so, and this is His nature. After He has properly afflicted His own, He shows Himself most benevolent and pours Himself out completely.* (*Luther's Works*, Vol. 3, p. 17)

• Wesley also stresses that the text is a witness to Justification by Grace: "If Abraham, who was so rich in good works, was not justified by them, but by his faith, much less can we" (*Commentary on the Bible*, p. 38).
• Calvin made it very clear that it is not faith that made Abraham righteous or saves us:

> *... when Moses says that faith was imputed to Abram for righteousness, he does not mean that faith was the first cause of righteousness, which is called the* efficient, *but only the* formal *cause... For it is especially to be observed, that faith borrows a righteousness elsewhere, of which we, in ourselves, are destitute.* (*Calvin's Commentaries*, Vol. I/1, p. 407)

• Martin Luther notes our need to depend solely on grace due to our own sinful pride:

> *There is nothing this nature of ours is less able to bear than its own honors and God's favors. Consequently, God turns His face away for a little while and leaves man to himself...*
> *God abhors the confidence we have with regard to ourselves. But it is a natural shortcoming that troubles all the saints, especially the greatest. As a result they sin against the first table.*
> (*Luther's Works*, Vol. 3, p. 4)

• The law of God needs to be taught precisely to facilitate this dependence:

> *The law and works do not justify; yet law and works must be taught and performed, in order that we may become aware of our wretched state and accept grace all the more eagerly.* (*Luther's Works*, Vol. 3, p. 26)

• In the same context (exegeting our text) he proceeds to proclaim the constancy of God's promise, despite appearances as Abraham seemed to experience:

> *But this is not because God may have changed His mind... His will to save us through His Son, to whose kingdom He has called us, remains steadfast and unchangeable; but this awareness of this mercy is removed for a time.*
> (*Luther's Works*, Vol. 3, p. 7)

• Regarding the promises of offspring and the nations which would spring from Abraham, Martin Luther wrote:

> *But sacred scripture points out very clearly that eternal and spiritual blessings are included in the material blessings. For we are not created like oxen and asses; we are created for eternity... Moreover, the material promises are like nuts and apples with which we attract children to ourselves. Thus we are led and attracted to the love of eternal things, and the hope of immortality is nourished, so to speak, by the material promises.* (*Luther's Works*, Vol. 3, p. 149)

• Commenting on the Psalm of the Day, John Calvin offers comments to help us understand the significance of God's promises:

> *... whatever benevolence, love, zeal, attention, or service, might be found among men, they are far inferior to the paternal mercy with which God encircles His people... for sooner shall the laws of nature be overturned a hundred times, than God shall fail His people.* (*Calvin's Commentaries*, Vol. IV/2, p. 460)

• Commenting on the covenant with Abraham story, John Calvin claims "there is no other method of living piously and justly, than that of depending on God" (*Calvin's Commentaries*, Vol. I/1, p. 444):

Whence the gratuitous kindness of God shines the more clearly, because, although men impede the cause of it by obstacles of their own, it nevertheless comes to them.

(*Ibid.*, p. 459)

4. Socio-Economic, Political, Psychological, and Scientific Insights
• The American middle-class has been badly squeezed. A 2010 "Annual Report of the White House Task Force on the Middle Class" notes the challenges include expensive child-care obligations, mounting student debt incurred for college costs, failure of middle-class to save adequately for retirement, and the shrinking of the job pool of jobs with adequate salary to provide a middle-class lifestyle. Add to this list we must consider rising health-care costs and inflation. (Today it requires about $486 to purchase what you could buy with $100 in 1973.)
• A 2011 *Time*/Aspen Ideas Festival poll revealed the pessimism that these dynamics have created. Sixty-eight percent of the public believed we are in decline and over half those polled think our children will be worse off than they are today when they become adults.
• A 2010 survey by Erasmus University revealed that America only ranked seventeenth among the happiest nations of the world, far outpaced by Denmark and Switzerland (the winners).
• Research by the Conference Board revealed in 2010 that only 45% of American workers were happy with their jobs.

5. Gimmick
The Second Sunday in Lent: A Sunday historically dedicated to nurturing holiness. What does God's establishment of the covenant with Abraham have to do with this Sunday and with us?

6. Possible Sermon Moves and/or Stories/Examples
• Relate the story with reference to all the bullet points of Exegesis (after the first bullet).
• Yahweh has delivered. His chosen people, the Jews, have their roots in Abraham, and for all the suffering they have endured, they continue to exist, even now in the land Yahweh promised. But it is less clear to American Gentiles that He is delivering on promises today.
• The promises of America, the "American Dream," today seem in shambles. Consider data in the first bullet point of Socio-Economic, Political, Psychological, and Scientific Insights and the second bullet point of that section for the First Lesson, Advent 1.
• In view of these harsh realities, it is little wonder that Americans are not as happy. Use the last three bullet points of Socio-Economic, Political, Psychological, and Scientific Insights. We need confidence, the confidence that comes from a belief that the future is in God's hands and then some excitement and hard work that results from that confidence.
• Suggest to the congregation that we have a witness to that sort of confidence in the future when we read our First Lesson. God has not abandoned the Jewish people, has not reneged on His promise to Abraham. That faithfulness was not contingent on Abraham's goodness.
• Cite commends by John Wesley and John Calvin in the fourth and fifth bullet points of Theological Insights.
• Martin Luther underscores these points, insisting that the reason we need to depend solely on God is that He knows that we are not worthy (keep in mind how we Americans are despairing over our fate, as if we did not deserve it). Don't trust in yourself; trust in God (see sixth bullet point of Theological Insights).
• This is truly a loving God, a shield and a friend. See quotes in the second and third bullet points of Theological Insights.
• Granted, things have not been easy for the Jews over the centuries. Likewise we cannot expect that everything will get better just because we hang around God in faith and rely on Him.

The African-American church has a refrain especially appropriate for us to remember those times (like today) when life does not seem to be going our way. It is said commonly in these circles: "God may not come when you want Him, but He's always on time."
• Use the eighth bullet point of Theological Insights. There is a constancy in God's love that never vanishes — that never gives up on us — no matter how much we go astray.
• When you hang around this loving, forgiving God who wants to make you His (like He made Abraham), much of the anxiety, the unhappiness we noted, gets addressed. It seems that people who spend a lot of time in God's presence are rewarded with the flow of the pleasurable brain chemical dopamine, which leads to happiness (see second bullet point of Socio-Economic, Political, Psychological, and Scientific Insights of Second Lesson, Advent 1).
• Living with God's promise and hanging around the Lord changes you. God's love and the joy that goes with it keeps you going, despite all the hassles, like the Jews have remained faithful despite their ups and downs. Use John Calvin's comments in the last bullet point of Theological Insights. The only way to live with piety and holiness, to live a life in seeking justice,

is in dependence of God, dependent in the graceful kindness that keeps shining no matter how much we try to block it. Also consider Martin Luther's comments in the second bullet point of Theological Insights of Second Lesson, Christmas.

7. Wrap-Up
God's grace and love changed Abraham's life, his destiny, despite all the hang-ups he and his heirs would continue to have. So it is with Christians confident in the fact that God's promise never fails. Then we can say like Martin Luther did when we are struggling with doubts and the tough times in American life:

> *The life of such a person and whatever he does, whether great or small and no matter what it is called, is nothing but fruit and cannot be without fruit... Everything such a person does comes easy for him, not troublesome or vexatious. Nothing is too arduous for him or too difficult to suffer and bear.* (*Luther's Works*, Vol. 24, p. 230)

Sermon Text and Title
"Hanging Around Jesus Changes You"
Philippians 3:17—4:1

1. Theological Aim of the Sermon and Strategy
To proclaim how despite our sin, Christ and the gospel change us (or will change us Eschatologically). Justification by Grace and Sanctification are presented.

2. Exegesis (see Introduction to Selected Books of the Bible)
• An exhortation by Paul urging the reader to imitate him and others who are faithful (3:17).
• Many live as enemies of Christ's Cross (3:18) and their end is destruction, as their bellies are their god (3:19).
• Christians have their homeland in heaven, whence we expect Christ to come (3:20). He will transform our bodies that they may be conformed to the body of His glory by the power that subjects all things to Himself (3:21). Justification as Intimate Union with Christ is suggested here.
• A closing exhortation to beloved readers to stand firm in the land (4:1).

3. Theological Insights (see Charts of the Major Theological Options)
• The text considers sin, Justification by Grace, Sanctification, and Eschatology.
• John Calvin explains the phrase "living as enemies of Christ's Cross" (3:18). This is living by carnal affections, thinking of nothing but the world (*Calvin's Commentaries*, Vol. XXI/2, p. 106).
• Martin Luther while preaching a sermon on this text made a similar point:

> *The world cannot conduct itself in any other way, when the declaration comes from heaven saying: "True you are a holy man, a great and learned jurist... and honorable citizen, and so on, but with all your authority and your upright character you are going to hell; your every act is offensive and condemned in God's sight. If you would be saved you must become an altogether different man; your mind and heart must be changed."* (*Complete Sermons*, Vol. 4/2, p. 349)

• Interpreting the law's role in working wrath (v. 15), Martin Luther writes:

> *Thus the law works wrath, that is, when it is not fulfilled, it shows the wrath of God to those who have failed to provide for its fulfillment.* (*Luther's Works*, Vol. 25, p. 279)

> *For the law, as long as it is without faith which fulfills it, makes all people sinners and establishes the fact they are guilty and thus unworthy of the promise, indeed worthy of wrath and desolation, and in consequence it turns the promise into a threat.* (*Ibid.*, p. 281)

• John Calvin nicely describes how the law leads to sin:

> *For such is the viciousness of our nature, that the more we are taught what is right and just, the more openly is our iniquity discovered.* (*Calvin's Commentaries*, Vol. XIX/2, p. 171)

• He nicely summarizes the faithful's total dependence on grace:

> *... when we are called by the Lord we emerge from nothing; for whatever we seem to be we have not, no not a spark of anything good, which can render us fit for the kingdom of God that we may indeed on the other hand be in a suitable state to hear the call of God, we must be altogether dead in ourselves.* (*Ibid.*, p. 175)

• He proceeds to add: "And this connection of faith with the word ought be well understood and carefully remembered; for faith can bring us nothing more than what it receives from the word" (*Ibid.*, p. 182).

- Luther proceeds to describe faith (what it does and why we need it):

  Faith is a divine work in us which changes us and makes us to be born anew of God, John 1(:12-13)... O, it is a living busy, active mighty thing this faith. It is impossible for it not to be doing good works incessantly... This knowledge of and confidence in God's grace [that faith provides] makes men glad and bold and happy in dealing with God and with all creatures. And this is the work that the Holy Spirit performs in faith. Because of it, without compulsion, a person is ready and glad to do good to everyone, to serve everyone, to suffer everything out of love and praise to God who has shown him this grace.

  (*Luther's Works*, Vol. 35, pp. 370-371)

4. Socio-Economic, Political, Psychological, and Scientific Insights
- Cross-bearing does not seem very popular in America these days. It goes against the grain of our desire for instant gratification. Witness the success of prosperity gospel preaching and the growth of congregations inspired by this ideology.
- Neurobiologists note that concentration on activities activating the frontal lobe of our brains, activities that get us away from acting on our immediate impulses (as presumably happens when we practice some self-denial in bearing crosses) leads to a consistent morality and is pleasurable as more dopamine is released in the brain (Andrew Newberg, *Why We Believe What We Believe*, pp. 187-188).
- Regarding adultery, *Cosmopolitan* magazine reports that 54% of married women have had at least one affair. The Jarvis Report on sexual behavior in America set the figure at 33% for married men. MSNBC had the figure of 21%.
- A Gallup poll conducted over a decade ago indicated that nearly 1 in 3 Americans suffer from low self-esteem.
- The Centers for Disease Control reported in 2008 that 10% of Americans suffer from clinical depression.

5. Gimmick
Read 3:18. Many are enemies of the Cross of Christ.

6. Possible Sermon Moves and/or Stories/Examples
- People don't want anything to do with the Cross of Christ. No surprise. Who of us wants to mess with death and suffering? That's just common sense.
- Elaborate on the first bullet point of Socio-Economic, Political, Psychological, and Scientific Insights.
- We want prosperity so badly because things are not very good in America. Note the last three bullet points of Socio-Economic, Political, Psychological, and Scientific Insights. Also see that section for the First Lesson. Note how a number of these points are occasioned by our desires to live as enemies of the Cross, to make bellies our god (3:18-19). Especially note the third bullet point of Socio-Economic, Political, Psychological, and Scientific Insights; first bullet point of that section for the First Lesson, Advent 2; data in this section for Second Lesson, Christmas.
- Lent is all about coming to terms with our unfaithfulness, with our waywardness, and love for our bellies. This is why we need to hear the Word of condemnation that Paul delivers in our lesson. Use the second through the sixth bullet points of Theological Insights. Especially start with Martin Luther's comments in the third bullet, noting how even the best of people deserve hell and need to become different people, totally changed in heart and mind.
- Paul's good news to the Philippians, to us, is that Christ is coming to transform us, so that we may be conformed to His body (3:21). Hanging around Christ changes you! It leads you to take up Jesus' Cross. Acknowledging our sin, denying our goodness is a kind of cross to bear. Paul and the gospel say that is good for us.
- Crosses in life make us all the more dependent on God's love. It is like the seventeenth-century Scottish clergyman Samuel Rutherford once put it: "How soon would faith freeze without a cross."
- Use the sixth and last bullet points of Theological Insights. John Calvin claims that when called by Christ we emerge from nothing. Around Jesus, nobodies become somebodies. Elaborate on how this confidence nicely addresses the issues of American unhappiness and depression noted in Socio-Economic, Political, Psychological, and Scientific Insights.
- Martin Luther had it right. We can be certain and confident, he said, because we are snatched outside ourselves, so we don't need to depend on ourselves, our strength, conscience, experience, person or works, and can depend on God, on the righteousness He gives, us, which is a lot more certain than we could ever be in ourselves (*Luther's Works*, Vol. 26, p. 387). Faith makes nobodies into somebodies.
- Faith in Christ, hanging around Jesus changes you and makes a difference in how you live your life. Use the last two bullet points of Theological Insights.
- Employ images of marital love transforming us as a way to describe how we are changed by our relation with Jesus. Consider Bernard of Clairviaux in the eighth bullet point of Theological Insights for the Gospel, Transfiguration and also images of Martin Luther in the fifth bullet point of this section of the Second Lesson of Christmas 1; second bullet point of Theological Insights for Second Lesson, Christmas (where he makes the case for not needing to be guided by the law).

7. Wrap-Up
No two ways about. We need to be changed in America in order to get out of the messes we are. Hanging around Jesus does it for us, transforms us into folks not willing to fall prey to the ways of the world, confident and secure enough to live with joy and for the good of others. (One could elaborate on the mental health this style of life offers by reflecting on the second bullet point of Socio-Economic, Political, Psychological, and Scientific Insights.) Hanging around Jesus changes you.

Sermon Text and Title
"The Gospel Says No to What We Love"
Luke 13:31-35

1. Theological Aim of the Sermon and Strategy
To proclaim a vision of the Christian life (Sanctification) that helps the faithful to find the golden mean between denying the things of the world and still using God's good creation for purposes God intended them.

2. Exegesis (see Introduction to Selected Books of the Bible)
- Jesus' message to Herod and His lament over Jerusalem.
- Having offered prophecies about the end of the age (vv. 22-30), some Pharisees urge Jesus to escape for Herod reportedly planned to kill Him (v. 31).
- Jesus refers to Herod as a "fox," that He will continue His work of healing but would finish on the third day (v. 32). Jesus seems to imply that Herod is cunning; reference to the third day may foreshadow His time in the tomb.
- Jesus says on the third day He will leave, because as a prophet He cannot be killed outside of Jerusalem (v. 33).
- Lamenting over Jerusalem Jesus bewails how it is a city that has killed the prophets. He would gather its children as a hen with her brood, but the town's citizens have been unwilling (v. 34). Jerusalem is left to its citizens, but they will not see Him until the time comes and they will bless Him (v. 35). Perhaps this prefigures the Palm Sunday Procession.

3. Theological Insights (see Charts of the Major Theological Options)
- The text can be construed as a depiction of the Christian life (Sanctification) as being "in the world, but not of it."
- Commenting on verse 34, John Calvin noted that "whenever the word of God is exhibited to us, He [God] opens His bosom to us with maternal kindness, and not satisfied with this, condescends to the humble affection of a *hen* watching over her *chicks*" (*Calvin's Commentaries*, Vol. XVII/1, p. 107).
- New Testament scholar Eduard Schweizer regards the texts as a critique of religious institutions, which like Jerusalem (v. 34), think they know all there is to know of God (*The Good News According to Luke*, pp. 231-232).
- At a number of points Martin Luther spoke of the Christian life as a walking of the golden mean between affirming the legitimate pleasures of the goods of the earth and their rejection. A great lover of music, he claimed that "next to the word of God, music deserves the highest praise..." (*Luther's Works*, Vol. 53, p. 223). And he saw in the behavior of dogs a model for how we should love God (*Luther's Works*, Vol. 54, p. 175). He was a wine lover too (*Luther's Works*, Vol. 54, pp. 71-72). Christians can enjoy the things of life with gladness:

> *Thus a Christian man who lives in this confidence toward God knows all things, can do all things, ventures everything that needs to be done, and does everything gladly and willingly.* (*Luther's Works*, Vol. 44, p. 27)

- Perhaps the very best comment the first Reformer offered on this matter of our openness and attitude to the goods of the earth appeared in 1523. He wrote:

> *As we have heard, a sincere Christian believer has all the possessions of God and is a child of God. The time of his life, however, is but a pilgrimage. For through faith the spirit is already in heaven... but God permits him to remain alive in the flesh and lets his body walk the earth in order that [a person] may help others and bring them to heaven too. Therefore we must use everything on earth in no other way than as a guest who travels across country, comes to an inn where he must spend the night, and takes nothing but food and lodging from the innkeeper. Thus we must also deal with temporal goods as if they did not belong to us.* (*Luther's Works*, Vol. 30, p. 35)

- John Wesley nicely describes what is entailed in taking up the Cross:

> *And every one that would follow Christ, that would be His real disciple, must not only deny himself, but take up His cross also. A cross is anything contrary to our will, anything displeasing to our nature.* (*Works* Vol. 6, p. 108)

- Augustine reminds us that Jesus' directive to take up the cross and follow Him is not hard or grievous, because He aids us (*Nicene and Post-Nicene Fathers*, First Series, Vol. 6, p. 408). Further elaborating on the meaning of this directive,

Augustine adds: "The world is loved; but let Him be preferred by whom the world was made. Great is the world; but sweeter is He by Whom the world was made" (*Ibid.*, p. 410).

4. Socio-Economic, Political, Psychological, and Scientific Insights
- Jesus' critique of the powers that He invites American Christians to consider are that people and institutions have too much and need to be challenged. A 2011 Gallup poll found that Americans rate lobbyists and major corporations (along with banks and financial institutions) as the entities with the most invalid power in America. When we note that lobbyists spent $3.5 billion in 2010 (not much higher than in the previous five years) and that in 2010 the top 25 U.S. corporations had a 63% increase in profits (while the top 1% of Americans control 42% of our wealth), it seems that perceptions of these entities' undue power is on target.
- The cult of self-fulfillment is still alive and well in America. This is made evident in a 2009 Gallup poll demonstrating that 3 in 5 Americans find divorce and sex outside of marriage morally acceptable. Most Americans also found having a baby outside marriage morally acceptable. Doing what feels good outweighs long-term commitments.

5. Gimmick
Depending on the region in which the sermon is given, note how being a Christian is not in the mainstream, makes you a bit of an oddball (on the east and west coasts). In other regions, note how although being a church-goer may be typical, it is not that way elsewhere in the nation. The historic theme of the Second Lesson in Lent (purity) does not make it easy to present Christian faith as an attractive option to the American public preoccupied with self-fulfillment or individual well being. (Note third bullet point of Socio-Economic, Political, Psychological, and Scientific Insights for data on the per durance of the cult of self-fulfillment in America.)

6. Possible Sermon Moves and/or Stories/Examples
- Highlight the theme of the Second Sunday in Lent (see Theme of Day). This theme is evident in today's Second Lesson and its call for our faithfulness to Christ's Cross, to realize that our homeland is in heaven and not in the things of earth (Philippians 3:17-19). Then note how this theme reflects in the gospel, as Jesus prophesies the destruction of Jerusalem, even of the temple (vv. 34-35).
- Note the significance of this bold prediction. For an ancient Hebrew, Jerusalem represented the epitome of civilization, all the good things in life. It was the place to go for action and not unlike how we think of Times Square and Manhattan.
- This helps frame Jesus' prophecy. To prophesy destruction of Jerusalem and its temple was like predicting a destruction or denial of the good life, of the good things in life. Was Jesus advocating an other-worldly, life-denying asceticism that simply will not wash in our context?
- Other examples of this theme appear elsewhere in Luke's version of Jesus. He is reported to have told His disciples to sell all their possessions and give away what was earned from their sale (12:33-34). Jesus seems critical of earthly goods and riches. So often He issued criticism of the rich and wealthy (6:24; 18:24-25).
- Is the life of a monk, giving up all earthly goods, the only way to live as a Christian? Is this what Jesus demands? Or perhaps those denominations that stress holiness and striving for perfection are more on target with Jesus' way. In fact, Jesus' way is a life-affirming way!
- We see this in Jesus' passions about Jerusalem expressed in the gospel story. Luke says He laments over Jerusalem (vv. 33-34). He loves Jerusalem! He would gather it under His wings like a hen with her brood! Elaborate on the second bullet point of Theological Insights. When we recall what Jerusalem connoted for the ancient Hebrew it is clear that Jesus loves the things of the world. Do not forget where He performed His first miracle — at a wedding (John 2:1-12). They are part of God's good creation!
- The First Lesson echoes this point. Note that the covenant God made with Abraham had to do with physical things – with children and the promise of land (Genesis 12:2-3, 7; 15:4-5, 18). Our Second Lesson makes a similar point, and the good things of the earth do not contaminate, that we need not renounce them. For Paul makes clear that even in heaven we will still have bodies (Philippians 3:21)!
- No, the things of the earth are not evil. Christians are people who know how to use them in the right way, to say "no" to them without rejecting them. Use the quotation by Augustine in the last bullet point of Theological Insights.
- In a way Christianity is a relation of the golden mean. We teach that God is three in one — both. Likewise we say that Jesus is two in one, human and divine. The golden mean. Push one side of the pole too hard and you lose the other. You need to affirm both.
- So it is with the things of the earth. Say "no" to them (never put them above God) but do not think they are evil. They can

be affirmed and even used. They are good in themselves, given by God but we risk our purity before God when we make them too important.

• Cite points by Martin Luther to make these points. Note the fourth bullet point of Theological Insights. Christians can do all things with gladness. The Christian life is a life-affirming mode of existence.

• Note Luther's image of the goods of the earth as the motel in which we stay on our travels. Use the fifth bullet point of Theological Insights. We do not own the things we have. They belong to God.

7. Wrap-Up

Relate the previous point to Justification by Grace Through Faith to the idea that all we have is a gift of God. This insight frees us up to use and enjoy earthly goods and pleasures, to enjoy and use them in all purity. Earthly goods are such pleasures when we use them with deference to their owner — to God. All we have is God and that insight makes the things of the earth different!

Lent 3
March 3, 2013

Revised Common	Isaiah 55:1-9	1 Corinthians 10:1-13	Luke 13:1-9
Roman Catholic	Exodus 3:1-8	1 Corinthians 1-6, 10-12	Luke 13:1-9
Episcopal	Exodus 3:1-15	1 Corinthians 10:1-13	Luke 13:1-9

Theme of the Day — Turn around and bear fruit! God will see to it. This theme meshes with the historic purpose of the Third Sunday in Lent, at which time in the ancient church candidates for baptism on Easter were given careful scrutiny.

Collect of the Day — Noting that God's kingdom has broken into our troubled world through Christ's death and resurrection, petitions are offered that we might hear and obey His word, bringing God's saving love to fruition in our lives. Again an emphasis on Predestination, Justification (by Grace), and Sanctification is evident.

Psalm of the Day *Psalm 63:1-8*

• Personal lament: a prayer for deliverance from personal enemies. Though attributed to David, *Elohim* is used to name God, rather than Yahweh.
• The Psalmist claims to thirst for God. He is sought in the sanctuary, where His power and glory can be beheld (vv. 1-2).
• God's steadfast love is said to be better than life. Consequently the Psalmist will praise Him, lifting up hands to call His name (vv. 3-4).
• With a satisfied soul the Psalmist joyfully praises God, for He has been a help, with a right hand that upholds Him (vv. 5-8).

Sermon Text and Title
"Heads Up You Backsliders: The Lord Is Moving On!"
Isaiah 55:1-9

1. Theological Aim of the Sermon and Strategy
To proclaim our sin, the need for repentance and the confidence we can have in God, who because of His very nature as Yahweh, is a God who forgives and keeps working on us for the better. Justification by Grace through Faith and Sanctification are then also proclaimed.

2. Exegesis
• A hymn of joy and triumph celebrating the approaching consummation of Israel's restoration written by Deutero-Isaiah in the sixth century BC near the coming end of the Babylonian Captivity.
• An invitation is made to a banquet (reminiscent of the banquet hosted by wisdom in Proverbs 9:3-6). Everyone who is thirsty and is poor is invited and challenges those who spend money that does not feed us. We should only eat what is good (vv. 1-2).
• Reference is made to the everlasting covenant with David, which the nations shall note because Yahweh has glorified the people. A renewal of this covenant seems promised (vv. 3-5).
• A call for repentance is issued, for when the people return to the Lord He may have mercy on them (v. 7).
• Yahweh proceeds to remark that His thoughts and ways are not the ways and thoughts of the people (v. 8-9).

3. Theological Insights (see Charts of the Major Theological Options)
• The text addresses the need for repentance (including our sin and neediness), but also proclaims the fulsome mercy of the Lord (Yahweh) (Justification by Grace).
• John Calvin noted powerfully the misery in which we find ourselves:

> *Those who are puffed up with vain confidence and are satiated, or who, intoxicated by earthly appetites, do not feel thirst of soul, will not receive Christ.* (*Calvin's Commentaries*, Vol. VIII/2, p. 156)

- Commenting on the text's meaning, Martin Luther directs us to "See how violently he [Isaiah] condemns every righteousness and all efforts and expenditures apart from grace" (*Luther's Works*, Vol. 17, p. 251).
- John Wesley nicely explains why God has the authority to issue commands:

> *Because God is the Lord, Jehovah, self-existent, independent, eternal, and the fountain of all being and power. Therefore He has an incontestable right to command us.* (*Commentary on the Bible*, p. 77)

- Calvin proceeded to praise God's graciousness:

> *He [Isaiah] shews that we are poor and utterly destitute, and that we have nothing by which we can become entitled to God's favour; but that He kindly invites us, in order that He may freely bestow everything without any recompense.* (*Calvin's Commentaries*, Vol. VIII/2, p. 157)

- All this including our repentance is God's work: "Besides, God does not command us to return to Him before He has applied a remedy to revolt…" (*Calvin's Commentaries*, Vol. VIII/2, p. 167):

> *When men despair or doubt as to obtaining pardon, they usually become more hardened and obstinate; but when they feel that God is merciful, this draws and converts them.* (*Calvin's Commentaries*, Vol. VIII/2, p. 170)

- Regarding the repentance called for, John Wesley noted, "Thirsteth. For the grace and the blessings of the gospel. This thirst implies a vehement, active, and restless desire after it" (*Commentary on the Bible*, p. 336).

4. Socio-Economic, Political, Psychological, and Scientific Insights
- The text refers to invitations to those who hunger and thirst (v. 1). We continue to be in dire straights regarding hunger. Worldwide, 925 million people were starving according to 2010, almost 1 in 7 of the 7 billion on the globe.
- In the U.S., over 10% of American households had low food security in 2008, a figure that has likely climbed since the recession.

5. Gimmick
Assume the character of a non church-goer with no use for the church, criticizing the hypocrites. Do the same with one who attends, but does little else, or one who attends but says he/she has done enough.

6. Possible Sermon Moves and/or Stories/Examples
- The First Lesson speaks of a banquet to which we are invited with lots of good food. Even those thirsty and poor, those who had been exiled in Babylon as a result of their (or their ancestors') unfaithfulness were made welcome (vv. 1-2). God makes a place for the undeserving, provides more than His people deserve!
- Our other lessons make similar points: In the Second Lesson, Paul warns the Corinthians to watch out, to avoid sin, lest they think they are so good they can't fall, the mistake made earlier by the Jewish people in Old Testament times (1 Corinthians 10:7-12). And in the gospel, Jesus calls on His flock to bear fruit (Luke 13:6-9).
- Ask the congregation if they are measuring up enough, doing enough to be worthy of God's goodness. Suggest that they/we might be as much backsliders as the three characters to whom you introduced the congregation at the sermon's outset. Elaborate on the similarities, regarding how often we judge others negatively or falsely and pharasaically claim we have done enough for God when in fact we have not really done that much.
- Use the second and third bullet points of Theological Insights to point out how far we have fallen short, how vainly and falsely confident we are in our own righteousness. Martin Luther offers a classical statement about the nature of sin, how it permeates all we do, and even in our outwardly good deeds.

> *For man cannot but seek his own advantages and love himself above all things. And this is the sum of all his iniquities. Hence even in good things and virtues men seek themselves, that is, they seek to please themselves and applaud themselves.* (*Luther's Works*, Vol. 25, p. 222)

- God is putting an end to this self-seeking narcissism. He calls us to repentance (v. 7), to becoming totally dependent on Him. He makes it so that even our repentance is His work. (Use sixth and seventh bullet points of Theological Insights.)
- Why does God operate this way? Why is He so accepting of us and our foibles? Our lesson reminds us that the ways and thoughts of the Lord are not our ways, that His ways and thoughts are higher than ours (vv. 8-9). His awesome holiness is so much greater than our goodness. That is why we cannot possibly measure up to Him.
- But God for all His awesome holiness will not give up on us, invites us to His banquet, and provides salvation for us. He calls on you and me to something better. Why? How are His thoughts and ways so higher than ours? It has to do with His nature, revealed in this lesson by His name — Yahweh.

- Review the meaning of the Hebrew word "Yahweh." It is literally translated "I am who I am." Note how in ancient Hebrew present tense and future tense are identical. Consequently Yahweh's name can as easily be translated "I will be who I will be."
- Unpack the implications of this linguistic turn: It entails that Yahweh is a God who is not static, not done creating. He is a God who is still making Himself, because it is His very nature to keep moving on! To know who God is, you need to look ahead to what happens in history.
- No. God is not done creating and that means that He is not through with us. That is why He cannot tolerate our selfishness and failure to bear fruit. To tolerate it would be a denial of His forward-looking nature.
- Too often like the two church-goers we met at the beginning of this sermon we think we are doing enough. Too often we put off changing our lives because we tell ourselves things are good enough. Get the congregation to recognize that the next time they think this way, they should remember that these are not the ways of our Lord, Yahweh (vv. 8-9), that He is a God full of mercy, a God who moves on and will not leave us alone in our sloth, selfishness, and laziness.

7. Wrap-Up

We have a God named Yahweh, a God who is constantly about the business of doing new good. This is a God who will make us thirsty, instill in us a restless desire and a hunger for Him, a desire and hunger to bear Him fruit. (Consider again the last bullet point of Theological Insights.) Head's up all backsliders. That God, the Lord, is moving on!

Sermon Text and Title
"Nobody's Too Good to Repent"
1 Corinthians 10:1-13

1. Theological Aim of the Sermon and Strategy

To proclaim our sin and the need for repentance but with understanding that we are totally dependent on God if we are to be turned around (Justification by Grace).

2. Exegesis (see Introduction to Selected Books of the Bible)

- Warning against overconfidence.
- Paul reminds the Corinthians that the Hebrew ancestors were all under the cloud (the presence of God [Exodus 13:21]) and passed through the sea and were "baptized" by these means (vv. 1-2; cf. Exodus 14:22). They also drank and ate from the same spiritual food and drink (vv. 3-4; Exodus 16:4; 17:6; Numbers 20:7-11). Reference here is to imply that they received something like baptism and the Lord's Supper.
- Despite the favored status of the ancient Hebrews, Paul reports God's displeasure with most of them, striking them down in the wilderness (v. 5; Numbers 14:24-30). This is an example for the Corinthians to deter their desire for evil (v. 6).
- Paul then urges the Corinthians to shun idolatry and sexual immorality, not to put Christ to the test and not to complain as many did (vv. 7-10). The evil that happened to them is an example (v. 11).
- If we think we are standing we must watch out lest we fall (v. 12). No testing overtakes us that is not common to all. For God is faithful and will not let us be tested beyond our strength. The testing provides the way out for endurance (v. 13).

3. Theological Insights (see Charts of the Major Theological Options)

- The text warns of sin and the need for repentance (Justification by Grace).
- Consider bullet points 2-5 as well as the last two bullets in Theological Insights for the First Lesson. For more on the nature of sin, see the last bullet point of this section for First Lesson, Ash Wednesday.
- Pope Benedict XVI has spoken on how any change in our lives is the result of grace:

    He [God] has loved us first, and He continues to do so; we too, then, can respond with love... He loves us, He makes us see and experience His love, and since He has "loved us first," love can also blossom as a response within us.
    (*God Is Love*, pp. 42-43)

- Famed theologian of the early church Clement of Alexandria wrote of repentance: "Repentance, then is an effect of faith. For unless a man believes that to which he was addicted to be sin, he will not abandon it..." (*Ante-Nicene Fathers*, Vol. 2, p. 353).
- John Calvin notes in connection with this text that we are totally dependent on God and likely to fall prey to problems if we are not. He wrote: "... a temptation, however, slight it may be, will straightway overcome us, and all will be over with us, if we rely upon our own strength" (*Calvin's Commentaries*, Vol. XX/1, p. 332).

- In much the same spirit, Calvin's sixteenth-century protégé John Knox wrote of repentance:

    ... to provoke in Godis electe a hatred of synne, and unfeyned repentaunce of the same; which cause, yf it were rightuouslie considred, were sufficient to make all spirituall and corporall troubles tollerable unto us. (*Works*, Vol. 3, p. 125)

- Famed modern theologian (a martyr in the Hitler persecution of his opponents) Dietrich Bonhoeffer described the outcome of repentance:

    Let us leave this... repentance worship service not with despondent hearts, but with joyous and believing hearts. Come judgment day — joyfully we wait for you since we shall see the merciful Lord and take His hand and He will love us. (*A Testament of Faith*, p. 230)

4. Socio-Economic, Political, Psychological, and Scientific Insights
- Regarding the text's reference to sexual immorality (v. 8), see the first bullet point of this section for the Second Lesson, Christmas; second bullet point of this section for the First Lesson, Epiphany 1; Second Lesson, Lent 2; last bullet point of this section for Gospel, Lent 2. For a detailed summary of the best image-shattering scientific data and bibliography regarding homosexuality, google my article on homosexuality in *Lutheran Forum* (2009).

    There is plenty of data regarding American idolatry (v. 7), evident in our materialism. See the second bullet point of this section for the Second Lesson and Gospel, Advent 2; Second Lesson, Christmas; fourth bullet point of this section for the First Lesson, Transfiguration.
- On Americans' unwillingness to recognize their sinfulness and need for repentance, see this section for the Second Lesson, Epiphany 4. The optimism most Americans have about our role in saving ourselves bespeaks a failure to acknowledge our sinful nature.

5. Gimmick
Explain the historic significance of the Third Sunday in Lent. This is a Sunday for us to scrutinize ourselves. Ask the congregation to consider how we are doing as Christians.

6. Possible Sermon Moves and/or Stories/Examples
- The portion of Paul's First Letter to the Corinthians read today gives us some clues for evaluating ourselves on the question of how we are doing as Christians. The answer: not very good.
- Review how Paul finds the Hebrews to have sinned, even though they had received signs of God's love, like Christians do today (vv. 3-6). Have the congregation consider that if the devoted followers of Moses sinned, is it any surprise that we sin too?
- Note our guilt on the issues Paul warned — idolatry and sexual immorality (vv. 7-8). Use the first bullet point of Socio-Economic, Political, Psychological, and Scientific Insights.
- No way we can avoid the concerns Paul raises, even those of us not caught up in the materialism and sexual license we have considered. Cite quotes in the last bullet point of Theological Insights for the First Lesson, Ash Wednesday, pointing out how we sin in all we do. Even love is self-serving and addictive; consider the data in Socio-Economic, Political, Psychological, and Scientific Insights for the First Lesson, Ash Wednesday.
- The health of our faith depends on recognizing these realities. (See second bullet point of Theological Insights for the First Lesson.) No two ways about it: We need to repent.
- Repentance is nothing more than a hatred of sin, not liking where we are headed with our selfishness and acquisitiveness. That all God wants. And we don't even have to do it. God's love, God's grace, does it for us. Use the third through sixth bullet points of Theological Insights.
- Ask the congregation what happens to you when sin is renounced in this way. It does not make you perfect. It does not mean that there will not still be temptations, that all the selfishness and all the materialism will vanish (v. 13). Use the quotation by Dietrich Bonhoeffer in the final bullet point of Theological Insights. Repentance leads to joy, because we know that God is taking us in His hand to change us, even if not every problem is solved.
- Use John Knox's quote in next-to-last bullet point of Theological Insights. When you know you are in God's hand, everything is tolerable.

7. Wrap-Up
Ask the congregation again if they wonder how they are doing, if they have the strength to withstand the temptations and tough things in life. Remind them of our God who is there to take each of us in His hand, to turn us around and never to let us go.

Sermon Text and Title
"Quit Trying to Figure Out Why"
Luke 13:1-9

1. Theological Aim of the Sermon and Strategy
To proclaim our sin and the need for repentance, but with understanding that we are all equally sinful and totally dependent on God if we are to be turned around (Justification by Grace and Providence).

2. Exegesis (see Introduction to Selected Books of the Bible)
• Jesus' teaching on repentance and the parable of the fig tree.
• Jesus receives reports that some Galileans had been slain by Pilate while worshipping in the temple (v. 1).
• Jesus responds, in contrast to prevailing Jewish attitudes of the day, that those slain were no worse sinners (v. 2). His hearers must repent or they will perish like these Galileans (v. 3). He makes the same point in reference to victims of a collapse of a tower in the Siloam section of Jerusalem (vv. 4-5). "Jesus rules out the dogma that particular indiscretions lead to particular disasters" (Eduard Schweizer, *The Good News According to Luke*, p. 219).
• In the parable Jesus relates a tale of a man with a fig tree which had borne no fruit (v. 6). He instructs His gardener to cut it down (v. 7). But the gardener pleads for time to fertilize it with manure, cutting it down if it fails to yield fruit (vv. 8-9).

3. Theological Insights (see Charts of the Major Theological Options)
• The text warns of sin and the need for repentance (Justification by Grace) by all, with reference to God's mysterious, hidden ways (Providence).
• Dietrich Bonhoeffer offers a penetrating observation about Jesus' main point in this text:

> ... He [Jesus] is telling them to stop all their guessing, their interpreting, their judging, and to put an end to their know-it-all attitude... So for Jesus this distressing newspaper report about the terrible events in the temple is nothing other than God's renewed, unmistakable call to those who hear it to repent and change their ways.   (*A Testament of Hope*, p. 244)

> From now on our situation will become dangerous. We are no longer spectators, observers, judges of these events. Now we ourselves the ones addressed, we are the ones affected.   (*A Testament of Hope*, p. 245)

• For more on the nature of sin, see the last bullet point of this section for First Lesson, Ash Wednesday.
• In his famed Heidelberg Disputation the Reformer wrote: "4. Although the works of God are always unattractive and appear evil, they are nevertheless really eternal merits" (*Luther's Works*, Vol. 31, p. 39). "20. He deserves to be called a theologian, however, who comprehends the visible and manifest things of God seen through suffering and the cross" (*Ibid.*, p. 40).
• Søren Kierkegaard often spoke of the paradoxical character of Christian faith, which is a function of the fact this it is a religion in which "the eternal truth and existence are placed in juxtaposition with one another." It creates objective and uncertainty and throws the believer back to his or her subjectivity (*Concluding Unscientific Postscript*, pp. 186-187). In fact, the audacious Christian claim that "the eternal truth has come into being in time, that God has come into being, has been born, has grown up, and so forth, precisely like any other human being" is said to be absurd (*Ibid.*, p. 188).
• Karl Barth echoes the great existentialist in speaking of the apparent absurdity of faith: "The Bible may seem absurd to us because it is not about us but about God" (*Word of God & Word of Man*, p. 43).
• Martin Luther sees in this foolishness a paradoxical God who hides Himself in a wonderful love, which paradoxically does not seek pleasure but is totally generous and giving:

> *23. The love of God does not find, but creates, that which is pleasing to it. [But] The love of man comes into being through that which is pleasing to it.*   (*Luther's Works*, Vol. 31, p. 41)

• This paradoxical, seemingly absurd love of God changes us, makes us attractive:

> *Rather than seeking its own good, the love of God flows forth and bestows good. Therefore sinners are attractive because they are loved; they are not loved because they are attractive.*   (*Ibid.*, p. 57)

4. Socio-Economic, Political, Psychological, and Scientific Insights
• A 2009 Pew Forum poll showed that nearly 1 in 5 American adults have no affiliation with organized religion. Presumably Christianity is crazy for many, if not most of them.

5. Gimmick

Note the latest natural catastrophe or crime in the community in which an apparently innocent party was victimized. Ask if the victims got what they deserved.

6. Possible Sermon Moves and/or Stories/Examples

• Jesus was addressing exactly this point in our Gospel Lesson today (v. 1). His conclusion: The events of history are not examples of God singling out the greatest sinners in order to settle the score with them (v. 2). Yet there is a sense in which we deserve the evil we get.

• Elaborate further, using the third bullet point of Exegesis. Add the second bullet point in Theological Insights, to make clear that the story is addressed to us and that Jesus is warning us about the need to repent, guessing about why bad things happen to people is a pointless activity and lots less important than tending to our own precarious, sinful situation.

• No two ways about it: We need to repent. Why? We sin in all we do.

• Introduce Jennifer Jones (a woman in the congregation who represents/exhibits the congregation's demographic profile for women). She is a regular attender in worship. Also introduce the community pillar Max Hartman (happily married, successful, representing the demographic of successful men in the broader community). Use the last bullet point of Theological Insights of the First Lesson, Ash Wednesday. Point out the concepts of concupiscence and selfishness to make the case that we cannot avoid sin.

• Return to Jennifer and Max, showing how selfishness undergoes Max's community service, how he likes the power and good feelings he gets helping people. Point out Jennifer's enjoyment of her reputation in town as a religious, nice, caring person. No two ways about it: Jennifer and Max sin in the very best of their deeds. It is like Martin Luther once wrote:

> *For man cannot but seek his own advantages and love himself about all things... Hence even in good things and virtues men seek themselves that is they seek to please themselves and applaud themselves... I say now that no one should doubt that all our good works are mortal sins.* (*Luther's Works*, Vol. 25, p. 222)

• Jesus uses the parable of the fig tree to call us to repentance, to bear fruit (vv. 6-9). Relate it to congregation. Use the sixth bullet point of this section for the Second Lesson, highlighting that repentance is nothing more than hating sin, that is all God's work.

• From this perspective, confident that having repented we are in God's hands (see last bullet point of Theological Insights for the Second Lesson), gives us assurance in considering the bad things that happen in life.

• Ultimately the bad things that happen to people have something to do with sin; they are punishments. But only in paradoxical, hidden ways and so we may as well quit trying to figure them out. Consider the fifth and fourth bullet points of Theological Insights. About all we can say is that the ways of God are a mystery and that the bad things in life somehow are a function of sin and can be used to wake us up and turn us around, though they're not what God wants.

• Perhaps we could think about God's governance over the bad things like a renowned band leader of a less talented band (Arthur Peacocke, as reported in Larry Witham, *Where Darwin Meets the Bible*, pp. 48, 288). The band leader is in control, the concert will happen and conclude successfully, but sometimes bad notes get hit, which ruin certain songs. That is how evil impacts the evils of nature. But just as a bad song can be an incentive to the performer to play the next ones better, so bad things can be an incentive to use to change.

• Cite the comments by Martin Luther in the last two bullet points of Theological Insights. God paradoxically uses the bad things that happen in nature to wake us up, and then continues to act paradoxically in the way He loves us not looking for good things in us, but making us something good.

7. Wrap-Up

This is what God does to us. He works through the bad things in life (especially the Cross) that He makes us attractive, not so much by making us better, but by His love for us. With that outlook on life, no need to try to figure out everything else!

Lent 4
March 10, 2013

Revised Common	Joshua 5:9-12	2 Corinthians 5:16-21	Luke 15:1-3, 11b-32
Roman Catholic	Joshua 5:9-12	2 Corinthians 5:17-21	Luke 15:1-3, 11-32
Episcopal	Joshua (4:19-24) 5:9-12	2 Corinthians 5:17-21	Luke 15:11-32

Theme of the Day   Rejoice: God saves us by his grace! Historically this Sunday in Lent was called *Laetare* (rejoicing Sunday), a time to relieve the austerities of Lent with a mood of celebration.

Collect of the Day   After praising God for His compassion and welcoming of the wayward, petitions are offered that we might be clothed with grace by our baptisms and be fed at the table of love by Christ. Justification (by Grace) and sacraments' role as a means of grace are emphasized.

Psalm of the Day   *Psalm 32*
• A personal Psalm of praise for healing, attributed to David. It is a Maskill, an artful song.
• Those whose transgression is forgiven are said to be happy (vv. 1-2). Since disease was regarded as punishment for sin, healing was regarded as testimony to forgiveness.
• The Psalmist describes his experience, construing his illness as God's work (vv. 3-4).
• The healing began after acknowledgment of the sin (v. 5).
• The Psalmist commends a similar faith to the congregation. We should offer prayer to the Lord when in distress. The wicked are tormented but steadfast love surrounds those who trust in the Lord (vv. 6-10).
• We are to be glad in the Lord and righteous (v. 11).

Sermon Text and Title
"A Fresh Look at Passover"
Joshua 5:9-12

1. Theological Aim of the Sermon and Strategy
To proclaim God's concern for freedom and liberation for the poor (Justification by Grace and Social Ethics, with a Preferential Option for the poor).

2. Exegesis
• One of the so-called post-Pentateuch historical books, Joshua tells the story of Israel's successful settlement in Canaan. It shares the theological perspective of Deuteronomy (see the analysis of its main points in Introduction to Selected Books of the Bible), and so may be a product of the seventh century BC reforms of King Josiah, though it clearly has roots in earlier oral local traditions about the settlement.
• Main Sections: (1) Introduction — describing Israel's entry into Canaan (1-5); (2) Conquest of the land that portrays the conquest as complete, as it purports to portray Israel at its obedient best (6-12); (3) Apportionment of the land to the tribes, sometimes reflecting a tension between land the tribes actually possessed and land they sought (13-19); and (4) Conclusion — including acts of Joshua, his farewell, and the covenant at Shechem (20-24).
• An account of the first Passover spent by the Hebrews in the Promised Land.
• Yahweh said to Joshua that on that day He had rolled away from the Hebrews the disgrace of Egypt (v. 9). Commemoration of the Passover in the Holy Land is described (v. 10).
• Apparently they had begun to farm the land and when that happened, the manna from heaven that had fed them stopped (vv. 11-12).

3. Theological Insights (see Charts of the Major Theological Options)
• A Christian reinterpretation of the Passover in light of compatibilities with its original Jewish meaning as a festival of freedom. As such the text can be read as a testimony to Justification by Grace and political freedom (Social Ethics).
• Early twentieth-century British rabbi Morris Joseph claimed that "Passover affirms the great truth that liberty is the inalienable right of every human being." It is "God's protest against unrighteousness, whether individual or national."

- Though the Jewish heritage clearly construes the Passover in view of its Social Ethical significance, there is a tradition in rabbinic literature of applying the festival to issues of individual spiritual freedom. Modern rabbis Arthur Waskow and Phyllis Berman write:

    And the issues [of the Passover Story] are not only macro-political, but apply also to the spiritual and psychological struggles of individual human beings confronting their own "internal pharaohs," when one aspect of the self takes over the whole person, twisting and perverting a person's humanity by turning other facets of the self into slaves that yearn for freedom and full integration.

- Like much of the Christian tradition, Martin Luther understood Christ as the fulfillment of the Passover, leading us out of the Egypt of death's and sin's captivity (*Luther's Works*, Vol. 13, p. 355).
- Luther offered a profound comment about Christian freedom:

    From this anyone can clearly see how a Christian is free from all things and over all things so that he needs no works to make him righteous and save him, since faith alone abundantly confers all these things.   (*Luther's Works*, Vol. 31, p. 356)

4. Socio-Economic, Political, Psychological, and Scientific Insights
- It is estimated that 12.3 million are enslaved today worldwide, in various surreptitious forms.
- Other examples of oppression are found in the first bullet point of this section for the First Lesson, Advent 3.
- Martin Luther King Jr.'s comments on freedom are most relevant for this text:

    … the essence of man is found in freedom. This is what Paul Tillich means when he declares, "Man is man because he is free," or what Tolstoy implies when he says, "I cannot conceive of a man not being free unless he is dead"… There is nothing in the world greater than freedom. It is worth paying for; it is worth losing a job; it is worth going to jail for.

    (*A Testament of Hope*, pp. 120, 144)

- Proponents of black theology (National Committee of Black Churchmen) add a similar affirmation, relating this sort of freedom to the essence of the gospel:

    The message of liberation is the revelation of God as revealed in the incarnation of Jesus Christ. Freedom IS the gospel. Jesus is the liberator!   (Milton Sernett, ed., *Afro-American Religious History* [1985 ed], p. 475)

- See the first bullet point of this section of the First Lesson, Lent 1 for details on how rituals enhance social solidarity.

5. Gimmick
Our First Lesson provides an account of the Hebrew people's first Passover in the Promised Land. Now what can that have to do with Lent and the Fourth Sunday in Lent's stress on grace? What does it all have to do with our Monday through Saturday lives?

6. Possible Sermon Moves and/or Stories/Examples
- Of course around Easter we think of Passover, as the first Holy Week seems to have transpired during Passover. In fact we think of the Last Supper as a Passover Meal. Today we need to look at Passover in a new way, the Jewish way. As a festival of freedom. From that perspective it has a lot to say to Christians and about this Sunday in Lent.
- Let's see what Jewish leaders say about their holiday. Cite the second and third bullet points of Theological Insights. They both stress that Passover is about freedom.
- Even Christians see Passover that way. Use Martin Luther's remarks in the fourth bullet point of Theological Insights regarding how Christ as fulfillment of the Passover is also about freedom from slavery and the captivity of sin.
- The Passover as a celebration of freedom. Note how badly we need that word in America, worldwide, today. Note the examples of bondage in the first two bullet points of Socio-Economic, Political, Psychological, and Scientific Insights.
- Make clear that in addition to bondage to these horrible forms of oppression, there is the oppression of anxiety and depression (see last two bullet points of Socio-Economic, Political, Psychological, and Scientific Insights for Second Lesson, Lent 2) and also enslaved to sin, to our insidious selfishness (see last bullet point of Theological Insights for the First Lesson, Ash Wednesday).
- To all these forms of oppression, we need freedom. It is the essence of being human. Use the observations of Martin Luther King Jr. in the third bullet point of Socio-Economic, Political, Psychological, and Scientific Insights.
- Christian faith is all about this sort of freedom. It is not a religion about the status quo, dedicated to defending traditional values and the establishment. At least that is not Christianity at its best, when the church is faithful.
- Not surprising given its roots in the Jewish Passover tradition. Of course Jesus Himself, as the fulfillment of that tradition (consider again Luther's point in the next-to-last bullet point of Theological Insights). In fact, Jesus' work on the Cross

was all about setting us free, not counting our sins against us (as today's Second Lesson [2 Corinthians 5:19] makes clear). Galatians 3 (v. 13) announces the freedom Christ has freed us from the law. Christian faith is all about freedom!

• Just as the Passover's tradition of freedom is not a "do your own thing" kind of freedom, but a freedom to protest the lack of freedom (see second bullet point of Theological Insights), so Christian faith is about the freedom to serve and liberate others.

• Dietrich Bonhoeffer reflected on how freedom is a freedom from myself and so a freedom for others. See last bullet point in Theological Insights for the First Lesson, Epiphany 4. In many ways he echoed Martin Luther's views on freedom: "A Christian is a perfectly free lord of all, subject to none. A Christian is a perfectly dutiful servant of all, subject to all" (*Luther's Works*, Vol. 31, p. 344).

• To the preceding witnesses, add the observations of the black theologians in the next-to-last bullet point of Socio-Economic, Political, Psychological, and Scientific Insights.

• Even the Passover ritual itself (and the Christian commemoration of it annually in connection with Lent and Easter) has implications for rendering Christians more inclined to social solidarity, since the more we worship together, the more we sing and praise together, the more trusting and the more concerned we become for each other, and then in turn for the broader community.

7. Wrap-Up
Passover is not just a holiday for Jews and a holiday about family meals. It is commemoration of freedom, a prod to Jew and Christian alike to get restless with the bondage around us, to thank God for our freedom and then to pray, yearn, and begin to work for everybody else's freedom too. Lent is a time for confessing our failure on that score. But the church historically has also wanted this Sunday to be a time to celebrate and thank God for that freedom too.

Sermon Text and Title
"A New Beginning"
2 Corinthians 5:16-21

1. Theological Aim of the Sermon and Strategy
To proclaim the fresh start grace makes in our lives (Justification by Grace and Realized Eschatology, including its implications for Sanctification). Our sinful condition also requires analysis.

2. Exegesis (see Introduction to Selected Books of the Bible)
• Further discourse on the ministry of reconciliation.

• Paul urges that from now on we regard no one from a human point of view; though we once knew Christ only from such a point, no longer will we know Him that way (v. 16). Reference here seems to be to knowing Christ as risen and not as the one put to death.

• Anyone in Christ is a new creation; the old has passed away (v. 17).

• Speaks of the newness coming from God who reconciled us to Him and given us the ministry of reconciliation (v. 18). In Christ, God was reconciling the world to Himself and not counting trespasses against us and entrusting the ministry of reconciliation to us (v. 19).

• This makes us ambassadors for Christ, since God is making His appeal through us. Thus Paul entreats readers to be reconciled to God on behalf of Christ (v. 20).

• For our sake, God made Christ to be sin so that we might become the righteousness of God (v. 21).

3. Theological Insights (see Charts of the Major Theological Options)
• The text addresses sin, Justification by Grace, Sanctification (as a new reality), and Realized Eschatology. The operation of God in paradoxical ways (Providence) is also suggested.

• The great Reformed theologian Karl Barth profoundly explains the nature of God's forgiveness evident in this text:

> *The act of the divine forgiveness is that God sees and knows this stain [of his sins] infinitely better than man himself, and abhors it infinitely more than he does even in his deepest penitence — yet He does not take it into consideration, He overlooks it, He covers it, He passes it by, He puts it behind Him, He does not charge it to man.* (Church Dogmatics, Vol. IV/1, p. 597)

• Describing the new life in Christ, John Wesley writes:

> *He has new life, new senses, new faculties, new affections, new appetites, new ideas and conceptions. His whole tenor of action and conversation is new, and he lives, as it were, in a new world. God, men, the whole creation, heaven, earth, and all therein*

appear in a new light and stand related to him in a new manner since he was created anew in Christ Jesus.
(*Commentary on the Bible*, p. 525)

• Famed New Testament scholar Rudolf Bultmann well explains why we need such a new beginning (our sinful condition):

... man forgets in his selfishness and presumption... that it is an illusion to suppose that real security can be gained by men organizing their own personal and community life. There are encounters and destinies which man cannot master. He cannot secure endurance for his works. His life is fleeting and its end is death. History goes on and pulls down all the towers of Babel again and again. There is no real, definitive security, and it is precisely this illusion to which men are prone to succumb in their yearning for security.
(*Jesus Christ and Mythology*, pp. 39-40)

• For other useful quotes pertaining to how a sense of the future (Realized Eschatology) changes human life, see last bullet point of this section for First and Second Lessons, Advent 1; Gospel, Epiphany 1; next-to-last bullet point of this section for the Gospel, Advent 1.
• Martin Luther explains how giving up such security is related to an awareness that like God we should not look at things from a human point of view. For His love does not operate as we would expect love to work. The Message of the Cross is that while human love comes into being through that which is pleasing to it, "the love of God does not find, but creates that which is pleasing to it" (*Luther's Works*, Vol. 31, p. 41).

4. Socio-Economic, Political, Psychological, and Scientific Insights
• A 2009 Pew Charitable Trust poll indicated that American optimism was not dead. It revealed that 62% of the public believed things would get better in the future and that their children would have better lives.
• On American attitudes contradicting our dependence on grace, see this section for the Second Lesson, Epiphany 4.
• The majority of Americans do not accept the necessary role of grace in saving us. A 2005 poll of the Barna Research Group found that 54% believe that people who are good earn salvation.

5. Gimmick
Ask the congregation if they can ever really start again fresh, whether new beginnings are possible. Conclude it is not normally possible. Note how bad marriages and bad parent-child relationships do not usually get better and how once institutions get established, they resist change. We are pretty dull, monotonous people!

6. Possible Sermon Moves and/or Stories/Examples
• Part of the reason that change is so difficult is because we have histories that shape us and our character. We are the sum total of what we have done or the choices we have made (Rudolf Bultmann, *Jesus Christ and Mythology*, p. 30). But we are not totally satisfied with the way things have happened in life. We wish things were different, better.
• Of course Americans have hope. Our feel-good, therapeutic social ethos and its media gurus say it is possible, especially if we buy the products, network, and make wise investments. But what we do will not provide this sort of security for which we yearn. Cite the fourth bullet point in Theological Insights. Note the warning of Romans 7:18b-19 that we are trapped by our past and cannot do what we wish we could do. Self-improvement will not alleviate our predicament.
• We want meaning and security in life. But all that we might accumulate will not provide this, do not really change us. We remain the same insecure, uncertain, boring, or too cocky and selfish jerks we always were. Besides, all we possess or accomplish will wither and die. We are all on the way to the grave.
• We want to forget these harsh realities. But it is good to be reminded of our dire circumstances during Lent. This is a season of repentance. Yet all the repentance in the world cannot change our circumstances and will not make us new. (Cite the first quote by Calvin in Theological Insights for the Gospel.) We can only have a new beginning if God gives it to us. And He has done that on the first Easter!
• In our lesson (v. 17) Paul makes this point about the new beginning we have. But how can this be, if you are stuck in a dead-end job, a failing marriage, have a bad child or a bad reputation in school? Ask Paul how he could lie to us. Note that Lent and Easter are times for us to confess our sin and disbelief and to confess how we have squandered all the new opportunities Jesus has given us.
• We have missed how God has changed us. This word was at the heart of Jesus' preaching of the kingdom of God coming near (Mark 1:15, a text that most historians agree is one of the most ancient, historically accurate accounts of Jesus' preaching and teaching). Repent and believe that the new has come and that the past no longer holds us in chains.
• This message is evident in the First Lesson's proclamation that the Hebrews are no longer slaves (Joshua 5:9). Also in our Gospel Lesson the prodigal son was given a fresh start (Luke 5:11b-32). When you hang around Jesus, new beginnings,

improved relationships, and more fulfilling ways of life just seem to happen. We see this word in the Second Lesson with the word that we are not to regard anyone from a human point of view (v. 16a). Anyone in Christ is a new creation; the old has passed (v. 17)! This new beginning is a glimpse of the end times.

• New beginnings, fresh starts, really are possible from God's point of view. Lent helps us see how that is possible. Lent is an unattractive time, filled with sobriety. Yet it opens the way to the Easter celebration. It is God's style to do things in surprising ways. This is what Paul means by calling us not to look at things from a human point of view (v. 16a). Don't look at things from a human point of view, because we are in a new time.

• God clearly does not do things our way and does not work in accord with our expectations. The way in which our Lord loves and forgives us makes that apparent. Cite the quotations by Barth and Luther in Theological Insights. God has put the past behind us. He does not love us like human love works. God loves the kind of person He is going to make us to be. Not *what is* but what *will be* is what He loves.

• Note John Wesley's description in Theological Insights of this new way of being in Christ, which the love of God creates.

7. Wrap-Up
Ask the congregation if they feel dead in life and need a new beginning. Remind them that there is much to celebrate this day and that they have a fresh start! It is just a matter of looking at life, at the people in our lives, like God does. It is time to stop being so hung up on finding what looks pleasing or what looks good. This is the new beginning that Paul and Jesus promise. The unattractive ways of God and His creatures really are beautiful and so is life!

Sermon Text and Title
"God Will Forgive You Before You Even Thought About It"
Luke 15:1-3, 11b-32

1. Theological Aim of the Sermon and Strategy
The proclamation of God's prevenient grace, a love that precedes all we can do for Him or for others (Justification by Grace). The implications for Sanctification (Good Works as Spontaneous) are also celebrated.

2. Exegesis (see Introduction to Selected Books of the Bible)
• Jesus' parable of the prodigal son.
• Surrounded as he was by tax collectors and sinners, Jesus is criticized by the Pharisees for the company He kept (vv. 1-2).
• The story of the man with two sons unfolds, the younger receiving his share of the father's property departs and squanders all the wealth (vv. 11-13).
• In need, working as a field hand feeding pigs (a shameful impure undertaking for a Jew), he resolves to return to his father to seek forgiveness (vv. 14-20a). His father sees him and welcomes him home (v. 20b). The son apologizes, saying he is no longer worthy to be the father's son but the father initiates a celebration on grounds that his "dead" son is alive (vv. 21-24).
• The elder son heard all this and learned his brother had returned and his father had initiated a celebration (vv. 25-27). He is angered and refuses to join the celebration (v. 28).
• The dutiful son confronts his father, reminding him that he had worked like a slave for him and never disobeyed, yet his father never had held a celebration for him and his friends (v. 29). His father responds that his eldest always had been with him and all that he has is his. A celebration was in order because the eldest son's brother who was dead has now come to life (vv. 31-32).

3. Theological Insights (see Charts of the Major Theological Options)
• The text testifies to Justification by Grace and the priority of grace over all forms of preparation.
• Noting God's extraordinary forgiveness and love John Wesley observed: "So does God frequently cut an earnest confession short by a display of His pardoning love" (*Commentary on the Bible*, p. 446).
• John Calvin nicely clarifies the sense in which the Father's forgiveness of the prodigal son was not conditioned by his repentance:

> *It is wretched sophistry to infer from this, that the grace of God is not exhibited to sinners until they anticipate it by their repentance... it is wrong to infer from this, that repentance, which is the gift of God, is yielded by men from their own movement of their heart.*
> (*Calvin's Commentaries*, Vol. XVI/2, p. 347)

- All the love that surrounds us now is by God's initiative, Martin Luther reminds us: "With these words one can apprehend God as He is to be apprehended. You do not seek Him; rather He seeks you…" (*Complete Sermons*, Vol. 2/1, p. 344).
- To a great extent Karl Barth agrees. He has pointed out that God does not owe it to the world to love it (*Church Dogmatics*, Index, p. 432).
- In another case Luther compares Christ's love to the sun, which "will not refuse to shine because I am lazy and would gladly sleep an hour or two longer." In the same way the light of God's love will keep shining on the hardhearted, even if we do not want to see it (*Complete Sermons*, Vol. 2/1, pp. 347-348).
- The gift, Luther claims, is like a child born in his or her parent's home, with a right to the inheritance by birth, though when the child grows into adulthood it naturally follows that the adult child will seek to increase the family inheritance: "[The child of the house] does not, first of all, gain the inheritance by our works; yet we must be co-laborers with the Father to increase it" (*Complete Sermons*, Vol. 2/1, p. 349).

4. Socio-Economic, Political, Psychological, and Scientific Insights
- For poll numbers that indicate how dramatically recent American spirituality contradicts the wisdom of the parable of the prodigal son, see this section for the Second Lesson.
- Comparing a December 2009 Gallup poll on whether religion can answer most of today's problems with results from a similar 1957 Gallup poll bespeaks growing secularization. In 1957 82% of Americans saw religion as relevant to the issues of the day. In the 2009 poll only 57% shared such an opinion.

5. Gimmick
Mark Twain is said to have called our Gospel Lesson, the parable of the prodigal son, the greatest story ever told. It is a great one, a powerful story of love!

6. Possible Sermon Moves and/or Stories/Examples
- Rehearse the parable in dramatic fashion. A familiar story.
- A story of love and like a lot of love stories (too often it happens with the love stories in which we are living) we may easily trivialize it, because of its familiarity. As a result we tend to ignore it. No surprise that this can happen when we remember that in love the brain is flooded with the pleasurable neurochemical dopamine, an amphetamine that is addictive (see last bullet point of Socio-Economic, Political, Psychological, and Scientific Insights for the First Lesson, Epiphany 2). Like any addiction we reach a saturation point, where we no longer get the high from the drug. That's why love fades, why we come to take God's amazing love for granted.
- What we need in these cases, therapists say, is to do new, fresh things in love. Well, let's take a fresh look at the love of God in this parable.
- God's love is not like the love that gives to get. It is the love of family member, the love of parent or a spouse (see second and third bullet points of Theological Insights for First Lesson, Epiphany 2, for references). It is a love filled with forgiveness and not the conditional forgiveness, the fickle love, like we see in different television shows, like *The Good Wife*. This is an unconditional forgiving love.
- Stress the idea of unconditional love. This goes against the grain about what a lot of Americans think about God. Surveys show we think you need to do something to please God: at least to ask for forgiveness. Cite data referred to in the first bullet point of Socio-Economic, Political, Psychological, and Scientific Insights. This is how we often mess up our understanding of Lent, as we sometimes think of it incorrectly as a period of repentance necessary in order to be worthy of the Easter blessings.
- That is not the way it is with God. Consider what happens in a loving relationship. Wonderful as these relationships are they are not without tensions and not without spats. But in a happy marriage, in a good parent-child relationship, they are not built on or maintained by the apologies of the offending partner. No, in real love, you love even when you are angry, that is even how it is with God's love.
- Use observations of John Wesley and John Calvin in the second and third bullet points of Theological Insights on how God forgives before we repent! We see this in the parable, as the father welcomed home the prodigal son before receiving his apology (v. 20b)!
- God takes the initiative in loving us, Martin Luther claims (see fourth bullet point of Theological Insights). Follow with observations of Karl Barth in the fifth bullet point of Theological Insights.
- Use Martin Luther's point about Christ's love being like the sun and not refusing to shine when we are lazy (next-to-last bullet point of Theological Insights). Elsewhere Luther says this light is a love that transcends all love, a great incomprehensible fire (*Complete Sermons*, Vol. 6, p. 187). God's light of love will keep shining on the hard-hearted, even if they don't

want it. That's the significance of God so loving the world. That light shines for *everyone*, even for unbelievers. That's the kind of love God has for the world. This is another example of God seeking us even when we do not seek Him.
• Hold on to that image, hold on to that love, the next time despair and doubt hit, the next time you are inclined to take this marvelous love for granted.

7. Wrap-Up
We never hear what happened to the prodigal son after he was forgiven, but Martin Luther and Augustine have some ideas, knowing what God's love can do. Use the last bullet point of Theological Insights for the former. Augustine speaks of the love of God setting our wills on fire leading us to love (*Nicene and Post-Nicene Fathers*, First Series, Vol. 3, p. 534). Touched by a love like this, we prodigal children of God can't help but start to make a difference in our church, families, and community! We have a lot to celebrate today. Just as God forgives us before we even think about it, so Christians caught up in that love will start doing good even before we think about it. What a wonderful love our God has for prodigal children like us.

Lent 5

March 17, 2013

Revised Common	Isaiah 43:16-21	Philippians 3:4b-14	John 12:1-8
Roman Catholic	Isaiah 43:16-21	Philippians 3:8-14	John 8:1-11
Episcopal	Isaiah 43:16-21	Philippians 3:8-14	Luke 20:9-19

Theme of the Day   With God, you get a new way up ahead.

Collect of the Day   The creator God who prepares a new way in the wilderness and whose grace waters the desert is addressed. Petitions are offered that we might have our hearts opened to be transformed by the new thing God is doing, so that our times might proclaim the extravagance of His love. Justification (by Grace) and Sanctification (the Spontaneity of Good Works) are emphasized.

Psalm of the Day   *Psalm 126*
- Prayer of deliverance from national misfortune.
- Reminiscence of the joy inspired by God's favor toward His people in the past (vv. 1-3).
- Prayer for such favor again (vv. 4-6).
- Those in mourning and oppressed shall experience joy (v. 6) and posits here a preferential option for the poor.

         or *Psalm 119:9-16*
- A wisdom Psalm, a meditation on the law of God but in the mode of a lament. The Psalm is in the style of an acrostic poem (each line beginning with a consecutive letter of the Hebrew alphabet).
- The verses read speak of the Psalmist's desire to learn and delight in the law of God. It is a way for youth to keep pure.

Sermon Text and Title
"All Your Burdens Are Just History: God Is Moving On!"
Isaiah 43:16-21

1. Theological Aim of the Sermon and Strategy
To proclaim how God wipes away all the sin and error of the past, forgiving us and freeing us for the future (Sin, Justification by Grace, Sanctification, and Realized Eschatology).

2. Exegesis (see Introduction to Selected Books of the Bible)
- Part of the promise of the restoration and redemption of Israel written by Deutero-Isaiah in the sixth century BC during the Babylonian Captivity.
- Having promised to break down the bars holding the Judeans, Yahweh say He makes a way in the sea and will not remember former things (vv. 16, 18). He promises to do a new thing, making a way out of the wilderness (v. 19).
- Also reminiscent of the Exodus wanderings He promises to water the wilderness, giving drink to His chosen people that they would declare His praise (vv. 20-21; cf. Exodus 17:1-7).

3. Theological Insights (see Charts of the Major Theological Options)
- The text addresses Providence, Sin, Justification by Grace, Sanctification (as a new reality), and Realized Eschatology.
- An African bishop of the early church, Cyprian of Carthage, interpreted the reference to God making a way out of waters (v. 16) and the new thing He would do in making a way out of the wilderness (v. 19) to refer to God rejecting the former way of anointing His people to baptism and God's new way of using water to give life (*Ante-Nicene Fathers*, Vol. 5, p. 511).
- For leads on quotations pertaining to how a sense of the future (Realized Eschatology) changes human life, see this section for the Second Lesson, Lent 4.
- By saying He will be our God, Calvin adds, the Lord offers us "His paternal favour, and declares that our salvation is become the object of His care; He gives us free access to Himself…" (*Calvin's Commentaries*, Vol. X/2, p. 133).

4. Socio-Economic, Political, Psychological, and Scientific Insights
- See this section for the Second Lesson, Lent 4.

5. Gimmick
In the previous week's sermon drawn from the Second Lesson, note that in some respects themes of the previous week repeat. Either way, ask the congregation if they have ever felt burdened by mistakes of the past and trapped by bad habits and regrets. Lent is a time for reflecting on such questions.

6. Possible Sermon Moves and/or Stories/Examples
• Our First Lesson has something to say about this range of issues. Read verses 18-19a. Note that God the Lord (Yahweh) is doing a new thing.
• Note that one of the Hebrew names for God, Yahweh, gives deep insight into the Bible's understanding of God. "Yahweh" may be translated "I am who I am" (Exodus 3:14). Since in the language of ancient Hebrew there is no distinction between present and future tenses, you could just as easily translate the Lord's name as "I will be who I will be." (If sermon noted in the Gimmick was used the previous week, put all these comments in the mode of "recall.") In other words, Yahweh is a God who is always on the move, ever becoming who He is, and leaving behind the past. This is the way Isaiah refers to our Lord today.
• Our First Lesson makes it very clear that God is doing a new thing. What is this new thing? We Christians read this prophecy in the context of the whole Bible, and so we can only read it as a prophecy concerning Jesus Christ. That is the way to think about the work of Christ. It is God's new thing!
• The incarnation and saving work of Christ we commemorate in Lent are not something God planned to do in eternity. They were not foreseen at the time of creation. The decision to have the eternal Son go to the Cross for human sin is a new thing, planned only after our fall into sin. In other words, the Cross and Incarnation are "emergency operations."
• We have a God who can change His mind, adjust His plans, and learn from experience. Such a God, for example, regretting He had made human beings (Genesis 6:6), who once repented (or changed His mind) concerning evil He had been planning against Israel for its sin (Exodus 32:14). A God who repented, who regretted that He had made Saul King of Israel (1 Samuel 15:35).
• That God changes His mind does not entail that He is fickle. He may change His mind about strategies. But you can count on Him to be faithful to His promises. Cite Romans 11:29 and note (based on Romans 9:6) that the Jews remain His chosen people.
• What is the payoff for everyday life? This picture of Yahweh helps us get to know Him better and makes Him more personal. A God who reacts to us as He does makes Him more like a friend. Then there is the best part of this God who is always moving on, knowing that this is a God who really does forgive our sins. It is right there in our First Lesson. Speaking through His prophet Isaiah, Yahweh says He will not remember the things of the past for He is doing a new thing. Read again verses 18-19a.
• God does not want us to remember the things of old and doesn't want us to remember what went before. Note the great comfort in these words. God does not want us to remember the old things and hurts of the past. He does not remember them either!
• Forgive and forget. That is the formula for perfect forgiveness. There is true forgiveness in God, in a way we cannot. Because in forgiving, God actually forgets (forgets our sin). It is as famed nineteenth-century Congregationalist minister Henry Ward Beecher (brother of Harriet Beecher Stowe) once put it: "I can forgive, but I cannot forget, is only another way of saying, I will not forgive. Forgiveness ought to be like a cancelled note — torn in two, and burned up, so that it never can be shown against one." The old things are forgiven: Read 43:25. God will not remember your sins. He has called us away from the Bible's demands and called us to a new life free of doubt, bad habits, and regrets.
• In calling us not to remember the former things, Isaiah paints a picture of a new way to live, free from the past, thanks to God's forgiving love. The same word is present in our Second Lesson: Read Philippians 3:7-9. Paul is willing to give it all up. The reality of being justified by God's grace entails that we let the past go. This is quite natural, for in forgiving our sin, God is indeed doing a new thing! He does not remember our old sins any more.
• What does all this talk about the new thing God is doing — about His forgetting our sin — have to with everyday life? Let the past go! Not because you have to but because it just makes sense.
• Why keep the old grudges and hurts? Why keep on with the old destructive habits and ways of thinking? Why let regrets paralyze you? The first-century Roman writer Syrus (Publius Syrus) said it well: "We may with advantage forget what we know."
• In our lesson, Yahweh, the God who is moving on, says that one of the new things He is doing is to form His people for Himself, so that they might become people who proclaim His praise (v. 21). Though first referring to the people of Israel, we should read these words as about you and me. We are no longer people stuck in our past. It no longer matters. We can't help but look ahead; we are brand new!

7. Wrap-Up
The old ways of the past can no longer harm us. They are gone! Liberated from all that has been destructive in our lives, we are God's new thing indeed.

Sermon Text and Title
"Giving It All Up for Jesus and What's Ahead"
Philippians 3:4b-14

1. Theological Aim of the Sermon and Strategy
To proclaim the renunciation of our sinful past that is overcome by Union with Christ (Sin and Justification by Grace) leading to Sanctification and resurrection (Eschatology).

2. Exegesis (see Introduction to Selected Books of the Bible)
• A warning to break with the past.
• Paul claims that if anyone had reason to be confident in the things of the flesh, he did. He proceeds to enumerate his Jewish pedigree and zeal as a persecutor of the church (v. 4b-6).
• Yet whatever gains he had in these ways, Paul has come to regard as loss because of Christ (vv. 7-8a).
• For Christ's sake, Paul claims to have suffered the loss of all things and regard them as rubbish in order to gain Christ and be found in Him, not having a righteousness of his own that comes from the law, but one that comes through faith in Christ (vv. 8b-9).
• The apostle claims to want to know Christ and the power of His resurrection by becoming like Him in His death, attaining the resurrection (vv. 10-11).
• Paul notes that he has not attained such death and resurrection but is pressing on to make it his own since Christ had made him His own (vv. 12-14).

3. Theological Insights (see Charts of the Major Theological Options)
• The text deals with Sin, Justification (as Intimate Union), Sanctification, and Future Eschatology.
• On renouncing all we can bring to Christ, consider the quotations by Luther and Augustine in this section for the Second Lesson, Lent 1.
• John Calvin wanted to make clear that Paul's comments about pressing on (vv. 13-14) do "not here call in question the certainty of his salvation…" (*Calvin's Commentaries*, XXI/2, p. 102).
• Calvin offered other comments pertaining to pressing on:

> *Paul, however, condemns here such looking back, as either destroys or impairs alacrity. Thus, for example, should any one persuade himself that he has made sufficiently great progress, reckoning that he has done enough, he will become indolent… or, if any one looks back with a feeling of regret for the situation that he has abandoned, he cannot apply the whole bent of his mind to what he is engaged in.* (*Calvin's Commentaries*, XXI/2, p. 102)

• Commenting on Paul's point about the law not giving righteousness, famed preacher of the early church John Chrysostom compared the law to dung, but noted that dung has a use as from it wheat is gathered (*Nicene and Post-Nicene Fathers*, First Series, Vol. 13, p. 235).
• Elaborating on the righteousness God has given us, making us his own, the famed preacher adds:

> *… He saw us in such guilt, He did not reject us; was not wroth, turned not away, hated us not, for He was a master, and could not hate His own creation.* (*Nicene and Post-Nicene Fathers*, First Series, Vol. 13, p. 238)

• Reflecting on this text, Martin Luther noted its good news: "Therefore a Christian, as a child of God, must always rejoice, always sing, fear nothing, always be free from care, and always glory in God" (*Luther's Works*, Vol. 29, p. 177).

4. Socio-Economic, Political, Psychological, and Scientific Insights
• See this section for the Second Lesson, Lent 4.

5. Gimmick
Invite the congregation to think about all they have done. That's just the past, Paul says in our lesson (vv. 7-8). Look at the past like twentieth-century American poet Paul Eldridge once wrote: "Praises for our past triumphs are as feathers to a dead bird."

6. Possible Sermon Moves and/or Stories/Examples
• Get over your successes. No matter how good you have been, how spiritual you are, how much you have accomplished, it does not matter.

• Americans do not want to hear this. Like Marvin and Harriet Thompson (name them accordingly and locate them age-wise, economically, and vocationally in accord with the prevailing demographics of the congregation), successfully situated in your community, with good reputations and even some influence in the community, they are proud of their accomplishments. (Cite survey data in Socio-Economic, Political, Psychological, and Scientific Insights that bear out the optimism Americans have, a sense of their goodness.)

• Know what Paul says to them (and to the whole congregation regarding them accomplishments). All we have been and done in the past is nothing but rubbish (v. 8b)!

• Why is what we have done rubbish? Famed New Testament scholar Rudolf Bultmann nicely explains why we need to get free from our past and why it is sinful. We come into every new situation, he claimed, as the person we became through previous decisions. But that suggests that our decisions are not really free but are determined by our past decisions. Truly to be free, we need to be free of our past (*History and Eschatology*, p. 44). Also see the leads in the last bullet point of Theological Insights for the First Lesson, Ash Wednesday, regarding our bondage to selfishness and sin. This mars the goodness of *anything* we have done!

• Use John Calvin's quote in the fourth bullet point of Theological Insights. It is essential that we not get preoccupied with ourselves, or we will take our focus off Christ!

• The answer to all this? When you give up yourself you wind up having your focus on Christ and that changes you.

• Jesus won't let us go. He will not reject us! Use the quotation by John Chrysostom in the next-to-last bullet point of Theological Insights. Christ sets us free from the need to justify our own existence and righteousness, based on what we have accomplished. That righteousness is nothing but bull; see John Chrysostom's comments in the fifth bullet point of Theological Insights. And in its place He gave us His own righteousness!

• With nothing left but Christ on whom to devote our attention, Paul speaks of our yearning to know Christ and the power of His resurrection and the sharing of His sufferings by becoming like Him (v. 10). This call for Union with Christ is most reminiscent of the image of a marriage to Christ. In marriage we become like our beloved spouse. Consider the quotations in the second bullet point of Theological Insights for Second Lesson, Christmas; fifth bullet point of that section for Gospel, Christmas 1.

• When you are engaged in a happy marriage, it changes you. After a while you almost forget who you were before that relationship! This is basically Paul's point, his prayer for us. The past is yesterday for one who has become like Jesus and been united to Him. It just doesn't matter ultimately any more. It's like American composer and poet John Cage once wrote: "We need not destroy the past. It is gone." The past, all our efforts at justifying our goodness pales in relation to Jesus. And with the pressures of having to prove yourself and our status gone, off our backs, life gets a lot sweeter (see the last bullet point of Socio-Economic, Political, Psychological, and Scientific Insights for First Lesson, Christmas 1).

7. Wrap-Up
Close with the quotation by Martin Luther in the last bullet point of Theological Insights. With the weight of the past gone, wrapped up in our relation with Jesus, there is nothing to fear, no more care, no wonder we sing songs in church. Urge the congregation to feel that joy and freedom right now, for when we are wrapped up in Jesus and His future, nothing but joy is left!

Sermon Text and Title
"Nothing Matters but Jesus' Future"
John 12:1-8

1. Theological Aim of the Sermon and Strategy
To proclaim God's Providential care, Justification by Grace in the midst of the poverty and meaninglessness of life (Sin), the impact of grace on our lives (Sanctification), and (Realized) Eschatology as an image for understanding Christian life.

2. Exegesis (see Introduction to Selected Books of the Bible)
• The anointing of Jesus' feet by Mary and Martha.

• Six days before the Passover (just prior to Palm Sunday [v. 12]), Jesus came to Bethany and the home of Lazarus whom He had earlier raised from the dead (v. 1; cf. 11:1-44).

• Jesus receives dinner with Lazarus at table and his sister Martha serving (v. 2).

- Lazarus' other sister Mary anoints Jesus' feet with perfume, wiping them with her hair, filling the whole house with good fragrance (v. 3).
- Judas Iscariot (identified as the one who would betray Jesus) objects that the expense for the perfume (a year's wage in that economy) was not used to help the poor (vv. 4-5). Parenthetically, Judas' apparently good motives are undermined and he is accused by the writer of the gospel as a thief of the common purse of the disciples of which he was the caretaker (v. 6).
- Jesus defends Mary, claiming she had bought the perfume for use on the forthcoming day of His burial (v. 7). He adds that the poor will always be with His followers, but they will not always have Him (v. 8).

3. Theological Insights (see Charts of the Major Theological Options)
- The text testifies to the priority of Christ over our present (sinful) circumstances and how a life of praise to Him leads the faithful to countercultural activities (Sanctification) that anticipates the kingdom of God (Eschatology).
- John Calvin advises that this text (vv. 24-26) entails that:

> *When, therefore, the godly are distressed by various afflictions, when they are pressed hard by the difficulties of their situation, when they suffer hunger, or nakedness, or disease, when they are assailed by reproaches, when it appears as if they would every hour be almost overwhelmed by death, let them unceasingly consider that this is a* sowing *which, in due time, will yield fruit.*
> (*Calvin's Commentaries*, Vol. XVIII/1, p. 28)

- Augustine comments on the fragrance that surrounded all the disciples as a result of the anointing of Jesus (v. 3). He claims that this perfume or ointment was righteousness. It give Jesus' followers a sweet odor (*Nicene and Post-Nicene Fathers*, First Series, Vol. 7, p. 280).
- Augustine would have us be on fire to despise the world, so that the whole of life becomes only vapor in comparison to love for eternal things (*Nicene and Post-Nicene Fathers*, First Series, Vol. 7, p. 287).
- Analyzing the condition of the world, John Calvin notes that "out of Christ, there is nothing but confusion in the world…" (*Calvin's Commentaries*, XVIIII/1, p. 36).

4. Socio-Economic, Political, Psychological, and Scientific Insights
- See the statistics on poverty in the first two bullet points of this section for the First Lesson, Advent 1.

5. Gimmick
This is a strange, troubling story. Relay it enthusiastically, trying to make the congregation feel that they are present for the events. Stress the criticism of Mary by Judas Iscariot (vv. 4-5) and Jesus' defense of her (v. 7).

6. Possible Sermon Moves and/or Stories/Examples
- A strange story and especially problematic are Jesus' words about the poor always being with us (v. 8). Small government proponents or those who blame the poor for their own problems seem to have a text here that authorizes neglect of the poor. What is it that Jesus intends?
- Over 1,500 years ago, Saint Augustine offered an insight about what this story might mean, what significance it might have for us. Cite the third bullet point of Theological Insights. The perfume with which Jesus was anointed (v. 3), he claimed was the sweet odor of righteousness. Jesus wears the righteousness God. This scent could make all the disciples smell good and nothing much matters after that!
- Jesus clearly has the Cross and perhaps His ascension in view as He says that He will not always be with His followers (vv. 7-8). The message: Enjoy Jesus while you have Him. He and His future are all that matter.
- The story starts to make sense when you look at it this way. Life sure is chaotic in our context. See references cited in Socio-Economic, Political, Psychological, and Scientific Insights for the First Lesson, Passion Sunday. Elaborate on these examples. Stress the sense that life is chaotic meaninglessness. We could remove poverty in this generation and it might return. We could build the great society of justice and harmony and our children or we ourselves could ruin it. All our accomplishments are so minute, our relationships so fragile, ultimately ending in separation (even if it is the separation of death). Little we have done will be remembered.
- Cite the quotations by John Calvin in the second and last bullet points of Theological Insights for further elaboration.
- Ask the congregation where we go from here. Note Augustine's comments in the next-to-last bullet point of Theological Insights. He would have us be on fire to despise the world so that the whole of life becomes only vapor in comparison to love for eternal things.
- On fire for Christ, scented with His righteousness, the turmoils of our day do not matter quite as much. We become more oriented to where Christ is headed. Use the Bultmann quote in Theological Insights from the Gospel, Epiphany 1, regarding how faith opens us to the future, freeing us from the past.

• American journalist William Allen White well expresses these sentiments: "I am not afraid of tomorrow, for I have seen yesterday and I love today."
• When Christians are with Jesus, they need not fear tomorrow, for reveling in Him, praising Him, they can love today. The turmoil of yesterday are just that. They don't count so much. Mary, it seems, really did have her priorities right in our story.

7. Wrap-Up
Easter is just two weeks down the road. Keep in mind our story as a model for your Lenten discipline, for your efforts to cope with the craziness of life. Get out the perfume of righteousness, shower Jesus with your praise, and then follow the odor of His righteousness into the future, to Easter, where there's a future that can make the present a little less chaotic and a little more a place of love. Nothing matters if you don't have Jesus' fragrance. Wish the congregation some happy sniffing this week, so that they do not miss the sweet smell of Jesus' righteousness and care for them.

Passion / Palm Sunday (Lent 6)
March 24, 2013

Revised Common	Isaiah 50:4-9a	Philippians 2:5-11	Luke 22:14—23:56
Roman Catholic	Isaiah 50:4-7	Philippians 2:6-11	Luke 22:14—23:56
Episcopal	Isaiah 45:21-25	Philippians 2:5-11	Luke (22:39-71) 23:1-49 (50-56)

Theme of the Day God's love shines through the cross and changes us.

Collect of the Day Three prayer possibilities are available. The first alternative praises God for His endless love in sending Jesus to take our nature and to suffer death. (The third alternative refers to the God of mercy and might who offers infinite life through the Passion.) Petitions are offered to enable sharing in Christ's obedience and victory. (The third alternative asks that we be gathered round the Cross and preserved until the resurrection.) Emphasis in these prayers in placed on Sanctification (with a bit more emphasis on grace in the third alternative). The second alternative focuses more on divine sovereignty, with the petition that the Holy Spirit keep the faithful in the joyful procession of those praising Christ. This alternative has more to say about Providence and the Holy Spirit, offering a freer, more joyful vision of Sanctification.

Psalm of the Day *Psalm 31:9-16*

• Prayer for deliverance from personal enemies and attributed to David. These verses are a cry for help. In view of Jesus' family ties to the Davidic line, the Psalm could be interpreted as a prophecy of His sufferings.
• Psalmist is in sorrow, scorned, broken, and the object of schemes (vv. 10-13).
• Prays for vindication that we may be saved by God's steadfast love. An awareness that our whole life is in God's hands (vv. 14-16).

Sermon Text and Title
"A God Who Never Stops Caring"
Isaiah 50:4-9a

1. Theological Aim of the Sermon and Strategy
To testify to God's kindness (a Forensic understanding of Justification by Grace) despite our sin.

2. Exegesis (see Introduction to Selected Books of the Bible)
• A work of Second Isaiah written soon before the fall of Babylon.
• A text taken from the Book of Consolation, a series of eschatological prophecies.
• This text is the so-called Third Servant Song. There is much dispute about the identity of the Servant in these songs (42:1-4; 49:1-6; 50:1-6; 52:13—53:12). Historically the church has claimed that an individual (the Messiah, and specifically Jesus) is the referent. Many scholars understand them to concern the role the nation of Israel would play in propagating God's mission.
• The Servant says that God made Him a teacher, to sustain the weary (exiled Israelites) (v. 4).
• The Servant does the Lord's bidding (v. 5) and accepted the insults received (v. 6).
• Using a law-court image, the Servant expresses unshakable confidence that God will vindicate Him (vv. 7-9).

3. Theological Insights (see Charts of the Major Theological Options)
• The text is best read in terms of Christology and God's faithfulness in Jesus' mission. Sin and evil do not have a chance.
• Commenting on this text, John Calvin offered some helpful insights:

> *The faithful servants of God, when they administer the doctrine of the word, cannot escape this condition, but must endure fights, reproaches, hatred, slanders, and various attacks from adversaries... Let them, therefore, arm themselves with steadfastness and faith.*
> (*Calvin's Commentaries*, Vol. VIII/2, pp. 55-56)

> *However that may be, He always watches carefully and runs to give aid; and even when we fly and resist, He calls us to Him, that we may be refreshed by tasting His grace and kindness.*
> (*Ibid.*, p. 54)

- Jesus' suffering is thus good news, Martin Luther claimed:

    > ... it hurts the Lord to see that we weep at the sight of His suffering. He wants us to be glad, praise God, thank His grace, extol, glorify, and confess Him; for through this journey we come into the possession of the grace of God.
    >
    > (*What Luther Says*, p. 180)

4. Socio-Economic, Political, Psychological, and Scientific Insights
- For examples of the weariness endured by Americans, see the second bullet point of this section for the Second Lesson, Christmas; Gospel, Advent 2; first bullet point of this section for the First Lesson, Lent 2; last bullet point of this section for the Gospel, Ash Wednesday; fourth bullet point of this section for the First Lesson, Transfiguration.

5. Gimmick
Identify the most pressing problematic issue facing your congregation, community, state, or the nation at large. Use any search engine to find statistics or poll data that supports your thesis that this is a problem. See Socio-Economic, Political, Psychological, and Scientific Insights for statistics on some of the key problems. Note that when Jesus and His work come into the picture this week, these realities — evil — do not stand a chance.

6. Possible Sermon Moves and/or Stories/Examples
- It was late in the sixth century BC in Israel (Judah) when our First Lesson was written. Times were no less dire. In fact, the nation of Judah was in decline, on its last legs, having been conquered by the Babylonians. (Try to draw connections with the analysis of the problems you have already discussed.)
- In the midst of this despair that we may feel over our challenges today, the writer of our lesson had a word of hope. He sang a song about a servant (whom we have come to call the Suffering Servant) who would become a teacher with a word to the weary, but who would suffer in contending with adversaries. We Christians have understood this to refer to Jesus, a messianic prophecy.
- Sustain the weary. Our lesson tells us to put our trials on Jesus, and he will take them on for us and comfort us with His loving and fresh insights (vv. 6-9).
- There is a reference in our text to the guilt we feel, from which God vindicates us (v. 9). Yes, there were things for the people of Judah about which to feel guilt. Review the third bullet point of Central Themes for the book of Isaiah. Note the similarities between their oppression of the poor, ill-considered foreign alliances, and a faith that was more ritualistic than committed to the will of God and our own early twenty-first-century ethos. Much of the weariness we feel (see Gimmick) is a function of our endless quest for "more, more, more" at the expense of the poor.
- The good news of this lesson of Palm Sunday is that God does not give up on us, despite our waywardness. That is the message of the day, as the fickle crowd that cheered Jesus when He came to town, and later called for His death, are those for whom Jesus died. Likewise God did not give up on the Judeans, despite all their missteps He promised to send the Servant to save them. (God did bail them out of Babylon after the Captivity.) He will do the same for us!
- Use the second quotation in the second bullet point of Theological Insights. No matter what we do, God is always watching us carefully, running to give aid even when we run and fly. He wants us to taste His grace and caring kindness. This Savior of ours loves us so much that He suffered and died for us, to give us life. That is what the coming week is all about.
- We don't see this kind of faithful love much in the movies or on television. This is why His love is so astounding, wonderful, and hard to believe. This is a love even better than Forrest Gump's faithful love. Sure, his lover had gone her own way, to a life of wild living and narcissism, not unlike us in relation to God. Forrest's love was in part a grateful response to his beloved's defending him from childhood tormentors. But the love God has for us is not in any way the result of anything we have ever done for Him.
- Having this God who never stops caring makes it a lot easier to cope with the weariness we feel in dealing with everyday life. Experiencing such love can get us away from ourselves, less concerned about needing to do or get things in order to prove our worth.
- Of course to have a God who never stops caring does not mean that you will never face problems. (Note the first quotation by Calvin in Theological Insights.) On the contrary, more than likely you will be exposed to all sorts of chiding, slander, hatred, and disdain for your values. At least we would still have the comfort of knowing that we gave a God who loves us so much that He sent us Jesus to suffer for us. Use the last Luther quote in Theological Insights. Jesus is hurt when we weep at His suffering. What love! He would rather see us happy and just praising Him.

7. Wrap-Up
Conclude by reiterating how God keeps running after us, determined not to lose us. This is a God who wants to refresh us

from our weariness (refer to the issue noted in the Gimmick and other pressing issues noted in the sermon) — a love that would rather see us joyful and praising Him than being sad about our sin. Some say we commemorate Passion Sunday today, commemorate Christ's suffering and death all week. However, Luther's right, Christ does not want tears this week. Instead wave the palms, celebrate, be joyful, and then in the long-term all the weariness and meaninglessness won't have a chance. We'll be too busy with joy and praise.

Sermon Text and Title
"God Doesn't Always Behave Like We Think He Should"
Philippians 2:5-11

1. Theological Aim of the Sermon and Strategy
To proclaim God's use of apparently contradictory means to accomplish good and give life (Providence and the Theology of the Cross). Insofar as the aim is to have us depend totally on God, Justification by Grace is also proclaimed.

2. Exegesis (see Introduction to Selected Books of the Bible)
• After being urged to love and be concerned with the interests of others (vv. 2-4), Paul exhorts the faithful to have the mind of Christ Jesus (v. 5).
• Christ is depicted (in hymn form) as divine, but as one emptying Himself into humanity and on the Cross (vv. 6-8). In turn, God has exalted Him (vv. 9-11).

3. Theological Insights (see Charts of the Major Theological Options)
• Christology, God's Providential use of Christ's apparently contradictory activity, and Sanctification (practice of love in the Christian life) are the center of the text. The text is most suggestive of Martin Luther's famed Theology of the Cross (God's use of apparently contradictory means in order to give life).
• Martin Luther well explains this Theology of the Cross in the following quotations:

> *For what is good for us is hidden, and that so deeply that it is under its opposite. Thus our life is hidden under death, love for ourselves under hate for ourselves... salvation under damnation, heaven under hell... And universally our every assertion of anything good is hidden under the denial of it, so that faith may have its place in God, who is a negative essence and goodness and wisdom and righteousness.* (*Luther's Works*, Vol. 25, pp. 382-383)

> *Therefore since [God] can make just only those who are not just, He is compelled to perform an alien work in order to make them sinners before He performs His proper work of justification. Thus He says: "I kill and I make alive; I wound and I heal."* (*Luther's Works*, Vol. 51, p. 19)

• Luther notes that all that Christ did (taking on human frailties and bearing our sin) He did not do because we were worthy of it (*Complete Sermons*, Vol. 4/1, p. 179).
• John Calvin speaks of the text alluring us to imitate Christ in humility with His example (*Calvin's Commentaries*, Vol. XXI/2, p. 54).
• He further noted that the human mind is averse to being abased, and yet this is highly desirable (*Ibid.*, p. 59).
• In much the same spirit Luther wrote:

> *A true Christian must have no glory of his own and must to such an extent be stripped of everything he calls his own... Therefore we must in all things keep ourselves so humble as if we still had nothing of our own. We must wait for the naked mercy of God, who will reckon us just and wise.* (*Luther's Works*, Vol. 25, p. 137)

4. Socio-Economic, Political, Psychological, and Scientific Insights
• New business trends with their stress on flexibility seem to make it difficult to measure success by standards of achievement. As much as anything, making sure that your image as a "winner" is established and maintained (Richard Sennett, *The Corrosion of Character*, pp. 78-80).
• Neurobiological research has demonstrated that the part of our brain, the prefrontal cortex, which most distances us from our own immediate needs as it is activated when we engage in projects bigger than ourselves (self-emptying activities), is especially involved in intimate relationships (Daniel Amen, *Change Your Brain, Change Your Life*, pp. 114, 264-267, 275-277).

5. Gimmick
In some respects, life hasn't treated us like we wish, has it? Elaborate on our disappointments and pain. Life is not like the

prosperity gospel preachers have promised. They say that God wants to give us prosperity in the here and now (Joel Osteen, *Your Best Life Now*, pp. 8, 10). God has not delivered on what they say. He has not seemed to answer all our prayers. We have all had loved ones die.

6. Possible Sermon Moves and/or Stories/Examples
• In fact, we have a God who does things just the opposite from what we would expect God to do. This is what Martin Luther called the Theology of the Cross. Passion Sunday (Palm Sunday) especially illustrates this view of God. Along with our Bible lessons the theme of this Sunday gives a powerful witness, some solace, when we suffer or despair. We have a God who uses death to give life, who uses despair and disappointment to give hope (see Deuteronomy 32:39).
• The Second Lesson provides a witness to these themes. Paul outlines how the eternal divine Son of God, though in the form of God, empties Himself to take the form of a servant (v. 7).
• Quote verse 8. Note that God works through lowly ordinary things, through vehicles that are apparently contrary to His aims. Through such lowly means, God achieves just the opposite, exalting Christ! Quote verses 10-11.
• The Palm Sunday/Holy Week sequence (much of it recorded in the Gospel Lesson) reflects God's propensity to confound us by doing just the opposite of what we would expect Him to do. The king, the creator of the universe, comes to Jerusalem — on the foal of an ass (Luke 19:35ff). The glory of God on a humble ass. A study of contrasts. God works through contrasts and opposites.
• More to the story and this pattern: The ordinary procession with Jesus on the colt is greeted in the big city as if it were the entourage of a king! The humble, ordinary-looking Jesus gets treated with the majesty that only a king deserves. God works through contrasts and opposites.
• Then it happened again. The crowd that met Jesus that day praised and cheered Him. They called Him their king (Luke 19:36-38)! Fickle people. Just five days later they deserted Him while others called for His death (Luke 23:18ff). Continue to note again how God is working through contrasts and opposites.
• The final act happens on the Cross when the crowd got its wish and saw Jesus put to death (Luke 23:33ff). The one who is God was humbled and met death on a Cross (vv. 6-8)! Yet on that Cross Jesus not only found life for Himself; forever His death became the passage to exaltation and life for others (vv. 9-11)! God has this thing about working through contrasts and opposites, about giving good out of bad things, and about showing strength in the midst of apparent weakness. He just doesn't behave like most Americans think a god should.
• Ask what all this has to do with everyday life. Passion Sunday and God's style of working good through contrasts and opposites, making good out of evil (what Martin Luther called the Theology of the Cross), explains the problems noted at the beginning of the sermon. (Reiterate points in the Gimmick.) It also helps explain why God often seems far away or irrelevant to everyday life. Passion Sunday and Holy Week teach us that God works in hidden ways (like He used death on a Cross to give life). God seems so powerless and distant sometimes, faith in Him seems to have made no difference in our lives, wracked as they are sometimes with death, disappointment, and pain, because our God is a God who works in hidden ways!
• Martin Luther once nicely explained why God operates in these hidden, surprising ways. Cite first quote in the second bullet point of Theological Insights. Because God is so grand as to contradict our sense of goodness and wisdom, He is only known through negations and opposites. Why does he operate that way? To exercise our faith. He makes us sinners.
• Here's the deal: By making Himself seem to be absent from us, making it appear that He is powerless and unable to help, God brings out our sin and unbelief. Note to the congregation their and the preacher's own doubts. We are a lot like the fickle crowd at the procession of Palms, who later called for Jesus' death. Cite the second quotation by Luther in the second bullet point of Theological Insights.
• Note the reference to humility in the preceding quote by Luther. We need to get ourselves out of the way in order to appreciate the fact that we are totally dependent on God, He alone saves us, and we bring nothing to the table when it comes to salvation. See the third bullet point of Theological Insights. Then use the last two bullet points of that section.
• Just makes sense: God hides Himself and does not seem to answer our prayers, so that we experience unfaith and realize we are not so good that we deserve good treatment. We get our false gods and false sense of security destroyed in the midst of our doubts.
• Psychologist M. Scott Peck thinks it takes a self-emptiness to hear or care for another: "We cannot let another person into our hearts and minds unless we empty ourselves. We can truly listen to him or truly hear her only out of emptiness." Mother Teresa, a believer who knew a good bit of this sort of love, explained it well: "Love, to be real, must cost, it must hurt, it must empty us of self."

7. Wrap-Up
The next time we feel those doubts or wonder about God, keep in mind that God doesn't always behave like we think He

should. He is a God who works through contrasts and opposites. He is making such doubts show us our lack of faith. But take heart: He is using those doubts to get us more ready to appreciate what He has done for us in saving us and using the doubts to change us. We need a God who doesn't behave like we think He should in order to prod us to appreciate Easter, the grace of God, love and life a little more!

Sermon Text and Title
"We're so Messed Up That We Don't Know What to Be Happy About"
Luke 22:14—23:56

1. Theological Aim of the Sermon and Strategy
An exploration of the depth of our sin, or tendency to take it and the magnificence of what Christ has done for us for granted. Christ's death for us (Justification by Grace) has the final word.

2. Exegesis (see Introduction to Selected Books of the Bible)
• Luke's account of the Passion from the Last Supper through the Crucifixion.
• At the Passover meal Jesus tells His followers that He desired to eat with them before He suffered, for He would not eat that meal until the Passover is fulfilled in God's kingdom (22:14-16).
• Likewise He took the cup, gave thanks, and had the faithful divide it among themselves on grounds that He would not drink the wine again until the kingdom comes (22:17-18).
• After uttering the words of institution of the Lord's Supper (22:19-20), He notes that one present would betray Him and woe to that one. (Refers to Himself as Son of Man, noting what befalls Him is determined.) The disciples begin to wonder who this is (22:23).
• A dispute arises among the disciples over who is the greatest. Jesus insists that the greatest among them must become like the youngest and a servant. He is among them as one who serves 22:24-27. He praises them as those who have stood by Him in His trials and He will confer a kingdom on them as the Father conferred it on Him. They will eat and drink at His table and sit on thrones judging the Tribes of Israel (22:28-30).
• Jesus speaks to Peter, prophesying his failure to confess Him before the cock crows the next morning, though Peter insists he will stand by Jesus (22:31-34).
• He asks the disciples if when He sent them out without material possessions they lacked anything. They said no (22:35). He tells them to get the resources they need now (22:36). Scripture (Isaiah 53:12) must be fulfilled in Him He claims (22:37).
• With the disciples He goes to the Mount of Olives (presumably Gethsemane), instructs them to pray that they may escape this trial He endures, and then withdraws (22:39-41).
• Jesus requests not to have to endure the upcoming trials, yet adds that His will should be subordinated to the Father's will (22:42). (It is reported but only in some manuscripts that He is comforted in His great anguish by an angel [22:43-44].)
• He finds the disciples asleep because of grief. He rouses them to pray more (22:45).
• The betrayal by Judas' infamous kiss of Jesus to an armed crowd (22:47-48). Kissing a rabbi as a greeting was a common sign of respect in that era. One of Jesus' followers takes armed action against the high priest's slave, but Jesus puts an end to the violence and heals the slave (22:49-51). He next allows the chief priests and officers of the temple police to seize Him, noting He was not arrested previously when teaching in the temple. He claims it is the hour of these adversaries, the hour of the power of darkness (22:52-53).
• Jesus is seized and led to Caiaphas the high priest. Along the way Peter denies Him when confronted by a female slave. Then he denies Jesus again and then the cock crowed (22:54-60). Jesus looks at Peter, and Peter remembering Jesus' prophecy of his failure to confess him, weeps (22:61-62).
• Jesus is beaten and mocked (22:63-65). The assembly of all the Jewish elders (the Sanhedrin) gathered and invited Jesus to tell them if He were the Messiah. Jesus claims that if He told them they would not believe (22:66-68). He claims as Son of Man He will be seated at the right hand of the power of God. When they ask Him if he is Son of God, Jesus simply says that that is what they say. The assembly claims in anger that Jesus had made idolatrous claims (22:69-71).
• The Sanhedrin brought Jesus before the local Roman governor Pilate, accusing Him of perverting the Jewish nations and of forbidding the payment of taxes to the emperor and claiming to be the messianic king (23:1-2). Pilate asks Jesus if he is king of the Jews and Jesus simply notes that that is Pilate's confession (23:3). Pilate then claims to find no basis for the accusations, but the Jewish crowds insist on His guilt, claiming He stirs up people with His teaching (23:4-5).
• Learning Jesus is a Galilean, Pilate turns Him over to Herod's jurisdiction. This pleases Herod who had hoped to see Him perform miracles (23:6-8).
• Herod receives no answers from Jesus, and the chief priest and scribes who are present continue to accuse Him (23:9-10).

The king and his soldiers treat Jesus with contempt and mock Him, finally putting an elegant robe on Him and returning Him to Pilate (23:11). From that point, Herod and Pilate, previously adversaries, formed a coalition (23:12).
• Pilate tells the crowd that neither he nor Herod finds Jesus guilty of perverting the people as charged by the Jews. He does not deserve death (23:13-15). Pilate proposes to flog Jesus and then release Him (23:16). A seventeenth verse, absent in most ancient manuscripts refers to Pilate being obliged to release someone for the Jews at a festival, though there is no historical evidence of such a practice.
• The crowd shouted for Jesus' death, calling for the release of Barabbas, a man imprisoned for starting an insurrection and murder (23:18-19). Pilate, wanting to release Jesus, addresses the crowd again, but the crowd shouts for crucifixion (23:20-21). The same scenario happens a third time (23:22-23). Finally Pilate relents, releasing Barabbas (23:24-25).
• On the road to the site of the Crucifixion, Simon, from the African district of Cyrene (a region with a large Jewish population) is made to bear Jesus' Cross (23:26). He is given no credit for undertaking this task, as it is imposed on him.

Many followed, among them women who beat their breasts and cried for Jesus. He comforts *them*, saying only that they should weep for themselves and their children (23:27-28). Jesus invokes the Hosea 10:8 reference to the blessedness of one without a child in view of the days that are coming. Proverbially He suggests that Jerusalem will endure a horrible fate (23:29-31).
• Also led to the Crucifixion site, the Skull, are two criminals who were to be put to death with Him, one on each side of Him (23:32-33). Jesus urges the Father that those involved be forgiven. His garments are divided by lot (23:34).
• He is mocked as the Messiah who cannot save Himself. Soldiers give Him sour wine with the same mocking mantra. An inscription of the charge, "King of the Jews," is placed on the Cross (23:35-38).
• He engages in dialogue with the two criminals crucified with Him, the one mocking Him for not saving all of them if He is the Messiah and the other rebuking such mocking on grounds that Jesus was innocent (23:39-41). He requests that Jesus remember him when Jesus comes into the kingdom, and Jesus responds with the promise that this criminal would join Him in paradise (23:42-43).
• Darkness envelops the land from noon until three (23:44-45a). This may be a reference to Amos 8:9-10 where mourning for an only son is related to the sun going down in daylight.

The curtain of the temple is reported to have been torn (23:45b), a miraculous event paralleling the natural miracle of the light.
• When dying, Jesus commends His spirit to the Father (23:46) (as per the Davidic Psalm 31:5) Unlike in Mark's version (15:34), Jesus trusts God to the very end. This leads a centurion to praise God and proclaim Jesus' innocence (23:47).
• The crowds witnessing these events seemed agitated (perhaps by a sense of guilt [18:13; cf. Zechariah 12:10]) (23:48). But Jesus' acquaintances stood at a distance (23:49).
• Respected member of the council, Joseph of Arimathea, expecting the immanence of the kingdom of God, asks for Jesus' body. Pilate receives verification of the death and gives Joseph the body (23:50-52).
• Women who had followed Jesus from Galilee see where the body is laid. They return and prepare spices and ointments (23:53-56).

3. Theological Insights (see Charts of the Major Theological Options)
• The text testifies to our sin, Jesus' faithfulness, and God's forgiving love.
• Martin Luther notes that Simon of Cyrene "is a pattern for all Christians, for they must bear the Cross of the Lord Jesus; and that it is not, however, on account of this bearing that their sins are forgiven" (*Sermons on the Passion of Christ*, p. 148).
• Luther also thoughtfully describes the depth of our sin that it distorts our entire outlook on the Passion account. He writes:

> *We should weep for ourselves, because sin has polluted us so, and because so terrible a judgment awaits us. But where is the man to be found who weeps? The deeper men sink into the slime of sin, the more secure and joyful they grow.*
> (*Sermons on the Passion of Christ*, p. 152)

> *Even as we are disobedient with reference to the first lesson, for no one weeps and none laments their sins; so do we disobey in regard to the second, for no one wishes heartily to rejoice over the dear Lord Jesus... Instead of laughing and exulting all our heart that Christ has died for us, we weep. Now, we either regard this rejoicing on account of Jesus as not superior to the more popular joys of the world... We weep and lament and despair, as though Christ had not paid for our sins.*
> (*Sermons on the Passion of Christ*, p. 153)

• Luther also sees in the Passion a testimony to Christ's "tremendous love" (*Complete Sermons*, Vol. 5, p. 372).
• In John Calvin's view Peter's denial may be applied to the whole church, those in fear and to comfort them (*Calvin's*

Commentaries, Vol. XVII/1, p. 260). "Let us therefore remember that our strength is so far from being sufficient to resist powerful attacks, that it will give way, when there is the mere shadow of a battle" (*Ibid.*, p. 261).

• His denial teaches us that "we shall never cease to fall, if the Lord does not stretch out His hand to uphold us" (*Ibid.*, p. 264). The brutal stupidity that holds us is perpetual. "Let us therefore know, that whenever any one has fallen, his repentance will never begin, until the Lord has looked at him" (*Ibid.*, p. 265).

• The account shows, in Calvin's view, that "the truth of God always rises superior to all obstacles raised by human unbelief" (*Ibid.*, p. 289). He also gives advice regarding how we can best meditate on and profit from Christ's death:

> *For if we are desirous to profit aright by meditating on the death of Christ, we ought to begin with cherishing abhorrence of our sins, in proportion to the severity of the punishment that He [Christ] endured. This will cause us not only to feel displeasure and shame of ourselves, but to be penetrated with deep grief, and therefore to seek the medicine with becoming ardour, and at the same time to experience confusion and trembling. For we must have hearts harder than stones, if we are not cut to the quick by the wounds of the Son of God, if we not hate and detest our sins for expiating which the Son of God endured so many torments.*
>
> (*Ibid.*, p. 290)

• Calvin sees significance in Christ being stripped of His clothes (15:24). By His nakedness we have obtained the riches that make us honorable in God's presence (*Ibid.*, p. 298).

• He adds that thinking of Christ being fought against by those surrounding the Cross gives us a remedy for overcoming temptations when we feel that the world is against us:

> *And, therefore, if we learn to raise our minds to God, it will be easy for us to look down, as it were, from above, and despise the ignorance of unbelievers; for whatever may be their strength and resources, still they know not what they do.*
>
> (*Ibid.*, p. 301)

• Calvin finds an important lesson in Joseph of Arimathea securing Jesus' body for burial:

> *We see then how the Lord in a moment forms the hearts to new feelings and raises up by a spirit of fortitude those who had previously fainted. But if through a holy desire to honour Christ, Joseph assumed such courage while Christ was hanging on the Cross, woe to our slothfulness, if, now that He has risen from the dead, an equal zeal, at least, to glorify Him do not burn in our hearts.*
>
> (*Ibid.*, p. 333)

4. Socio-Economic, Political, Psychological, and Scientific Insights

• For social sins to abhor, see the references in this section for the First Lesson.

• For evidence of Americans' positive self-image of themselves, belief that they are good, see *New York Times* magazine, May 7, 2000, revealing that 73% of the population believe we are born good. No reason to think that this optimism has been tempered in the past decade.

5. Gimmick

Nobody much likes the story of Jesus' final week on earth. We commemorate it year after year, but Easter looks a lot better. The palms we distribute this Sunday help us dodge the reality of Holy Week a little. But most of it is distraction. Why not? We don't like to see what we look like during Holy Week. For that reason we are not really prepared for Easter when it comes; rather, we are inclined to regard it as just another routine Holy Week. We don't want to go through this preparation for Easter, because to see our lives from the perspective of the Cross isn't pretty.

6. Possible Sermon Moves and/or Stories/Examples

• Call the roll of those who failed. The disciples foolishly squabble over who is the greatest (22:24-27). Several of them fall asleep while Jesus had asked them to pray (22:39-45), Judas Iscariot betrays him (22:47-48), and Peter denies him (22:54-60). The crowds who had cheered him on the first Palm Sunday want Him crucified (23:4-5, 21, 35; cf. 19:37-38). But even when they got what they wanted, it did not seem to satisfy them (23:48).

• Note how in a sense, we do the same, as we squabble over or compete for the power positions in the church or the community, as we sleep late and miss church or the church meeting. Maybe it happens when we miss a chance to witness to Jesus with our friends or coworkers, meeting critical comments about Christianity and the church with silence. No, the story of the Passion is about us.

• Most of the time we don't want to hear that word, do our best to repress it. See the second bullet point of Socio-Economic, Political, Psychological, and Scientific Insights. Note the first quotation by Martin Luther in the third bullet point of Theological Insights regarding how the deeper we sink into the slime of sin, the more secure and joyful we grow. Perhaps that is why we are not moved as we should be by Jesus' great sacrifice.

- John Calvin offers some deep insights at this point into the Cross and our relationship to it. Cite the seventh bullet point in Theological Insights. Calvin had it right. To appreciate the meaning of Christ's death and the good news of Easter in all their depth, you need to begin by contemplating sin.
- Let's do that in even a bit more depth. Our story illustrates with even more profundity how badly sin has messed us up. We're so messed up that we don't know what we want. As famed modern theologian Karl Barth once put it: We are so crooked that we even think crookedly about our crookedness [sinfulness] (*Church Dogmatics*, Vol. IV/1, p. 361).
- Another significant twentieth-century American theologian Reinhold Niebuhr said that sinful human beings are like onions. You have to peel a lot of skin to get to what is edible in the onion. But the closer you get below the layers, the more pungent the onion is. It is like that for us. Once you peel off our pretensions of righteousness (skin deep), you get to the depth of the onion, which is just intolerable to taste and be around (*Justice & Mercy*, p. 90).
- Ask the congregation if Niebuhr is not right. We might look all right on the surface, but we are downright intolerable at the depth of who we are.
- Luke reports that on the way to Golgotha Jesus dialogued with a number of women in the crowd who were crying and hitting themselves (23:27). Jesus said they had their priorities wrong at that point and that they should be crying not for Him but for themselves (23:28ff)! In other words, even Jesus' faithful followers are so messed up that they don't know what to be happy about.
- Use Martin Luther's comments on this subject in the first quotation in the second bullet point of Theological Insights. We weep for Jesus when we should be crying about our sin and messed up lives. In fact, we should be laughing and celebrating over what Jesus did for us on the Cross. This is why we call this Friday "Good Friday!" Also consider John Calvin's comments in the next-to-last comments in Theological Insights.
- Note Luther's comment in the fourth bullet point of Theological Insights and Calvin's comment in the second quote of the second bullet point of that section for the Second Lesson.

7. Wrap-Up

On the Cross we see God's "tremendous love." This is a love that is not stopped by us no matter how hard we resist, no matter how messed up we are, it comes after us, working to change us, to save us. Jesus turns our tears into laughter, so we come to cry for the right reasons (our sin and selfishness) and celebrate for the right ones (His hanging on the Cross). We have a lot to celebrate this week and every week, so let's be sure we show up for the right parties!

Maundy Thursday / Holy Thursday
March 28, 2013

Revised Common	Exodus 12:1-4 (5-10) 11-14	1 Corinthians 11:23-26	John 13:1-17, 31b-35
Roman Catholic	Exodus 12:1-8 (11-14)	1 Corinthians 11:23-26	John 13:1-15
Episcopal	Exodus 12:1-14a	1 Corinthians 11:23-26 (27-32)	John 13:1-15 or Luke 22:14-30

Theme of the Day In the presence of Christ!

Collect of the Day Two options are available. In the first, petitions are offered that Christ's commandment to love one another be written on our hearts and we be given the will to serve others. Sanctification as exhorted is here emphasized. The second alternative, after referring to Christ's establishing a new covenant in the Lord's Supper and showing us the dignity of service, petitions that God grant that by the Holy Spirit the aforementioned signs refresh us and speak to our hearts. This alternative emphasizes the sacraments and the Holy Spirit.

Psalm of the Day *Psalm 116:1-2, 12-19*
• A thanksgiving for healing.
• God praised for hearing us (vv. 1-2).
• Reference to lifting the cup of salvation (v. 13) reminds us of the Lord's Supper.
• Reference to being a servant of the Lord, the child of a serving girl (v. 16) could be applied to Jesus (especially the v. 15 reference to how precious the death of the faithful is to the Lord).

Sermon Text and Title
"Celebrating Passover"
Exodus 12:1-4 (5-10) 11-14

1. Theological Aim of the Sermon and Strategy
To clarify the nature of the Lord's Supper in light of precedents in the Jewish festival of Passover. Testimony is given to the love of God that unites Christians and Jews (Justification by Grace) and to the theme of freedom (implicit also in the Jewish celebration of Passover) (Social Ethics and Sanctification).

2. Exegesis (see Transfiguration)
• P's version of the establishment of Passover. This follows the account of the final plague the Lord worked against Pharaoh, which does not succeed in liberating the people (ch.11).
• The month of Nissan (March-April) is to be designated the beginning of the year (v. 2).
• On the tenth of that month, each family is to take a lamb or share a lamb with their closest neighbor and divide the lamb (vv. 3-4). The lamb is to be one year old and without blemish (v. 5).
• Instructions are given to put blood of the lamb on the doorposts and lintel of the houses of the people (these were the holy places of a house). The lamb was to be eaten the night it is killed, and instructions are given on how it is to be prepared and what is to be eaten (vv. 7-9). The lamb is to be entirely consumed, save remains to be burned the next morning (v. 10).
• Instructions are given on the attire one is to have when eating the lamb. It should be consumed hurriedly (v. 11).
• Passover explained, how the Lord would strike down the first born of all living things in Egypt, but the blood on the door posts would be a sign for him to pass over that house so the plague would not destroy them (vv. 12-13).
• Henceforth the day was to be one of remembrance, a celebration of perpetual observance (v. 14).

3. Theological Insights (see Charts of the Major Theological Options)
• Consideration of the Lord's Supper as well as Satisfaction Theory of Atonement and their relation to Justification by Grace, Social Ethics (construed as freedom/liberation), and Sanctification (construed as thankful pilgrimage).
• See the quotations about the Passover by Jewish rabbis in this section for the First Lesson, Lent 4.
• John Wesley notes that as the Passover lamb was killed not just to be looked upon but to be eaten, so "we must by faith make Christ ours, so we do that which we eat, and we must receive spiritual strength and nourishment from Him, as from

our food, and have delight in Him…" (*Commentary on the Bible*, p. 72).
• With reference to the perpetual observance of Passover, Wesley adds: "As long as we live we must continue feeding upon Christ and rejoicing in Him always, with thankful mention of the great things he has done for us" (*Commentary on the Bible*, p. 72).
• Early African monk Macarius the Egyptian (who influenced Wesley) notes that just as the Hebrews having observed the Passover leave, so individuals, having received the life of the Holy Spirit and eaten the Christ the Lamb, progress and move on (*Pseudo-Macarius*, p. 236).

4. Socio-Economic, Political, Psychological, and Scientific Insights
• A 2007 poll of the Anti-Defamation League reveals that there is still a core of 12% of the American public maintains hard-core Anti-Semitic attitudes.
• See this section for the First Lesson, Advent 3, for leads on obtaining statistics for prevailing social trends from which we need liberation.

5. Gimmick
Greet the congregation with "Shalom." Repeat the term. Note how strange a way this Jewish greeting seems to be in a Christian church. Yet it is fitting in view of the First Lesson's account of the Passover. Fitting in view of the relationship between Passover and the Lord's Supper we commemorate today.

6. Possible Sermon Moves and/or Stories/Examples
• Review what Passover is the Jewish festival celebrating their escape from bondage in Egypt. First Lesson tells the story. When Egyptians would not let the people of Israel go, despite the miracles God had given Moses to perform, the Lord sent the angel of death to kill all the first-born males in the land. To the people of Israel He told them to smear lamb's blood on their doorposts so that the angel of death would pass over their houses and not kill their first-born males.
• This was the last straw for the Egyptians. They gave the Israelites their freedom. And because the people of Israel did not have time to make bread with yeast, they had to make bread without yeast for their trip to freedom (vv. 15, 17-20).
• We know that the Last Supper transpired in connection with the Passover (John 13:1). It seems that it was during the sacred Passover Meal, which Jews call Seder, that Christ first instituted Holy Communion. We see this tight Jewish-Christian connection even clearer when the nature of the Seder meal is considered.
• Review (educate congregation of) characteristics of the Seder. First night of Passover all the members of a Jewish family sit down at the kitchen table for dinner (like Jesus and His disciples did). On the table is a roasted shinbone, which serves as a reminder of the slaughtered Passover lamb, an egg symbolizing the awakening of nature to spring, and bitter herbs to remind Jews of their slavery in Egypt. During the meal the meaning of each of these items is explained by the head of the family. Haggadah, the story of the Passover, is read.
• These are not the only elements involved in the Seder meal. On the table sits three matzot — the unleavened bread — which reminds Jews of the speed with which their ancestors had to leave Egypt. Here we have the clearest overlap with Christian faith. It was this bread Jesus used in the Last Supper and on that table sits cups of wine, which Jesus also used at the Last Supper.
• Using something that was already part of the Jewish faith and then changing or expanding its meaning was Jesus' style. This is evident in His establishment of Holy Communion.
• In fact, this has been God's game-plan throughout history. He elected the Jews to be His chosen people and through them planned to save us all. So He gave them many of the elements of salvation (promise of the Messiah, the law, the word of God's forgiving love, and the Seder) and then sent Jesus as a Jew with the express intention of taking the very best in Judaism and then modifying it so all people could more clearly know of God's love. That is exactly what Jesus has done. To this day, the faith Christ creates in us, the faith we know as Christianity, is like the flower whose seed was Judaism. That's how closely the two religions are related: Christianity is the flower, and Judaism is the seed.
• Review the significance of these points of contact. First, note that when we receive communion we are participating in a ceremony with roots that are centuries older than Christianity and the institution of the Last Supper. We not only receive Christ's body in this meal; we also celebrate the real meaning of the Passover, which is freedom — the promise that freedom and salvation are not just for the Jews, but for everyone.

At every Seder meal, Jews place an extra cup on the table, one more than the family needs. This extra cup is also filled with wine, symbolizing that someday everyone will enjoy the freedom Jews received at the Passover and with the Jews, will enjoy salvation.
• Our own Christian Lord's Supper conveys this theme. When eating the bread and wine we are reminded that salvation

is not just for us and that God's love is for everyone. We realize that we are celebrating exactly what the Jews celebrate at Passover — the freedom and redemption of all humanity! The only difference is that while Jews celebrate it as a promise from God, we celebrate it as a done-deal.

• The links between Christian and Judaism are even more evident. It may be that the guys present in the church are not wearing a *yamacah* (the little Jewish skull-cap worn by adult males). We may not keep a kosher kitchen. But we are as much a Jew as Benjamin Netanyahu, Larry King, or Dustin Hoffman, because we have received the same promises of freedom and salvation as they have. We are as much children of Abraham as they are.

• No room, then, in the church for anti-Semitism. Every time Christians make fun of Jews we are really showing hatred of ourselves. Christians are tied with Jews in a relationship that can never be destroyed. Destroy the seed, and you kill the flower too.

• The Bible teaches that there will always be Jews, right up to the second coming. Note relevant verses in Romans 9-11. The seed that is Judaism must continue to flourish if the flower — Christianity — is to survive!

7. Wrap-Up
Invite members to reflect on the relation between Christian and Jewish faith. When receiving Communion remind the flock that they are celebrating the real meaning of Passover — the promise of freedom that comes with God's love. Come and get that love.

Sermon Text and Title
"The Presence of Christ's Body!"
1 Corinthians 11:23-26

1. Theological Aim of the Sermon and Strategy
To help the faithful appreciate the way in which the Lord's Supper renders Christ present.

2. Exegesis (see Introduction to Selected Books of the Bible)
• After critiquing certain reportedly aberrant practices in the Corinthian church pertaining to the celebration of the Lord's Supper (vv. 17-22), Paul reports Jesus' words of institution, which he claims to have received from the Lord (v. 23).
• The words of institution for the sacrament are reported (vv. 24-25).
• Paul reports that as often as the bread and cup are eaten and drunk, we proclaim Christ's death until He comes (v. 26).

3. Theological Insights (see Charts of the Major Theological Options)
• The doctrines of the Lord's Supper and Sanctification receive attention. The text also addresses the unity of all Christians (and so the nature of the church).
• Preachers should consider the official doctrinal statement of their denomination regarding the nature of Christ's presence in the sacrament.
• For Martin Luther, preaching on this text, the sacrament serves to keep Christians united in one mind, doctrine, and not faith, not each being his own kernel of grain…" (*Complete Sermons*, Vol. 6, p. 45).

> *… Christ used bread and wine for His supper because as many kernels, each having its own body and form are ground together, becoming one bread, so every human being is an individual kernel, that is, his own person and a separate creature. But because we all are partakers, we are all one bread and body and are called one lump.* (*Ibid.*)

> *He claims that Christ instituted the sacrament to keep Christians together so that they would know nothing but Jesus Christ.* (*Ibid.*, p. 46)

• The Reformer also speaks of what the sacrament has to offer for everyday life:

> *But our Lord Christ desires that just as your greed speaks to you and preaches to you endlessly of money and goods, or power and honor, in the same manner you would let yourself be drawn and led into that life, and think on your Redeemer, who died on the Cross for you; and so set your heart on fire, that you desire to be with Him, being weary of this world.* (*Ibid.*, p. 47)

4. Socio-Economic, Political, Psychological, and Scientific Insights
• Rituals like the sacraments seem as capable of facilitating the flow of pleasurable dopamine as spiritual reflection (Andrew Newberg, *Why We Believe What We Believe*, p. 189).
• See the section for First Lesson, Lent 1, for details on how rituals/sacraments enhance social solidarity.

5. Gimmick
Read the words of institution (vv. 24-26). Ask the congregation what this means.

6. Possible Sermon Moves and/or Stories/Examples
• Describe the position of your denomination on the relation of Christ's presence to the bread and wine. Preachers should use the official doctrinal statement of their denomination to make their points.
• For those teaching that Christ is really and bodily present (esp. Lutherans and some Episcopalians), analogies for how bread can be Christ's body and still be bread (two at once) should be provided. Among these analogies might be a burning coal (both fire and coal), a burning iron, or an embrace of lovers (both a hug and love really present).
• Explore the so what. For traditions that teach a symbolic view of the sacrament, stress the joy of a pleasant memory, now love can be transmitted when we recall a loved one. In the case of those embracing the idea of the sacrament as a seal, note how good it is to have an encounter with a loved one, how much better to discourse with the loved one than merely to rely on a memory. This transpires when the Holy Spirit raises our soul out of the body to meet Christ in heaven (the position held by Presbyterian, some Methodist and Episcopal proponents of this view of the sacrament).
• For those who hold the real presence position, make clear that this view is not a cannibalism, insofar as it entails that we actually swallow Jesus. Present it more as a physical embrace (as Jesus' affirmation of our bodies) or as an intimacy a lot like sexual intercourse. Note how the actual physical embrace enhances relations much more than words sometimes.

7. Wrap-Up
Call on parishioners to come to the altar, not with fear or unnecessary seriousness, but to come with joy. For waiting is a loving God, ready (for proponents of the Symbolic View) to create more pleasant memories; for proponents of the Sign View, to fellowship with Jesus, or ready to clasp us in His arms and tell of His love (the Real Presence view)!

Sermon Text and Title
"Worship God on His Own Terms"
John 13:1-17, 31b-35

1. Theological Aim of the Sermon and Strategy
A proclamation of God's love for us shown in the Passion understood as a humble love (Justification by Grace) and how it might inspire such loving by us (Sanctification).

2. Exegesis (see Introduction to Selected Books of the Bible)
• The story of the events of the Last Supper.
• Before the Passover festival, Jesus knew it was time for Him to depart and go to the Father. Loving those who were His, Jesus is said to have loved them to the end (v. 1).
• Notes the devil had already put the idea of betraying Jesus in Judas Iscariot's heart (v. 2).
• Jesus is said to come from God, receiving all things from the Father, and knows He is to return (v. 30). He proceeds to wash the disciples' feet (vv. 4-5).
• Peter protests against his Lord washing his feet. Jesus responds that unless one is washed they will have no share of Him (vv. 6-9). The atonement is here prophesied.
• Jesus says the disciples are clean, but not all of them, indicating His knowledge of His betrayal (vv. 10-11).
• Jesus explains the significance of His washing the disciples' feet, though He Himself was their teacher and lord. It is an example to the disciples (vv. 12-15). Servants are not greater than their master, nor messengers greater than the one who sent them. If these things are known there are blessings if they are done (vv. 16-17).
• After further discourse and the identification of Judas as His betrayer (vv. 18-20), Jesus leaves the room of the supper. He notes that now the Son of Man has been glorified and God glorified in Him (vv. 31b-32).
• Jesus adds that He will only be with the disciples a little longer. They cannot go with Him (v. 33).
• He gives them a new commandment — to love one another as He has loved them (v. 34). By this everyone will know who His disciples are (v. 35).

3. Theological Insights (see Charts of the Major Theological Options)
• The washing of the disciples' feet by Jesus is analyzed as a sign of the Passion and of God's love for us (Justification by Grace) as well as a sign for Christian living (Sanctification).
• John Wesley contends that Jesus' insistence on washing the disciples' feet (v. 8) referred to the fact that if He does not wash

us in His blood we have no communion with Him (*Commentary on the Bible*, p. 466).
• Wesley also adds that Jesus sought to teach a lesson of humble love (*Ibid.*).
• John Calvin saw the washing of feet as a testimony "that the love with which He embraced them [His disciples] was firm and lasting; that, though they were deprived of His presence, they might still be convinced that death itself would not quench this love" (*Calvin's Commentaries*, Vol. XVIII/1, p. 54).
• Regarding Peter's sin of not wanting his feet washed (v. 8), Calvin notes:

> *In short, until a man renounces the liberty of judging as to the works of God, whatever exertions he may make to honour God, still pride will always lurk under the garb of humility.* (*Ibid.*, p. 57)

• About our human condition he writes: "… every man thinks more highly of himself than he ought, and despises almost every other person" (*Ibid.*, p. 60).
• We are to love the weak, he adds:

> *… the man who does not think of associating with weak brethren, on the condition of submitting mildly and gently even to offices that appear to be mean, claims more than he has a right to claim, and has too high an opinion of himself.* (*Ibid.*, p. 61)

• The Reformer also reflects on the awesomeness of the Passion:

> *Even at the present day, the remembrance of the Cross of Christ is sufficient to make us tremble, were we not instantly met by the consolation, that He triumphed in the Cross, having obtained a victory over Satan, sin, and death.* (*Ibid.*, p. 73)

4. Socio-Economic, Political, Psychological, and Scientific Insights
• American life is infected by the malady of self-promotion. It is thought to be the only way to succeed in American life. For good examples just google "self-promotion as a key to success" to see the astounding number of sites devoted to this topic.
• A 2008 Barna Research Group poll revealed that 88% of the American public felt accepted by God. But this is clearly not in line with the biblical witness insofar as an earlier 2004 poll revealed that only 25% of the public believed salvation was by grace alone. This confidence in acceptance is clearly not an unconditional confidence for most Americans.

5. Gimmick
John's version of the Last Supper is a lot different form the other gospels. He devotes much attention, not to describing the institution of the Lord's Supper, but instead about Jesus washing the disciples' feet. What does this story have to do with the Passion, with the sacrament we commemorate tonight, and with worship? Quite a bit. It's all about humble love.

6. Possible Sermon Moves and/or Stories/Examples
• Our lesson says that Jesus having loved His own loved them to the end (v. 1b). He loves you and me to the end. John goes on to tell us that Jesus knows that the Father had given all things into His hands (v. 3b). *All* things are in Jesus' hands.
• Then it happened: Jesus got up, took off His robe, tied a towel around himself, poured water, and began to wash the disciples' feet. He even used the towel he had on to dry their feet (vv. 4-5)! The Lord of the universe, the one who has all things in His hands, washes the feet of His followers!
• Keep in mind that according to John this action by Jesus was part of the Passover celebration (v. 1). Keep in mind that this was part of the Jewish worship. Somehow Jesus wanted to make it clear that God is to be worshiped with this kind of humble love.
• Cite John Wesley's observation in the second bullet point of Theological Insights. We cannot worship God apart from celebrating what Christ has done for us on the Cross.
• We don't praise God like He wants if we are not focused on how His blood has made us clean! Cite the data in Socio-Economic, Political, Psychological, and Scientific Insights. This accounts for why though Americans claim to be "spiritual," worship attendance is in decline. We obviously are not inclined to worship God in the right way insofar as our confidence in God is not based on what Jesus did for us, but instead on how good we are.
• Urge the congregation to give a lot of thought to the issue of how much their faith is focused on Jesus' saving work rather than what they do for Him. Even those of us who claim to be Christian are more often than not Deists (believers in a judging God who demands obedience) than Christians (dependent on Christ and grace for all that happens that is good). Tonight is a good time to be sure we worship Christ the way He wants.
• John Calvin makes another important point about worship. Use quote in the fourth bullet point of Theological Insights. He makes it clear that when you have tasted the sort of humble love we have been describing, it provides such a wonderful sense of its firmness and endurance that even when Christ is not present that love is not quenched. Stress how this point enhances

worship. Even if we do not physically observe Christ in worship (lack His presence), a focus on this love of His makes faith in this love more certain! Doesn't matter so much if Jesus is not physically present when His love is present!

• This is a love that can change you and change America with all its self-seeking. Review again the data in Socio-Economic, Political, Psychological, and Scientific Insights.

7. Wrap-Up

America needs the kind of love this style of worship invokes. French enlightenment scholar Blaise Pascal tells us why. He says that Christ loves us more ardently than we ever loved our self-seeking foulness (*Pensées*, p. 315). In the presence of this compelling love Jesus has for us, worship life changes and so does life!

Good Friday
March 29, 2013

Revised Common	Isaiah 52:13—53:12	Hebrews 10:16-25 or Hebrews 4:14-16; 5:7-9	John 18:1—19:42
Roman Catholic	Isaiah 52:13—53:12	Hebrews 4:14-16; 5:7-9	John 18:1—19:42
Episcopal	Isaiah 52:13—53:12 or Genesis 22:1-18	Hebrews 10:1-25	John (18:1-40) 19:1-37

Theme of the Day   How the Cross changes everyday life.

Collect of the Day   Two alternatives are provided. In the first, petitions are offered to God to look with loving mercy on the family of faith. In the second, petitions are made that we who have been born out of Christ may find mercy at all times. Justification by Grace is the theme of both prayers.

Psalm of the Day   *Psalm 22*
• A lament prayer for deliverance from mortal illness, attributed to David.
• Cry for help and defense of forsakenness (vv. 1-2) quoted by Jesus on the Cross (Mark 15:34). This suggests the Psalm can be read as applying to Jesus' Passion.
• Other references foreshadowing the crucifixion (vv. 6-7), His being poured out like water as enriched by evil-doers (vv. 14, 16) and His clothes being divided (v. 18).
• The Psalm concludes with a vow of the sick one to offer a formal thanksgiving in the temple on recovery (vv. 22, 25). The hymn to be sung follows (vv. 23-31). Among its references to praising God include acclamation and affirmation of His hearing cries of the afflicted (v. 24), caring for the poor (v. 25), as well as receiving praise from the whole earth (v. 27), from the dead (v. 29), and from posterity (vv. 30-31). This praise could be applied to the God who raised Jesus.

Sermon Text and Title
"The Servant Who Shares It All!"
Isaiah 52:13—53:12

1. Theological Aim of the Sermon and Strategy
To proclaim that in His atoning work (Satisfaction Theory), Christ gives all He has to the faithful (Justification by Grace as Intimate Union); an Actuality View of what Christ's work accomplishes is presupposed. The social (Social Ethical) implications of this are also examined.

2. Exegesis (see Introduction to Selected Books of the Bible)
• Another text which is the work of Second Isaiah, written soon before the fall of Babylon.
• The text is taken from the Book of Consolation, a series of eschatological prophecies.
• This is the so-called Fourth Servant Song. For a description of these songs, see First Lesson for Palm Sunday.
• The first ten verses of chapter 53 are a congregational reflection on the Servant. Other verses in chapter 52 and the last two of chapter 53 purport to be God's word.
• This song is about God exalting His disfigured Servant (52:13, 15; 53:12a).
• Although in its historical context the song is intended to depict Israel's restoration, several passages (see below) can be read as prefiguring Christ's atoning work.
• The Servant is said not to have a desirable appearance (53:2). He was despised and rejected (53:3).
• The Servant also bore our infirmities (53:4) and was wounded for our transgressions. He took the punishment that made us whole (53:5).
• His death is said to have been a perversion of justice (53:8).
• Yet it was the will of the Lord to crush the Servant. It was an offering for sin (53:10). He makes many righteous (53:11).
• He bore the sins of many (53:12).

3. Theological Insights (see Charts of the Major Theological Options)
• The text testifies to Christology and the atonement (perhaps a Classic View). Justification by Grace (esp. but not exclusively, as Intimate Union) is presupposed.
• Another way to read the text in relation to its context in the Christian Bible would be to focus on Christ and the atonement (esp. the Satisfaction Theory).
• Reference in verse 11 connotes Christ's work of justifying us.
• On the extraordinary character of what Jesus had done, Martin Luther, while lecturing on this text, wrote:

> *Therefore the prophet leads us so earnestly beyond all righteousness and our rational capacity and confronts us with the suffering of Christ to impress upon us that all that Christ has is mine.* (*Luther's Works*, Vol. 17, p. 221)

This makes it a challenge in his view truly to believe this work of Jesus: "We can preach and uphold this passage in public, but we can only believe it with difficulty" (*Ibid.*, p. 222).
• The Reformer follows with some practical advice about accepting this witness:

> *Our nature is opposed to the function and power of Christ's Passion... We must clearly transfer our sins from ourselves to Christ... Hence you must say: "I see my sin in Christ, therefore my sin is not mine but another's. I see it in Christ."* (*Ibid.*, p. 223)

4. Socio-Economic, Political, Psychological, and Scientific Insights
• For social sins to abhor, see the references in this section for the First Lesson, Passion Sunday.

5. Gimmick
Review the historical background on the text, referring to the first three bullet points of Exegesis.

6. Possible Sermon Moves and/or Stories/Examples
• This ancient prophecy has a lot to say to us today. We hunger for better times, no less than the ancient Hebrews did. Review the social challenges we face referred to in Socio-Economic, Political, Psychological, and Scientific Insights.
• Elaborate on an analysis of Western society propounded by French existentialist Albert Camus written half a century ago that is still timely. He speaks of forgetting the fate of humanity for the delusion of power:

> *Impatience with limits... despair at being a man [human], have finally driven them to human excesses. Denying the real grandeur of life, they have had to stake all on their own excellence. For want of better to do, they deified themselves and their misfortunes began; these gods had their eyes put out.* (*The Rebel*, p. 305)

The people of Western society "no longer love life" he claims (*Ibid.*). We clearly need relief, a way out of the mess.
• It's for our mess that Jesus died. Our impatience, despair, human excesses, idolatry, and injustice to fellow humans is why He died.
• How can this not very good-looking, slightly deformed Servant (that's what the prophet says about Him in 53:2 and 52:14), one who suffered (53:5) do us any good?
• Our lesson tells us. We already knew it. He bears our infirmities (53:4) and bore our sins (53:12). The result: He made many righteous (53:11)! All our sin is taken away. Jesus makes us righteous in that sense. Use the last bullet point of Theological Insights.
• Martin Luther elaborated on this point with regard to the Cross' significance in freeing us from the agonies of death:

> *But Christ takes our place and innocently endures death, terror, and hell, so that through Him and in Him we escape all this. Through His undeserved and innocent death He saves us from the rightful death that we deserved, that is, from the sins whereby we merited death and hell.* (*Complete Sermons*, Vol. 5, pp. 402-403)

• Luther did a nice job summarizing precisely what happens on the Cross, what Christ the Suffering Servant did for us. He shares all that He has! Use the first quote in the fourth bullet point of Theological Insights.
• Emphasize "all." Christ gives us *all* that He has! The righteousness and sinlessness of God is now ours. The love and compassion for humanity is now ours. As Martin Luther put it elsewhere, the Father's favor and grace are now ours (see *The Book of Concord* [Kolb and Wengert, eds.], p. 440).
• Armed with all this, life cannot but get better. With God's eternal perspective (1 Timothy 1:17), we will be more oriented to the future and less fearful of death, sharing His creativity (Psalm 104; Genesis 1) more appreciative of life, sharing in His righteousness (v. 11; Exodus 9:27) less selfish and driven to excess, and sharing His passion for the poor (Psalm 35:10; Luke 18:22) less likely to be satisfied with injustice. The Servant who on the Cross shares with us all that He and the Father have

has a big impact on our everyday lives and on how we live and think outside the walls of the church. In making these gifts available by the Cross, today really is a "Good Friday"!

7. Wrap-Up
In the same spirit, turn-of-the twentieth century Christian businessman and Pentecostal missionary John G. Lake wrote: "The wonder is that Jesus purposed to make your heart and mine just as sweet and lovely and pure and holy as His own." Good Friday makes this aim of Jesus a done deal. With the sweet, lovely, and pure heart that God has given you and me on the Cross, life just yearns to be changed for the better. Simply note to the congregation that this gift is theirs.

Sermon Text and Title
"Look What Happened on the Cross"
Hebrews 10:16-25

1. Theological Aim of the Sermon and Strategy
To give special attention to the implications of Christ's atoning work (construed as Satisfaction Theory) for unity of human beings (Sanctification).

2. Exegesis (see Introduction to Selected Books of the Bible)
- After a brief citation from Jeremiah (31:33-34) concerning the New Covenant ushered in by Christ the high priest (vv. 16-18), exhortations to the faithful are offered.
- Forgiveness of sin and writing the Lord's laws on the hearts and minds of the people are the essence the New Covenant (vv. 16-18).
- Reference is made to the blood of Jesus giving confidence to enter the sanctuary [the presence of God] through the curtain (which is said to refer to His flesh) (vv. 19-20).
- Jesus is said to be a great priest (v. 21). As a result the faithful can approach a public confession in full assurance for their hearts are clear from an evil conscience (vv. 22-23).
- Calls for provoking each other to love and good deeds (v. 24). Would have the faithful not neglect meeting together (unlike some who do not) for the end time is approaching (v. 25).

3. Theological Insights (see Charts of the Major Theological Options)
- A discussion of the atonement (esp. Satisfaction Theory, implied by designating Christ a priest who performs sacrifice of sin, but since it is not clear to whom the sacrifice is paid, the text could be interpreted in the mode of the Governmental Theory) and Justification by Grace as well as their implications for unity (Sanctification and the church).
- John Wesley noted while commenting on verse 20 that:

    As by rending the veil in the temple, the holy of holies became visible and accessible, so by wounding the body of Christ, the God of heaven was manifested and the way to heaven opened. (*Commentary on the Bible*, p. 568)

- John Calvin describes Christ as the fountain of all holiness and righteousness (*Calvin's Commentaries*, Vol. XXII/1, p. 236).
- About the admonition to hold fast our faith (v. 23) the Reformer writes:

    For we hence first learn, that our faith rests on this foundation, that God is true, that is, true to His promise, which His word contains; for that we believe, the voice or word of God must precede... for except God promises, no one can believe. (*Ibid.*, p. 238)

- Calvin regards verse 25 as addressing the need to cultivate unity, which is so difficult because human beings tend to set themselves above others, for "those who seem in anything to excel cannot well endure their inferiors to be on an equality with themselves" (*Ibid.*, pp. 240-241).
- The great preacher of the early church John Chrysostom, commenting on verse 24 and its exhortation to provoke one another to love and good deeds, proclaimed: "For if a stone rubbed against a stone sends forth fire, how much more soul mingled with soul!" (*Nicene and Post-Nicene Fathers*, First Series, Vol. 14, p. 455). The connection of people sparks the flames of love.

4. Socio-Economic, Political, Psychological, and Scientific Insights
- A 2010 Gallup poll revealed more polarization in America over politics than ever before. Eighty-eight percent of Democrats

approved Obama administration politics, while only 23% of Republicans agreed. The most recent presidential election did little to reduce this tension.
• Blacks and whites continue to be divided in the way they see the world. A 2008 CNN/*Essence* magazine poll revealed that while 43% of African Americans regard racism as a serious problem, while only 11% of whites polled agree. Nearly half of them claim it is not a serious problem.

5. Gimmick
Americans (human beings) are very divided. Cite data in Socio-Economic, Political, Psychological, and Scientific Insights. Some of the divisions are the result of who we are (ethnicity, gender, age). Other divisions have to do with what we believe. Good Friday is about overcoming these differences.

6. Possible Sermon Moves and/or Stories/Examples
• Ask the congregation to consider whether they feel America is divided. Ask them to confess the tensions they feel with those in the church, in the community, and in their workplaces. Good Friday is a time when we confess our sins, for they are the very reason Christ went to the Cross.
• Divisions like we have been considering are consequences of how you look at life. When we are in conflict, it is a function of making judgments about our neighbor and finding them wanting. We are evaluating our reality in accord with certain rules of behavior and being. It is living under the law, certain demands that people need to live up to or you judge them. This is the Old Covenant (Exodus 19:5) that our lesson says has been replaced by Christ's sacrificial work.
• But today, on the Cross, our lesson says that Christ the high priest has ushered in a New Covenant (v. 15). This New Covenant is characterized by forgiveness, not by judgment (vv. 17-18)! Cite John Calvin's comment in the third bullet point of Theological Insights.
• Our lesson elaborates further on this point. This New Covenant gives us direct access to God (vv. 19-20), and so a full assurance of being free from an evil conscience (vv. 22-23)! Freed from judgment we are also free from judging others.
• Good Friday is about the end of being judgmental. For God is not judgmental about us. When you are not judgmental of others, you don't find yourself divided anymore from others.
• In line with this thinking, the author of our lesson proceeds to note that with this new way Christ's sacrifice has created, we are to look for ways to provoke each other to good deeds, meeting together and encouraging each other (vv. 24-25). Christ's sacrificial work on the Cross brings us together and overcomes the divisions noted previously.
• What happened on the Cross is that Jesus died for us all. The divisions are gone (unless we introduce them again)! Political arguments, racial and gender differences did not matter to Jesus on the Cross. Should they matter to us?
• Martin Luther talks about those who rely on Christ being carried on His shoulders (*Luther's Works*, Vol. 29, p. 226). We are all on His shoulders. Not much room to fight when you are all sitting on the same shoulder.
• Forgiveness of sin on Good Friday does other things in our lives. The Cross abolishes all the old, petty divisions and that makes life better.
• The ancient Greek poet Aesop said it well: "In union there is strength." Likewise the nineteenth-century American poet George Pope Morris: "United we stand, divided we fall."
• Note the last bullet point in Theological Insights, John Chrysostom's point about how mingling together can put us on fire (for God and for each other). Urge the congregation to consider how much fire could be lit among us in the coming year by rubbing our souls together, made possible by the unity the Cross creates.

7. Wrap-Up
No two ways about it. Life is so much better, so much more in harmony, we are so much more unified, because Jesus put us all on His shoulders and died for each and every one of us.

Sermon Text and Title
"What's Good About Good Friday?"
John 18:1—19:42

1. Theological Aim of the Sermon and Strategy
A proclamation of God's initiative in saving us, regardless of how we respond, and the implications of that awareness for life. Some attention is also given to the nature of sin that threatens to becloud these insights.

2. Exegesis (see Introduction to Selected Books of the Bible)

- John's version of the Passion narrative, Jesus' arrest, trial, and crucifixion.
- Following His high priestly prayer (ch. 17), Jesus and the disciples reportedly journey to Kidron Valley, between Jerusalem and the Mount of Olives (18:1). Judas leads soldiers, temple police, and Pharisees to arrest Him (18:2-3).
- Jesus asks them whom they seek and when His name is mentioned, He uses a phrase suggestive of his identification with God (with the name Yahweh), "I am He" (Exodus 3:14; Isaiah 43:10-11, 25). His arresters do obeisance (18:4-8a).
- He urges that his followers be released to fulfill earlier prophecies that He would lose no one (18:8b-9; cf. 6:39; 17:12).
- Jesus stops Peter from trying to free Him (though Peter did cut off the ear of one of the high priest's men [vv. 10-11]).
- Jesus goes before Annas, the father-in-law of High Priest Caiaphas, who had (vv. 48-50) advised that it would be better to have Jesus killed as representative of the people of Israel than to have the people and the temple attacked by the Romans (18:13-14).
- Peter denies Jesus outside the gate of the high priest's courtyard. Another disciple known by the high priest enters the courtyard (18:15-18).
- Unlike other gospel accounts where Jesus first sees the Sanhedrin (on John's account He had already been judged by them [11:47-53]), Jesus simply is judged by former High Priest Annas. In the interrogation Jesus claims that all know or have heard of His teaching (18:19-21). He is struck for insubordination and sent to Caiaphas (18:22-24).
- Peter denies Jesus again after being accused of being a follower by a relative of one whom he had injured defending Jesus (18:25-27).
- Jesus is brought to Roman Governor Pontius Pilate. Jews do not enter the headquarters lest they become unclean for Passover celebrations (18:28).
- Pilate tries to have the Jews punish Jesus themselves, but they note that they are not permitted to inflict capital punishment (18:29-32).
- Pilate questions Jesus asking if He is king of the Jews. He notes His kingdom is not of the world and that His followers are not defending Him (18:33-36). More emphasis is placed by Mark on the charge of Jesus' kingship than in other gospels.
- After more exchange with Jesus, during which Pilate surmises that Jesus has claimed to be a king but failed to comment on the truth of His testimony, he offers Jesus' release to the Jews. The crowd prefers the release of Barabbas the bandit (18:37-40).
- Pilate has Jesus flogged and mocked by clothing Him with king-like attire (19:1-2). He is mocked, called king of the Jews (19:3).
- Pilate claimed to find no case against Jesus. But chief priests and police call for His crucifixion (19:4-7), Jesus' claim to be Son of God is the reason given for their call.
- After this exchange, Pilate is fearful. He further interrogates Jesus. Jesus refuses to answer some questions (19:8-9).
- Angered, Pilate threatens Jesus with the power he has over him. But Jesus responds that Pilate's power is dependent on God. The one who handed Jesus over is said to be guilty of a greater sin (19:10-11).
- Pilate then tries to release Jesus, but the Jews claim that Jesus is the enemy of the emperor (19:12-13). Announcing Jesus as the Jews' king, asking if He should be crucified, he finally hands Jesus over to the crowd at noon (19:14-16). Jewish custom was to slaughter Passover lambs on the day of preparation at noon for the festival.
- Jesus carries the Cross to Golgotha (Aramaic for "skull"). He is crucified between two others, with an inscription on the Cross, "Jesus of Nazareth, the king of the Jews." Many read it (19:17-20).
- Chief priests try to have the inscription changed to make it clear that it is only that Jesus claimed to be king of the Jews. Pilate refuses their protest (19:21-22).
- On His crucifixion, Jesus' clothes are divided by soldiers and they cast lots for His tunic, in fulfillment of Psalm 22:18 (19:23-24).
- In the presence of his mother, her sister Mary of Clopas, and Mary Magdalene, Jesus speaks to the disciple He loved (identity uncertain) to care for her (19:25-27).
- Knowing the end is near, Jesus sought to fulfill scripture (Psalm 69:21) by receiving sour wine in the response to his thirst (19:28-29). He then proclaims it is finished and dies (19:30).
- Because the Sabbath would dawn in the morning and Jews did not want bodies left on the cross, Pilate ordered the legs of the crucified broken (19:31-32). No need to do that to Jesus, who was already dead (19:33). Instead his side was pierced (19:34). Eyewitness testimony is claimed (19:35). Scripture is thereby fulfilled, with reference to not breaking bones of God's chosen (as Passover sacrifice cannot have bones broken, as per Exodus 12:46) (19:36). Jesus being pierced is said to fulfill Zechariah 12:10 and its claim that the one pierced will be mourned at the end (19:37).
- Joseph of Arimathea, a secret disciple of Jesus gets permission from Pilate to take Jesus' body (19:38). With a leader of the Pharisees Nicodemus (see 3:1-15) they embalm the body and lay it in a tomb (19:39-42).

3. Theological Insights (see Charts of the Major Theological Options)
• Focus on sin and Justification by Grace through Faith, with some attention to their implications for Christian life (Sanctification).
• Concerning Peter's zeal in defending Christ, John Calvin issues a helpful warning:

> *... Christ condemns everything that men dare to attempt out of their own fancy... Warned by so striking an example, let us learn to keep our zeal within proper bounds; and as the wantonness of our flesh is always eager to attempt more than God commands, let us learn that our zeal will succeed ill, whenever we venture to undertake any thing contrary to the word of God.*
> (*Calvin's Commentaries*, Vol. XVIII/1, pp. 194-195)

• Regarding Peter's repeated denials of Christ, Calvin notes how symptomatic it is of our ways of sinning:

> *Thus it happens to many persons every day. At first, the fault will not be very great; next, it becomes habitual, and at length, after that conscience has been laid asleep, he who has accustomed himself to despise God will think nothing unlawful for him, but will dare to commit the greatest wickedness.* (*Calvin's Commentaries*, Vol. XVIII/1, p. 203)

• About this episode Martin Luther adds: "For it is so very rich in comfort for all poor sinners, that a great man, an apostle, suffers such a fall and yet receives grace and forgiveness" (*Complete Sermons*, Vol. 5, p. 404).
• The Reformer also reflects on how easily the world dismisses such love:

> *Nevertheless, the dear, pleasure-loving world goes merrily along, takes none of this to heart, is lazy, cold, unthankful, and despises this great treasure.* (*Complete Sermons*, Vol. 5, p. 473)

> *If someone came to my rescue in an emergency, when death threatened by fire or water, I would have to be a wretch not to feel grateful toward him... Should we not respond, my Lord Jesus Christ suffered for me; therefore in return I will love Him... It is terrible for anyone to despise such a love!* (*Complete Sermons*, Vol. 5, p. 474)

• Noting that Christ was stripped of His clothes (19:24), Calvin notes "Christ was stripped of His garments, that He might clothe us with righteousness…" (*Calvin's Commentaries*, Vol. XVIII/1, p. 230).
• Luther also well summarizes the significance of the Cross:

> *But Christ takes our place and innocently endures death, terror, and hell, so that through Him and in Him we escape all this. Through His undeserved and innocent death He saves us from the rightful death which we deserved, that is, from the sins whereby we merited death and hell.* (*Complete Sermons*, Vol. 5, pp. 402-403)

4. Socio-Economic, Political, Psychological, and Scientific Insights
• As recently as 2009 a Gallup poll revealed that nearly one half of the public believed the observance of moral values was poor. Seven in ten Americans thought that the state of moral values was getting worse the poll revealed.
• Yet Americans still think they are basically good, as if Jesus got a good deal with us. This belief in our own goodness is evident in a 2005 Barna Research Group survey indicating that a majority of Americans (54%) believe that people who are good earn salvation. In 2000, 74% of Americans claimed that the Bible teaches that God helps those who help themselves.

5. Gimmick
What is good about Good Friday? The first reaction is "not much." Most of the time we just focus on Jesus' suffering and death. Sometimes we think of our own sin, the sin that led to His crucifixion.

6. Possible Sermon Moves and/or Stories/Examples
• Human beings are not put in a good light in John's version of the story. We see the scheming to retain power by Annas and Caiphas (18:13-14, 19-24), in Pilate's scheming to give the crowd what it wants, against his better judgment (18:28—19:16). We may also see ourselves in the mob mentality of the crowd (18:13-14) and the materialism of the soldiers dividing Jesus' clothes (19:23-24). Sin is a lot like John Calvin once described it: Use the third bullet point of Theological Insights; also see the third bullet point of Theological Insights for Gospel, Ash Wednesday.
• What's good about Good Friday? There is a sense in which this should be a day to reflect on our sins and how we have blown it. But not if such lines of thought have the final say. If that happens, we may miss the main point of Good Friday that Jesus went to the Cross for slobs like us. (Of course, given the realities American culture, we are not likely to have that problem, as Americans tend to think of themselves as basically good. See last bullet point of Socio-Economic, Political, Psychological, and Scientific Insights.)
• The main point about Good Friday is that it is not about us; it is about Jesus. We lose that if we are too hung up on ourselves and our sin. Because in that case we can too easily get in the mindset that now that I've confessed my sin, Jesus will forgive me. Forgive me because of my deep spirituality. But what if I have not been sorry for my sin, not been repentant enough?

That can cause doubt. Then Good Friday is not so good.
• Amazingly, none of the characters in the narrative in our Gospel Lesson from John asked for forgiveness. And yet Jesus went to the Cross for them!
• The good news of today is that God loves us so much that even before we ask for forgiveness, even before we seem to care about Him, He cared about us! Even when we do not care about Him, He cares for us. Good Friday is good news!

7. Wrap-Up
Will this good news make a difference? Use the second quotation in the fifth bullet point of Theological Insights. Pope Benedict XVI has said that on the Cross we see the power of self-giving goodness in action. This is a love that does to us what the medieval mystic Saint Catherina of Genoa said it would: A love so pure and clear that it separates ourselves from ourselves, consumes all that we love which is less than God, setting us on fire so that nothing remains in us but a yearning for God's love (O'Brien, *Varieties of Mystic Experience*, p. 191). Oh how this Friday is so good that it takes us away from our sinful selves and immerses us in the love of God!

The Easter Season

The Meaning of the Season
• The festival commemorating Jesus' resurrection (Easter Sunday) and the fifty days (seven Sundays) of celebration that follow.
• The season includes Ascension Day on its fortieth day.
• The English name for the festival is derived form the Anglo-Saxon goddess of springtime and dawn.

The Origins of the Season
• Probably widely celebrated in the church by 100 AD, originally beginning with a Saturday night vigil followed by baptisms.
• After much controversy, the Council of Nicea established the date of the festival — the first Sunday after the first full moon following the onset of spring. The Eastern church has a different time for celebrating the festival as it employs the Julian, rather the Gregorian Calendar like Protestants and Catholics do.

The Mood of the Season
• Expressed by the season color, white — a season of celebration and joy, commemorating the purity we have in Jesus' resurrection.

Preaching Strategies
• To proclaim the good news of Jesus' conquest of sin, death, and evil, as well as of God's forgiving love. Related to this strategy should include efforts to help hearers recognize that they have been given a fresh start.
• To affirm parishioners with the word of God's forgiving love, to revel in the joy of such a spirituality.
• To examine what this self-confidence can mean for everyday living.

Easter Sunday
March 31, 2013

Revised Common	Acts 10:34-43	1 Corinthians 15:19-26	John 20:1-18
	or Isaiah 65:17-25	or Acts 10:34-43	or Luke 24:1-12
Roman Catholic	Acts 10:34, 37-43	Colossians 3:1-4	John 20:1-9
Episcopal	Acts 10:34-43	Colossians 3:1-4	Luke 24:1-10

Theme of the Day   The resurrection: Its reality and impact.

Collect of the Day   Two alternatives are provided. In the first, after praising God for delivering us from death, petitions are offered to make us die daily to sin so we might live forever in the joy of resurrection. The focus in this prayer is on Sanctification. In the second alternative, we pray that there be an increase in our hearts and minds of the risen life we share in Christ and that we grow toward the fullness of eternal life. This prayer also focuses on Sanctification (with a growth in grace profile).

Psalm of the Day   *Psalm 118:1-2, 14-24*
- A thanksgiving for deliverance in battle. One of the Egyptian Hallel Psalms used after the Passover meal.
- Praise to God and His love (vv. 1-2, 16).
- Reference to not dying but living, to be punished but not being given over to death (vv. 17-18) foreshadowing the Cross-resurrection sequence. Likewise the concluding call to rejoicing (v. 24) suggests this Easter reading.
- Reference to the gates of righteousness and the gate the righteous enter (vv. 19-20) implies the outcome of Easter, the righteousness associated with Justification by Grace (Romans 3:21-26).
- The Christological interpretation further reflects in verses 22-23 and its reference to the stone the builders rejected. This is frequently attributed to Christ in the New Testament (Matthew 21:42; Acts 4:11; 1 Peter 2:7).

Sermon Text and Title
"Easter Makes Us One!"
Acts 10:34-43

1. Theological Aim of the Sermon and Strategy
To proclaim the universal character of the resurrection, to examine its Social Ethical implications (esp. attitudes toward immigrants and the poor).

2. Exegesis (see Introduction to Selected Books of the Bible)
- Peter's confession of the gospel justifying his efforts to convert the Gentile Cornelius in Caesarea. Cornelius summons Peter as a result of a vision (vv. 3-6), and Peter had a similar vision (vv. 7-17). Peter visits Cornelius and then proceeded with the confession (eventually culminating in the pouring out of the Spirit on Peter and other Gentiles, as well as their baptisms [vv. 44-46]).
- Peter refers to God showing no partiality, finding acceptable all with faith (vv. 34-35).
- Proceeds to recount the ministry of Jesus who preached peace and did good, healing all who were oppressed by the devil (vv. 36-38).
- Testimony is also given to Christ's death on a tree and His resurrection, appearing to witnesses with whom He ate (vv. 39-41).
- He is reportedly commanded by these witnesses to preach and that who believe receive forgiveness of sin (vv. 42-43).

3. Theological Insights (see Charts of the Major Theological Options)
- The universal offer of grace provided in Christ's atoning work is affirmed, along with the implications of this theological reality for Social Ethics (esp. regarding American attitudes toward immigrants and the impoverished).
- John Wesley noted, "[God] Is not partial in His love… He is loving to every man and wills that all men should be saved" (*Commentary on the Bible*, p. 480).
- Preaching on this text, Martin Luther calls it a "comforting message, a gospel of joy and grace, a message not accusing,

threatening and terrifying with a vision of God's wrath for our sin, as did Moses with his doctrine of the law" (*Complete Sermons*, Vol. 4/1, p. 195).
• Martin Luther King Jr. powerfully explained how Christ's work brings people together and the social and ethical implications of this. In 1967 he wrote:

> *But in Christ there is neither Jew nor Gentile. In Christ there is neither male nor female. In Christ there is neither Communist or capitalist. In Christ, somehow there is neither bound or free. We are all one in Christ Jesus. And when we truly believe in the sacredness of human personality, we won't exploit people, we won't trample over people with the iron feet of oppression, we won't kill anybody.*
> (*A Testament of Hope*, p. 255)

4. Socio-Economic, Political, Psychological, and Scientific Insights
• For data on black poverty and American views toward immigrants, see the first bullet point of this section for the First Lesson, Advent 3; last bullet point of this section for the Second Lesson, Epiphany.
• A 2007 *Detroit News* poll found that nearly half of the local white population preferred to live in an all-white neighborhood. For indications that crossing racial lines for social life and friendship are also not characteristically encouraged from the African-American side, see Beverly Tatum, *Why Are All the Black Kids Sitting Together in the Cafeteria*.
• Note African/black roots of the Bible, evident in the assigned Psalm.

5. Gimmick
What Martin Luther King wrote in 1963 is still true today: "We have learned to fly the air like birds and swim the sea like fish, but we have not learned the simple art of living together as brothers [and sisters]."

6. Possible Sermon Moves and/or Stories/Examples
• Cite data in the first two bullet points of Socio-Economic, Political, Psychological, and Scientific Insights.
• Peter gave a sermon one time that speaks to these concerns. Here's the background on the sermon. He had been summoned to Caesarea, a port on the Mediterranean Sea about fifty miles to the northwest of Jerusalem, by Cornelius, a devout Gentile who was also a commanding officer in the Roman army (vv. 5-8, 17-23). Meanwhile Peter had had a vision teaching him that the Gentiles were not unclean (vv. 10-16).
• This miraculous series of events had led the apostle to give up his Jewish practices of maintaining social distance from Gentiles lest such fraternization render him impure and displease God (v. 28). He began socializing with Cornelius and his emissaries (vv. 23, 27, 29). And now we pick up with the sermon he delivered explaining why this behavior transpired.
• What of Easter? We are getting to the point. Peter does it for us.
• In his sermon explaining God's Will to overcome barriers he invokes the resurrection (vv. 35ff). Get it? For Peter, Easter is all about overcoming barriers. Jesus rose for all!
• Peter makes this point to some extent when he says *everyone* who believes in Christ receives forgiveness of sins (v. 43)!
• Everyone. Easter breaks down the barriers. Christ rose for all.
• Cite the text by John Wesley above in Theological Insights. This word that God is not partial in His love truly entails that Easter is for everybody.
• We need this word to help break down barriers in America, to become a nation that is committed to our unity. Cite Martin Luther King Jr.'s quote in Theological Insights. A nation that continues trampling people, oppressing them, and failing to celebrate our unity contradicts the good news of the empty tomb.
• Speak to the complaint that we are no longer a nation divided by race or ethnicity. Reiterate points made in the first bullet point of this section. With regard to the second bullet point of Socio-Economic, Political, Psychological, and Scientific Insights, note that though we may get along with folks of other ethnicities on the job or at meeting, we don't typically socialize. Sunday at worship time remains the most segregated hour in this "Christian" nation of ours. We keep bashing those immigrants who don't speak English and "those welfare chiselers," who more than likely are of a different ethnicity than ours.
• This sort of inclusivity, rooted in God's love for all, is good for us — good for America. Reiterate the quotation by King in the last bullet point of Theological Insights. A selection of the following quotes on the virtues of such inclusivity respectively by Canadian librarian Judith Umbach, literacy coordinator Joe Bishop, and teacher Joseph Petner might be employed:

> *A peaceful world is an inclusive world.*

> *If we're going to live up to our potential, then we need to be inclusive of everybody.*

> *The idea of becoming and membership, being part of a community, is a basic human need... To include everyone is to open up those possibilities for learning and appreciating our humanity.*

An inclusive nation, prodded by the church's Easter word of inclusivity, will be a happier, nicer place.
• In view of all the benefits that being inclusive like Jesus and Peter were, it is obvious that Martin Luther had it right. The Easter word is a comforting message. (Use the Luther quote above in Theological Insights.) What a comforting message to know that everyone can have forgiveness of sin. No one has priority.

7. Wrap-Up
Easter proclaims that everyone is a forgiven sinner. And forgiven sinners like us, no longer burdened by fear of punishment on account of sin, can be brave. We can be brave because we know that we are acceptable in God's sight, and that Jesus has overcome all the roadblocks. We can also be brave because we are all in this together, all heirs of the resurrection. And in this unity, there is strength.

Note to the congregation that we celebrate Easter each Sunday, since the reason for worshiping Sunday (rather than the Jewish Sabbath Saturday) was to commemorate the resurrection. Thus Easter is not over for us after today. So the unity created by Easter is a year-round thing for us. To celebrate Easter all year is to celebrate it and work with others in unity!

Sermon Text and Title
"Why the Resurrection Makes Sense"
1 Corinthians 15:19-26

1. Theological Aim of the Sermon and Strategy
To explain the logic of Jesus' resurrection, how everything we know about Him entails that He must have risen, and what difference this proclamation can make.

2. Exegesis (see Introduction to Selected Books of the Bible)
• Paul continues to address the question of whether there is a resurrection of the body in response to some who deny it (v. 12) by considering its significance. These verses also describe the second coming.
• He claims that if for this life only we have hoped in Christ we are to be pitied (v. 19). This may be a Jewish proverb.
• The reality of Christ's resurrection is asserted as the first fruits of the general resurrection (v. 20).
• Since death came through a human being, the resurrection must also come through a human (v. 21). As all die in Adam, so all are made alive in Christ (v. 22).
• An order is posited: First Christ's resurrection, then at His coming for all who belong to Him (v. 23). Then the end comes, when Christ turns over the kingdom of God to the Father after destroying every ruler and power (dominating powers). The last of these is death (vv. 24-26).

3. Theological Insights (see Charts of the Major Theological Options)
• The text addresses the reality/factuality of the resurrection of Jesus and Eschatology. A Classic View of Atonement is presupposed.
• An argument that Christ's resurrection must have transpired insofar as it is a logical consequence of the Bible's witness to who He is (the resurrection and the life) was developed by Hans Frei in his *The Identity of Jesus Christ*, pp. 139-152. In many respects this is a kind of Ontological Argument, after the genre of Anselm, in his *Proslogion*, applied to Christ's resurrection.
• Martin Luther contends that in order to believe the resurrection of Jesus we must transcend feeling and understanding.

> *For reason does no more than merely to observe the facts as they appear to the eye, namely, that the world has stood so long, that one person dies after another, remains dead, decomposes, and crumbles to dust in the grave.*
> (*Luther's Works*, Vol. 28, p. 69)

• Luther points out that the world has nothing to offer compared to the marvels of the resurrection:

> *Behold, thus we must view our treasure and turn away from temporal reality that lies before our eyes and sense. We must not let death and other misfortune, distress and misery, terrify us so. Nor must we regard what the world has and can do, but balance this against what we are and have in Christ. For our confidence is built entirely on the fact that He has arisen and that we have life with Him already and are no longer in the power of death. Therefore let the world be mad and foolish, boasting of and relying on its money and goods.*
> (*Luther's Works*, Vol. 28, p. 111)

> *The world knows nothing of such consolation of such a defiant boast, although it does boast of and pride itself on its possession of much money and goods, great honor, friendship, power. But I challenge you to name one to me who could fend death off or work his way out of death with all that.*
> (*Luther's Works*, Vol. 28, p. 133)

- Luther proceeds to describe the risen Lord in compelling ways:

    Therefore, if you believe in Christ, you must not flee from Him or be frightened; for here you perceive and see that His whole heart, mind, or thinking are intent only on rescuing you from all that assails and oppresses you and on placing you with Christ over everything.
    (*Luther's Works*, Vol. 28, pp. 139-140)

- In this context he paints an inviting picture of our relation with God at the end:

    Behold, that is the consolation we derive from yonder life, that God Himself will be ours and that He will be everything to us. For picture to yourself all that you would like to have, and you will find nothing better and dearer and worth wishing for than to have God Himself, who is the life and inexhaustible depth of everything good and of eternal joy.
    (*Luther's Works*, Vol. 28, p. 146)

4. Socio-Economic, Political, Psychological, and Scientific Insights
- The idea that a hypothesis central to investigation (like the resurrection of Jesus is for Christian theology) may function as an unproven supposition as long as such a supposition allows us to account for new data is an accepted norm of scientific investigation. See Thomas Kuhn, *The Structure of Scientific Revolutions*.
- Insofar as spiritual experience stimulates the release of dopamine in the brain, it seems to result in the faithful experiencing more energy (Andrew Newberg and Mark Waldman, *Why We Believe What We Believe*, esp. p. 187; Daniel Amen, *Change Your Brain, Change Your Life*, esp. p. 81).

5. Gimmick
Read verses 19-20. Proclaim enthusiastically: Christ is risen! Then ask, "Is it true?"

6. Possible Sermon Moves and/or Stories/Examples
- Note the importance of the resurrection stories. Had Jesus not risen it is likely His cult would have faded into oblivion with His death. Only because of reports of His resurrection did Jesus' small group of followers keep His word alive.
- Report the words of famed modern German theologian Wolfhart Pannenberg: "The answer to the question 'Did Jesus really rise from the dead?' is absolutely decisive for any Christian proclamation and for Christian faith itself."
- For all its importance and the weight Christianity has put on it through the ages, the resurrection of Jesus has come to be viewed as an embarrassment, not unlike how the belief was under fire in Paul's day. Note he perceived the need to assert it in face of skeptics (v. 20). Ask the congregation if they have not struggled with the belief that a dead body could come back to life. Historians say it did not happen!
- Concede (give permission to congregation to believe) that there may be some things in the Bible that did not happen literally as reported. (Cite texts preacher can get away with in his/her context. Consider Jonah account or Genesis 6:2-4.) But the resurrection of Jesus is not one of these texts whose literal character can be dodged. If you can't accept the resurrection you can't go along with everything else that Christian faith says about Jesus.
- The Bible says this elsewhere in John (11:25), Jesus calls Himself the resurrection and the life. In Romans (1:4) Paul says that Jesus was designated Son of God by the resurrection! Get the point? You do not know the Jesus portrayed by the New Testament if He has not risen. The logic of Christian faith entails that if you accept the authority of the Bible, if that is where you know Jesus and you accept its version of Him, then it makes no sense to deny that Jesus is risen.
- This is not a blind faith. Historical evidence actually proved that Jesus has not risen would force us to reject the claim that the Easter events actually had happened. To say that the resurrection is true in this way is not any different from Americans claiming democracy is good or that reality is composed of atoms and that life evolved. None have been proven until data emerges that challenges these views of reality, they are accepted.
- We may not have proven the resurrection of Jesus but no one has proven Atomic Theory, Evolution, or the goodness of democracy either. So let's stop being so uncertain or uneasy in our faith. Shout the phrase, *Jesus is risen!* We have no more reason to be shy about believing Jesus' bodily resurrection than we do about accepting Atomic Theory, the Theory of Evolution, or singing the praises of democracy. The resurrection makes sense.
- Ask the congregation if Jesus has risen. Find ways to encourage a positive response. Then ask the question of "so what."
- Paul gives an answer in our lesson. Death has been destroyed, he claims (v. 26). Later in the chapter from which our lesson is taken he claims that all things have been subjected to the Son so that God may be all in all (v. 28). What a treasure Easter is. We need no longer to fear death or anything else. Use quotations by Martin Luther in the fourth bullet point of Theological Insights.
- The preacher should confess that he/she and perhaps congregants do not have this confidence, this new life Jesus' resurrection provides. Good to note that we are not really new like the risen Lord, but still caught in sin, too concerned with our own

lives and not enough concerned with others. Too concerned with our own well being and too fretful about dying.
• But Easter promises serenity, a new life of which Christ is the first fruit. A life in which we don't crave the things of the world so much anymore. Use quotations in last two bullet points of Theological Insights. Also consider 2 Corinthians 5:17; 6:9-10.

7. Wrap-Up
Easter testifies to the fact that we have a God who is wholly devoted to rescuing us for all that assails us and made us people who care nothing for the world except Jesus. When we get caught up in that way of living then all the doubts about the resurrection wither. Catch the Easter vision that Jesus has His whole heart and mind and thinking on you, all He wants is to rescue you and then the importance of the things of the world will wither and the common sense of the Jesus' Easter resurrection will make even more sense.

Sermon Text and Title
"Be Sure You Don't Miss the Risen Lord!"
John 20:1-18

1. Theological Aim of the Sermon and Strategy
To examine our lethargy (Sin) regarding the Easter message and to proclaim the need to encounter and have fellowship with the risen Lord (Justification as Intimate Union with Christ).

2. Exegesis (see Introduction to Selected Books of the Bible)
• The Johannine resurrection account.
• In accord with the Synoptics (except Luke 24), Mary Magdalene is given credit for first recognizing the resurrection (or the empty tomb) (v. 1). John's version is the only gospel to claim that this happened to her alone.
• She runs to tell Simon and Peter and "the one whom Jesus loved (John or the Christian community for which the gospel was written). She reports that the body must have been removed (v. 2). The two disciples hurriedly proceed to the tomb, with the one whom Jesus loved getting there faster than Peter (vv. 3-4).
• At first only seeking the linens which had wrapped the body of Christ, the disciples enter the empty tomb, and not understanding the biblical promises regarding the resurrection, they return home (vv. 5-10). This is the empty tomb tradition of the resurrection account, evidenced especially in Mark 16:1-8. The Johannine author weaves this together with the appearance tradition (stories of actual encounters with the risen Lord in the verses that follow).
• Mary remains outside the tomb weeping and angels sitting where the body of Jesus laid comfort her. She professes her agony over where the body has gone (vv. 11-13).
• With these words, Jesus appears. She does not recognize Him and His efforts to comfort her at first (vv. 14-15).
• Jesus then calls her name, and Mary recognizes Him (calling Him "rabbi"). Jesus asks her not to hold Him, because He has not yet ascended to their Father, to their God (vv. 16-17). She goes and reports these things to the disciples, claiming she had seen the Lord (v. 18). John does not make clear if the disciples actually believed her testimony, since a personal appearance later in the day to them is reported (vv. 19-23).

3. Theological Insights (see Charts of the Major Theological Options)
• An examination of our sin (failure to experience the joy and excitement of Easter) and the need to be encountered by the risen Christ.
• John Calvin claims that Peter's response to Mary's news shows that "the spirit of God works in the elect in a secret manner" (*Calvin's Commentaries*, Vol. XVIII/1, p. 250).
• Calvin also contends: "... Christ is born in us, and that we, on the other hand, are born in Him..." (*Ibid.*).
• The Reformer also notes how the reference to the disciples not knowing the testimony of Hebrew Scripture regarding a resurrection is a useful instruction today and that by our carelessness we are ignorant of what scriptures reveal regarding Christ (*Ibid.*, p. 252).
• Calvin also addressed Mary's initial failure to recognize Jesus:

> *In Mary we have an example of the mistakes into which the human mind frequently falls. Though Christ presents Himself to our view, yet we imagine that He assumes various shapes, so that our senses conceive of any thing rather than of the true Christ; for not only are our powers of understanding liable to be deceived, but they are also bewitched by the world.* (Ibid., p. 257)

- But in Calvin's view Mary also gives us clues about how faith works:

    Thus in Mary *we have a lively image of our calling, for the only way in which we are admitted to the true knowledge of Christ is, when He first knows us.* (*Ibid.*, p. 258)

- The father of existentialist philosophy, Søren Kierkegaard, insisted that there can be no disciples at second-hand, that the faithful must become contemporary with Christ (*Philosophical Fragments*, pp. 81ff).
- Martin Luther points out how awesome verse 17 is where Jesus identifies His Father with the Father of His followers. Those who deserted Him and so merit punishment share His Father and God (*Complete Sermons*, Vol. 1/2, p. 200)!

4. Socio-Economic, Political, Psychological, and Scientific Insights
- The failure of the male disciples to understand what had happened that first Easter, and that it was to Mary that Jesus appeared, opens the way to a sermon on "It Takes a Woman," extolling female spiritual leadership.

5. Gimmick
Mary Magdalene had told them. The tomb was empty. She and Peter and the disciple whom Jesus loved ran to the tomb (vv. 1-6). They saw the linen wrappings which had clothed the body. Though they believed, they did not understand and went home (vv. 8-10).

6. Possible Sermon Moves and/or Stories/Examples
- Tell the congregation to take off their shoes. They are on holy ground! Then like Peter and John we will all go home, not really understanding it all, not much changed.
- Ask why these disciples did not believe these women. Why we too often do not act like we believe them. The idea that someone could revive from the dead is so foreign to reason and our natural ways of understanding the world. As the great theologian of the last century Karl Barth once put it: Jesus Christ (and so the resurrection) is "truly beyond our comprehension" (*The Epistle to the Romans*, pp. 279-280).
- It is tempting to blame Peter's and John's disbelief in Mary's testimony on first-century sexism. This is a sexism still permeating our culture today. But it is not the whole story in their disbelief about the joyous Easter message. Peter's and John's unbelief has to do with our own failure to take the joyful word of Easter to heart and to live that way every day of our lives.
- Easter Sunday is a glorious day. Note the joy of a filled church and how many are surrounded by loved ones. Even if we are missing a loved one, this day seems to give peace of mind. God seems so real, and so does the resurrection.
- It will not be that way next week. Perhaps it will not be present tomorrow. Next Sunday the joy and peace will be gone. The church will be empty by comparison to today. Prophesy that even those present will not feel the Easter joy. We will not be quite as certain about the resurrection. Down the road, months ahead, there may even be times when the events of our lives will lead us to doubt God and His goodness, make us wonder about the truth of the resurrection. Like Peter and John we will come to regard the story of Mary about the empty tomb as an "idle tale." Like Peter and John we will not believe. Those on planning to be in worship next Sunday are already walking down Peter's and John's path to disbelief. We do not believe Mary Magdalene either. Why not?
- To answer this question, we need first to look at how highly trained students of the Bible proceed in dealing with the accounts of Jesus' resurrection. Note the two separate, originally independent traditions of resurrection stories — the empty tomb tradition and the appearance tradition. See the fourth bullet point of Exegesis. Both of these traditions (dating back to times before the Bible's composition) are present in John's gospel, right here in this lesson.
- Why is this academic biblical scholarship relevant to us? There seems to be a recurring pattern in the stories about the empty tomb. Disbelief makes itself evident in these instances. We see it in our lesson today but we also see it in the story of Doubting Thomas (John 20:24-25) and also in the gospels of Mark (16:1-8) and Luke (24:1-11). It is only when Mary and the disciples see Jesus that belief really happens (vv. 14-15, 19-23)! Only when Jesus is encountered is faith made certain.
- Ask the congregation if they see the point. It explains why the disciples did not originally believe the story of the resurrection. They only heard about the empty tomb. They had not actually yet experienced the risen Lord!
- This is our problem today. Too many of us only meet the risen Lord once or twice a year (sometimes just on Christmas and Easter). All we know is the story of the empty tomb.

    Where is He? Where can we meet the risen Lord? He is here every Sunday. He is present, Jesus told us, wherever two or three are gathered in His name (Matthew 18:20). He is present now. And He is also present when you pray at home and read your Bible.
- Suggest to the congregation that if doubts about God came their way, if they feel apathetic and not excited about Christian

faith, then chances are that like Peter and John on that first Easter they have only heard the *stories* about the resurrection and have not actually been in the presence of the risen Lord enough. If you are a regular church-goer, maybe the problem is that you have not been paying enough attention to your meetings with the risen Lord.

  Note the next-to-last bullet point of Theological Insights. Not to encounter Christ regularly is to try to be a disciple at second hand and that does not work.

• When you get involved regularly in the life of the church, spend time with Jesus at home through prayer and reading the Bible, doubts about the resurrection fade.

7. Wrap-Up

Conclude with reflections on how we can gain confidence in Jesus' resurrection and in the joy and fulfillment that goes with it. Then you gain the wonderful assurance of the Easter faith in our risen Lord. Use the next-to-last bullet point of Theological Insights for the Second Lesson. Remind the congregation to be sure they don't miss the risen Lord.

Easter 2
April 7, 2013

Revised Common	Acts 5:27-32	Revelation 1:4-8	John 20:19-31
Roman Catholic	Acts 5:12-16	Revelation 1:9-13, 17-19	John 20:19-31
Episcopal	Acts 5:12a, 17-22, 25-29	Revelation 1:(1-8) 9-19	John 20:19-31

Theme of the Day   God and the resurrection have their way with us. Historically this was the first Sunday during which newly baptized members would be admitted into the fellowship as full members of the church, and so this theme of life being determined by something bigger than we are is most appropriate.

Collect of the Day   Petitions are offered to the Lord of life who reaches out to us amid our fears that by the Spirit's breath our faith in God's mercy might be revived and that we be strengthened to be Christ's body. A prayer focused on Justification and Sanctification along with prayer for the Church (Body of Christ).

Psalm of the Day   *Psalm 118:14-29*

• A Psalm of praise, offering thanksgiving for deliverance from battle.
• Yahweh is said to be the Psalmist's strength, for He has become his salvation (v. 14). Glad songs of victory are sung by the righteous (v. 15a).
• The right hand of the Lord is exalted for He is valiant (vv. 15b-16). This may be an ancient victory song.
• The Psalmist claims that he will live to recount Yahweh's deeds. For though punished severely by the Lord, He did not give him over to death (vv. 17-18). Messianic images seem to appear here and in the preceding bullet point (*Calvin's Commentaries*, Vol. VI/1, p. 391).
• Urges that the Lord open the gates of righteousness (vv. 19-20). Reference to gates could suggest that the previous verses were processional songs.
• Thanks Yahweh for answering and becoming our salvation (v. 21).
• The stone that the builders rejected has become the chief cornerstone (v. 22). This verse is frequently quoted in the New Testament (Matthew 21:42; Acts 4:11; 1 Peter 2:7). This is said to be Yahweh's doing, and it is marvelous in our eyes (v. 23).
• Verses of the choir's acknowledgment of what the Lord has done (vv. 23-25). (This is said to be the day the Lord made, and so we are to rejoice [v. 24]. The Lord is asked to save us, a phrase which in Hebrew is "Hosanna" [v. 25].) John Calvin wrote on these verses:

> *The call to the exercise of gratitude, which immediately follows, is intended to warn us against yielding to the madness of our enemies, however furiously they rage against us, in order to deprive us of the joy that Christ has brought to us.*
>   (*Calvin's Commentaries*, Vol. VI/1, p. 395)

• A suppliant is admitted with a choral blessing of praise (vv. 26-27). References to binding the festal procession with branches is a liturgical direction (v. 27b). The suppliant then makes his act of thanksgiving (v. 28).
• The choir responds with praise, regarding Yahweh's goodness and love (v. 29).

                          or *Psalm 150*

• A hymn of praise, marking the end of the Psalter.
• In each verse different modes of praise of Yahweh *Elohim* are commended (vv. 1-5).
• Everything that breathes is to praise the Lord (v. 6).

Sermon Text and Title
"The Easter Word and the Spirit Open the Door to Everyone"
Acts 5:27-32

1. Theological Aim of the Sermon and Strategy
To proclaim Justification by Grace through Faith, the work of the Holy Spirit, as well as the freedom and confidence this word offers to defy worldly authority (Social Ethics).

2. Exegesis (see Introduction to Selected Books of the Bible)
• Report of the proceedings of the Sanhedrin on the arrest of the apostles and Peter's witness in that context.
• The high priest questioning the apostles notes the strict orders given them against teaching Christ's name, and yet this had been disobeyed (vv. 27-28).
• Peter responds that God must be obeyed rather than human authority (v. 29). He proceeds to note that the God of the patriarchs had raised Jesus whom Jewish authorities had killed (v. 30). God is said to have exalted Jesus as leader and Savior to give repentance to Israel for forgiveness of sins. On behalf of all the apostles Peter claims to have witnessed this along with the Holy Spirit whom God has given to those who obey (vv. 31-32).

3. Theological Insights (see Charts of the Major Theological Options)
• A testimony to Justification by Grace, that salvation is a work of God through the Holy Spirit and not a matter of works of the law. The word of God's critique of earthly authority (Social Ethics) is also suggested.
• John Wesley claims that this text testifies to the fact that "God alone forgives sins" (*Commentary on the Bible*, p. 476). Martin Luther agreed that the entire Book of Acts was written to attest to Justification by Grace. He adds: "The entire book treats of nothing else than that the Holy Spirit is not given through the law but is given through the hearing of the gospel" (*Luther's Works*, Vol. 26, p. 204).
• In the same spirit, John Calvin insists that references to repentance in the text (v. 31) must be seen as a work of God changing our heart by His Spirit (*Calvin's Commentaries*, XVIII/2, p. 218).
• For more quotations on God's initiative in saving us, see the fourth and fifth bullet points of this section for the Gospel, Lent 4.
• On the importance of making the testimony of Justification by Grace, famed seventeenth-century French philosopher Blaise Pascal wrote:

Then Jesus Christ comes to tell men that they have no enemies but themselves, that it is their passions that cut them off from God, that He has come to destroy these passions, and to give men His grace. (*Pensées*, p. 164)

• Martin Luther added more about the benefits of this doctrine:

This knowledge of and confidence in God's grace makes men glad and bold and happy in dealing with God and with all creatures. And this is the work that the Holy Spirit performs in faith. It is impossible for it not to be doing good works incessantly.
(*Luther's Works*, Vol. 35, p. 370)

• Regarding the Holy Spirit, famed twentieth century theologian Karl Barth defined it as "the awakening power in which Jesus Christ has formed and continually renews His body…" (*Church Dogmatics*, Vol. IV/1, p. 643). Augustine refers to the Spirit as the love that binds together Father and Son (*Nicene and Post-Nicene Fathers*, First Series, Vol. 3, p. 100).
• John Calvin spoke of the courage that comes from this awareness that God cares for us:

Hence the more any one has found the kindness of God, the more courageously he ought to proceed in the discharge of his office, and confidently to commit to God his life and his safety, and resolutely to surmount all the perils of the world.
(*Calvin's Commentaries*, Vol. XIV/2, pp. 94-95)

4. Socio-Economic, Political, Psychological, and Scientific Insights
• John Calvin stresses the willingness of Peter to challenge the illicit use of authority by leaders. He writes:

We must obey God's ministers and officers if we will obey him. But so soon as rulers do lead us away from the obedience of God, because they strive against God with sacrilegious boldness, their pride must be abated that God may be above all in authority. (*Calvin's Commentaries*, Vol. XVIII/2, pp. 214-215)

Consider present issues over which our leaders have led us away from obedience to God. A few examples might be gay marriage, tax breaks for the rich while Social Security, Medicare, and Medicaid are reduced, as well as recent anti-immigrant legislation.
• Americans seem to have a difficult time endorsing the reality of the Holy Spirit; see the second bullet point of this section for the Second Lesson, Epiphany 1.
• For poll data indicating a tendency for Americans to compromise grace, see this section for the Second Lesson, Epiphany 4.
• Neurobiological research indicates that belief in a loving God, one not making demands, seems to enhance feelings of security and compassion. Presumably this is related to how such a focus demands less exercise of the parietal lobe and so results in freer-flow of the amphetamine-like brain chemical dopamine in the front part of the brain, which is associated with more sociable behavior and happiness. (Andrew Newberg and Mark Waldman, *How God Changes Your Brain*; see last two bullet points of this section for the Gospel, Easter 5.)

5. Gimmick
Life is so uncertain around tax time, especially in view of the economic instabilities of the last years. Last week's Easter celebration seems in the distant past. There were a lot of uncertainties and threats circulating in first-century Palestine, especially for followers of the way (the first Christians). Elaborate on the Jewish leadership's concern to maintain the purity of Jewish faith during this era of Roman occupation (motivated by good reasons [maintaining purity of the faith] and by the leaders' concern that a failure to keep order would reflect negatively on them in the eyes of the Roman authorities).

6. Possible Sermon Moves and/or Stories/Examples
• Leaders of the church had been summoned by the Sanhedrin (the official Jewish court, made up of seventy priests, scribes, and elders, presided over by the high priest). They had defied previous warnings by their Jewish leaders to stop teaching in the name of Jesus Christ (vv. 27-28; cf. 4:18).
• Note that Peter as the leader offered the response. Rehearse last bullet point of Exegesis. Note especially the proclamation of the resurrection. There is an Easter faith here.
• Use the second bullet point of Theological Insights to stress that the witness Paul gives is a testimony to Justification by Grace. Elaborate on how Peter's and the other disciples' defiance of an exclusive reliance on the Jewish Torah, but to witness to Jesus' role in giving forgiveness of sin (v. 31), was a testimony to the fact that works of the law do not save. Consider the quote by Luther in the second bullet point of Theological Insights.
• The witness to the role of the Holy Spirit is also significant here (v. 32). The Spirit's role in getting us to repent and bringing us to faith is another way of making clear that Peter's preaching is a critique of salvation by works. Develop the points in the quote by Luther in the second bullet point of Theological Insights and in the sixth and seventh bullet points of that section. On God's initiative in salvation, follow the leads in the fourth bullet point of the section.
• Comments about what the Holy Spirit is could be included. See the next-to-last bullet point of Theological Insights.
• Ask what this has to do with us and with the uncertainties and instabilities we face. Reiterate issues noted in the Gimmick. Note that a belief that we are saved by God in Jesus Christ, that the Holy Spirit has brought us this gift affords a confidence that leads to courage. Note how Peter and the disciples courageously witnessed to their faith before critics among the Jewish leaders on the Sanhedrin.
• Saved by God's work, the Spirit and grace doing the heavy lifting, takes the pressure off. Nothing can stop the good from happening when we realize that God will have His way with us.
• Use the comments by Pascal and Luther in the fifth and sixth bullet points of Theological Insights. The awareness of God's loving dominance over our lives frees us from all our enemies and gives us confidence. Assure the congregation that this confidence and joy can be theirs.
• A loving God gives the courage to stand up to the powers that be (see Calvin's reflections in the first bullet point of Socio-Economic, Political, Psychological, and Scientific Insights and the last bullet point of Theological Insights). Note some of the ways in which we might be called on to challenge the authority of political and ecclesiastical leaders today. Driven by the love of God and the Holy Spirit, no way we can let authorities drive us away from what God wants!

7. Wrap-Up
The faith of Peter and the first apostles in the loving character of a God who opens the way to salvation for all, along with the joy and confidence that goes with it, can be ours. Note the scientific basis for why such a faith in a loving God leads to feelings of joy, security, and compassion for society, provided in the last bullet point of Socio-Economic, Political, Psychological, and Scientific Insights. The good news of Easter, the good news of God's love, will have its way with you this week, can give us the courage to challenge what's wrong with America. Urge the congregation to remember and believe what happened last week, and all these things can happen to them!

Sermon Text and Title
"The Power of the Resurrection"
Revelation 1:4-8

1. Theological Aim of the Sermon and Strategy
To proclaim how Eschatology illuminates Christian life in the present (Justification and Sanctification) and providing confidence and peace. A Classic View of the Atonement is also deployed.

2. Exegesis (see Introduction to Selected Books of the Bible)
• An introductory salutation to the seven churches of Asia Minor that would receive the seven letters exposited in the book (1:9—3:22).

- The typical Greek formula of salutation at the outset of the lesson refers to God in a tri-fold way (He who is, was, and is to come). Reference to seven spirits may allude to angelic beings or to energies of the Spirit (v. 4b).
- The greeting refers to Jesus Christ in a tri-fold way; He is identified as ruler of kings, is said to love, and to free us by His love. Making us a kingdom of priests implies affirmation of the priesthood of all believers (vv. 5-6).
- Poetic testimony follows (vv. 7-8). Reference to the coming with the clouds and as the one who will make all the earth's tribes wail is an allusion to Daniel 7:13 applied to Jesus' Eschatological coming. God is said to be the beginning and the end.

3. Theological Insights (see Charts of the Major Theological Options)
- The text teaches Christ's lordship, Justification by Grace, Sanctification, the priesthood of all believers, and Realized Eschatology, with a future dimension. The characteristics of the coming kingdom include love and the sharing of power. As such, insights are given into the benevolent way in which God governs history (Providence).
- Karl Barth provides insights about Christ's kingly rule (he refers to Him as "the royal man"), what the kingdom looks like:

> *Our starting-point here is the first and final fact that the being of this royal man Jesus was not only identical with the glory of God in the highest... but also identical on earth with peace among men as the object to of the divine good-pleasure.*
> (*Church Dogmatics*, Vol. IV/2, p. 158)

- Barth sees Jesus' royalty as evidenced in "the pronouncedly revolutionary character of His relationship to the orders of life and value current in the world around Him" (*Ibid.*, p. 171).

> *... as long as there is history at all [the orders of life and value] enjoy a transitory validity in the history of every human place... This is how He Himself deals with them, not in principle, not in the execution of a programme, but for this reason in a way which is all the more revolutionary, as the one who breaks all bonds asunder, in new historical developments and situations each of which is for those who can see and hear — only a sign, but an unmistakable sign, of His freedom and kingdom and over-ruling history.*
> (*Ibid.*, p. 173)

- Martin Luther offered reflection on the context for this text and the book of Revelation as a whole:

> *Some of the know-it-alls are even doing that very thing. They see heresy and dissension and shortcomings... And so they decide offhand that there are no [true] Christians... They ought to read this book [Revelation] and learn to look upon Christendom with other eyes than those of [their] reason... In a word, our holiness is in heaven where Christ is, and not in the world before men's eyes... If only the word of the gospel remains pure among us... we shall not doubt that Christ is with us, even when things are at their worst. As we see here in this book, though through and beyond all... evil... Christ is nonetheless with His saints, and wins the final victory.*
> (*Luther's Works*, Vol. 35, pp. 410-411)

- Regarding the apparent reference to the last judgment (vv. 7-8) Luther wrote:

> *Even if your sin and your conscience plague and oppress you and you stand in awe of God's judgment, you must realize that all has been changed and that judgment has been abolished. Instead of harboring fear of the final judgment you must yearn and long for it.*
> (*Luther's Works*, Vol. 22, p. 364)

4. Socio-Economic, Political, Psychological, and Scientific Insights
- A 2006 Pew Forum on Religion and Public Life revealed that 1 in 5 American Christians do not believe in Christ's second coming.

5. Gimmick
Shout the phrases, "Christ is risen! Risen indeed!"

6. Possible Sermon Moves and/or Stories/Examples
- The pastor should note how he/she prophesied last week that the joy and confidence in the reality of Christ's resurrection would not be as real today. We do not feel the enthusiasm of last Sunday. Doubts may even emerge about whether Christ really has risen. At least we may wonder where the fruits of the resurrection are.
- The book of Revelation can help us struggle with these doubts. It was written to Christians who felt some anxiety about their faith. We may not be enduring the persecution they were, but we know some of their anxiety.
- Cite Martin Luther's quote in the fourth bullet point of Theological Insights. Revelation is a book that testifies that even when evil, sloth, and lack of enthusiasm emerge, they cannot win. Christ has won the final victory!
- Luther also refers to the fact that our holiness is in heaven where Christ is. Christ has won the victory over all doubts, sin, and evil. Christ is victorious!

- Review the last two bullet points of Exegesis. Not only is it revealed that Christ is ruler of all the earth's kings (v. 5). But later in the chapter (not part of our lesson) He is revealed as risen and having the keys of death and hell (v. 18). See the second bullet point of Theological Insights.
- Christ lives forever! Recall Luther's comment that Christ has won the final victory over death and hades. This is the antidote to our doubts, apathy, and lack of commitment to our faith. The formula is simple: We need to experience the risen and victorious Christ, need some encounters with His glorified self as He will be at the end of time, and then all the doubts will vanish. With this vision of Christ's ultimate conquest in view, we are ready to persevere and endure all the doubts and moments of weak faith. Use Luther's observations in the last bullet point of Theological Insights.
- Ask if it is really true. If Christ has conquered, why is there still so much apathy, hypocrisy, and doubt in the church? Why so much disbelief among Christians about His second coming? (See Socio-Economic, Political, Psychological, and Scientific Insights.) Why is there evil in the world?
- The preacher does well to confess struggling with these questions. The book of Revelation gives cues. Here and in chapter 12 we see the risen Christ proclaimed or shown to be victorious over sin and evil. But then elsewhere like in chapters 20, 13, and 9 (as well as in v. 9 of the lesson) we find acknowledgments of the fact that sin and evil are still in the world.
- John and our Lord seemed to feel that the people to whom Revelation was addressed would be comforted in their suffering and doubts by glimpses of Christ's heavenly glory. That is their main point: Our faith and enthusiasm for it can be invigorated by glimpses of His heavenly glory. Christ is victorious in heaven (in an ultimate sense) but the war isn't over yet on earth.
- Use the analogy of the war being won after a crucial battle (like after Gettysburg, the North was a sure victor in the Civil War, after D-Day the Allies could count on victory in Europe in World War II), though a lot of serious battles and loss of life remain. This is the sense in which Jesus is victorious. Jesus' heavenly reality of exaltation, His resurrection, guarantees that sin, evil, apathy, and the like have been vanquished. This is the power of His Easter resurrection. Yet just as the American soldiers in World War II had many hard battles to fight, with lives lost and so the skirmishes with sin, death, evil, and apathy remain. But they can't win!
- Use the third bullet point, relying on Karl Barth's observations about how the heavenly vision of Christ is a revolutionary perspective that shatters and renders relative all the historical orders of life and value.

7. Wrap-Up

Conclude with reflection on the power of the resurrection and of this vision of Christ's heavenly [Eschatological] glory. On Easter Christ won the major battle, though there is still the war to fight. How can we fail to be enthusiastic? Because with Christ in the battle with apathy, sin, evil, injustice, and death, we cannot lose! Urge the congregation to keep in mind this insight, the power of the resurrection, in the hassles of this week ahead.

Sermon Text and Title
"The Easter Message: Peace in the Midst of Our Chaos"
John 20:19-31

1. Theological Aim of the Sermon and Strategy

To indict our sin (including doubts like Thomas) and proclaim forgiveness (Justification by Grace) as well as Sanctification (our mission to forgive sins) which often manifests in hidden, not dramatic ways.

2. Exegesis (see Introduction to Selected Books of the Bible)

- Accounts of Jesus' resurrection appearances and the story of Doubting Thomas.
- The text begins reporting on Easter a gathering of disciples locked in a house for fear of the Jews. The risen Jesus enters and gives them a peace greeting (v. 19). The disciples rejoice (v. 20).
- Jesus then commissions the disciples, gives them the Holy Spirit and the power to forgive and retain sins (vv. 20-23).
- Thomas was not present and expresses doubts about Jesus' resurrection (vv. 24-25).
- In a gathering the following week, Jesus again appears and has Thomas feel His body. Thomas confesses his faith (vv. 26-28). Jesus asks him if he only has believed because he saw Jesus. The Lord adds His blessing for those who have not seen Him yet believe (v. 29).
- The author reports that Jesus did many other signs in the presence of the disciples not reported in the gospel (v. 30). The ones reported are provided, he writes, that readers may believe that Jesus is the Messiah, Son of God, and through believing have life in His name (v. 31). This verse is understood as the gospel of John's statement of purpose.

3. Theological Insights (see Charts of the Major Theological Options)
• Another text addressing sin, Justification by Grace, and Sanctification (our task in forgiving sins).
• John Calvin notes that the Holy Spirit was given to the disciples so that in the other tasks assigned they might not think that they have drawn on any resources in themselves (*Calvin's Commentaries*, Vol. XVIII/1, p. 270).
• He adds that given the commission the disciples received to forgive sins (v. 23) "believers may be fully convinced, that what they hear concerning the forgiveness of sins is ratified, and may not less highly value the reconciliation that is offered by the voice of men, than if God Himself stretched out His hand from heaven" (*Ibid.*, p. 272).
• Regarding Thomas' disbelief, Calvin writes:

> *Besides, this obstinacy of Thomas is an example to show that this wickedness is almost natural to all men, to retard themselves of their own accord, when the entrance to faith is opened to them.* (*Ibid.*, p. 274)

• Martin Luther and Søren Kierkegaard referred to sin in terms of *Angst* (a German term that translates "despair") (*Luther's Works*, Vol. 13, p. 7; *The Sickness Unto Death*, pp 147ff).
• Martin Luther claims Christ standing among the disciples, though the door was closed, "denotes nothing else than that he is standing in our hearts…" (*Complete Sermons*, Vol. 1/2, p. 354). Luther adds that Christ's coming through closed doors indicates that he does not break or displace the heart (*Ibid.*, p. 355).
• The Reformer also notes that "if you look to Christ and believe on Him, no evil that may befall you is so great that it can harm you and cause you to despair" (*Ibid.*, p. 357).
• He adds that Jesus offering peace to the disciples (v. 19) is a function of the fact that on earth there is little peace:

> *For the devil will not allow a Christian to have peace; therefore Christ must bestow it in a manner different from that in which the world has and gives, in that He quiets the heart and removes from within fear and terror, although without there remain contention and misfortune.* (*Ibid.*, p. 380)

• We have been made priests, he notes, to proclaim forgiveness of sins to each other (*Ibid.*, p. 398).
• Luther sees even in the Doubting Thomas story an illustration of the power of the resurrection (*Ibid.*, p. 409). Thomas becomes an entirely different man (*Ibid.*, p. 411). The story of Thomas, he adds elsewhere, is written "for our sakes that we may learn how Christ loves us, and how amiably, fatherly, gently, and mildly he deals with us and would deal with us" (*Complete Sermons*, Vol. 6, pp. 58-59).
• To the author's comments in verse 31 that miracles are reported and that readers may believe, Calvin wrote:

> *I reply, no other use is here assigned to the miracles than to be aids and supports of faith; for they serve to prepare the minds of men that they may cherish greater reverence for the word of God, and we know how cold and sluggish our attention is, if we be not excited by something else.* (*Calvin's Commentaries*, Vol. XVIII/1, p. 281)

4. Socio-Economic, Political, Psychological, and Scientific Insights
• On American disbelief about Justification by Grace, see this section for the First Lesson.

5. Gimmick
Note that God does not seem as real as He was this time last week. The joy and peace of the Easter celebration seems gone. The events of the past week have not helped as we got back to the grind.

6. Possible Sermon Moves and/or Stories/Examples
• We might not say that the days since Easter were filled with fear. Yet as sinners, scarred by sin, we live with fear or despair every day. Explain the idea of sin as angst, in the fifth bullet point of Theological Insights.
• Preoccupied with ourselves, our addiction to self-gratification or concupiscence (see last bullet point of Theological Insights for the First Lesson, Ash Wednesday) underlies all we do. We cannot escape ourselves. This is not a joyful affirmation of ourselves. It is a fear of not being able to maintain ourselves.
• Life is so uncertain. Here today; gone tomorrow. Behind it all is the fear that we are devoting a lifetime to empty, meaningless undertakings. Even if we do the right things, we might fail. It makes no difference ultimately, since someday (in two or three generations after our deaths) no one will remember who we were. Our heirs will not know us or remember us, and we will have lived for naught. Our days seem so humdrum sometimes, for they remind us that ultimately life counts for naught.
• Depressing, frightful reflections. We try to repress them but such feelings are constant and make us so uncertain about life and ourselves. Insecure as we are it is little wonder that we devote so much (undue) attention to ourselves, becoming selfish and concupiscent. This is why sin is deemed angst. Self-concerned like we are, it is little wonder that Thomas did not

believe the accounts of Jesus' resurrection without seeing it himself (vv. 24-25). Use John Calvin's comments in the fourth bullet point of Theological Insights.

• Turn to the text. Use (in dramatic fashion) the second bullet point of Exegesis. Use the sixth bullet point of Theological Insights to discuss the significance of Jesus entering the room though the door was closed. Jesus penetrates through the walls of our fear and self-doubts.

• When He enters He wishes the disciples peace. There was nothing extraordinary about this. Just an ordinary greeting. Yet the Hebraic term *Shalom* connotes completeness or fullness. One with "peace" is complete and has all that is needed. Jesus fills up the emptiness of the faithful. He gives them the Holy Spirit (v. 22)!

• Filled with the Spirit, our lives are no longer empty and incomplete. Then Jesus gave the disciples meaningful tasks to do, a mission (vv. 21-23). Use the third bullet point of Exegesis. No longer need we be so centered on ourselves and fearful. For in the mission of proclaiming the forgiveness of sins we have something meaningful to do with our lives.

• The problem is that although what happened to the disciples has happened to us, for we have the same commission as they to forgive sin and proclaim it, we do not always feel this peace but continue to experience the angst and chaos we previously described. This is why the doors to our lives are locked (v. 19). As noted (reiterate fifth bullet point of this section), Jesus penetrates through the barriers we erect. This is what He does with the Doubting Thomases in us too. Use comments by Calvin (fourth bullet point of Theological Insights) and of Luther (tenth bullet point of Theological Insights). Jesus lovingly tends to our doubts. Thomas represents us, someone caught up in the fear and chaos but someone Jesus pursues, lovingly deals with us, and even gently changes.

• No, we don't obviously change. Christ's appearances do not change the pattern of our lives. The old fears, hang-ups, and chaos are still around. But they are no longer as influential; Christ's peace holds sway.

• Consider the following quotation by Martin Luther about how Christ and the Easter message enter our lives:

> *... [Christ] does not come with a great voice, with storm and commotion, but very orderly; not changing nor breaking anything in the outward affairs of human life... Thus He does not derange and displace anything in man, neither his sense not his reason; but He illuminates and changes for the better his heart and reason.* (*Complete Sermons*, Vol. 1/2, p. 384)

7. Wrap-Up

Outwardly Christ's resurrection does not change our lives much. The old fears and hang-ups remain but Christ's peace has come and filled our hearts in a truly miraculous way. In the midst of chaos in everyday life we have peace of mind. In Christ our lives count for something. The anxiety, despair, and chaos of life cannot overcome!

Easter 3
April 14, 2013

Revised Common	Acts 9:1-6 (7-20)	**Revelation 5:11-14**	John 21:1-19
Roman Catholic	Acts 5:27-32, 40-41	**Revelation 5:11-14**	John 21:1-19
Episcopal	Acts 9:1-19a	**Revelation 5:6-14**	John 21:1-14

Theme of the Day   Amazing grace — historically this has been a Sunday to celebrate the goodness of God.

Collect of the Day   Petitions praising God's majesty and might are offered, followed by requests that we be inspired by the resurrection to follow Jesus. Sanctification by grace is again emphasized.

Psalm of the Day   *Psalm 30*
• A personal Psalm of praise, attributed to David, offering a thanksgiving for healing as a song of dedication for the temple, it was probably used at Hanukkah.
• Yahweh is praised for healing the Psalmist, bringing him up from Sheol (the pit) (vv. 1-3).
• The congregation is invited to join in the thanksgiving. God's anger is said to be for a moment, but His favor a lifetime (vv. 4-5).
• The story of what happened to the Psalmist follows (vv. 6-12). Before he became ill he had been secure (vv. 6-7).
• Claims there was no profit in his death or going to the pit, for the dust cannot praise God (v. 9).
• The Lord has turned the Psalmist's mourning into dancing, clothing him with joy so he could forever praise the Lord (vv. 11-12).

Sermon Text and Title
"We Don't Do It: God Does"
Acts 9:1-6 (7-20)

1. Theological Aim of the Sermon and Strategy
To proclaim that God saves us by His forgiving grace (Justification by Grace) and would help us get this word out (Sanctification/Evangelism).

2. Exegesis (see Introduction to Selected Books of the Bible)
• The account of Paul's conversion (slightly different versions are found in 22:4-16 and 26:9-18; cf. Paul's version in Galatians 1:13-17).
• Still known as Saul, a persecutor of the way (Christianity), it is reported that he asked the high priest in Jerusalem for letters of introduction to the synagogues in Damascus, so if he found any belonging to the way he might bring them to Jerusalem (vv. 1-2).
• Near Damascus a light flashes round him and a voice questions why Saul has persecuted him (vv. 3-4). Saul asks who the Lord is and learns it is Jesus, who instructs him to proceed to Damascus and do what he is told to do (vv. 5-6).
• Those traveling with Saul were speechless, having heard the voice but seen no one (v. 7). Saul's vision was gone, for three days seeing nothing and not eating or drinking (vv. 8-9).
• In Damascus a disciple named Ananias dwelt. In a vision the Lord summons him to go to the house of Judas where Saul was residing (vv. 10-11a). Saul while praying had had a vision that Ananias would heal him (vv. 11b-12).
• Ananias protests knowing the persecution Saul had led in Jerusalem (vv. 13-14). God responds, indicating that Saul will be His instrument to bring His name to the Gentiles (v. 15).
• Ananias responds to the command and the healings take place with the promise made that Saul be filled with the Holy Spirit (vv. 17-20).

3. Theological Insights (see Charts of the Major Theological Options)
• The narrative witnesses to God's initiative in saving us (Justification by Grace).
• Martin Luther believed that the story of Paul's conversion demonstrates that there is no need for special revelation. He writes:

Our Lord God does not purpose some special thing for each individual person, but gives to the whole world — one person like the next — his baptism and gospel. (*Complete Sermons*, Vol. 7, p. 271)

• John Calvin sees the account as a testimony to "the most excellent mercy of God, in that that man [Paul] is reclaimed unto salvation contrary to the purpose of his mind…" (*Calvin's Commentaries*, Vol. XVIII/2, p. 368):

We are all wicked and cruel naturally; therefore, in that we are turned to God, that cometh to pass by the wonderful and secret power of God, contrary to nature. (*Calvin's Commentaries*, Vol. XVIII/2, p. 372)

• Regarding God's use of Ananias (vv. 10ff), Calvin writes:

This is assuredly no small honour whereunto it pleaseth God to exalt humankind, as when he chooseth our brethren from amongst us to be interpreters of His will; when as He causeth His holy oracles to sound in the mouth of man, which is naturally given to lying and vanity. (*Calvin's Commentaries*, Vol. XVIII/2, p. 374)

• The Genevan Reformer also notes Ananias' protests (vv. 13-14) as an illustration of our weakness of faith (*Calvin's Commentaries*, Vol. XVIII/2, p. 379). "If any man object that the Lord speaketh not at this day in a vision [as He did to Ananias], I answer that forasmuch as the scripture is abundantly confirmed to us, we must hear God thence" (*Calvin's Commentaries*, Vol. XVIII/2, p. 380). All our excuses are gone.

• With regard to the ministry of Ananias to Paul, the famed preacher of the early church John Chrysostom proclaimed: "Nothing is more frigid than a Christian, who cares not for the salvation of others" (*Nicene and Post-Nicene Fathers*, First Series, Vol. 11, p. 133). "It is not possible for the light of a Christian to be hid…" (*Ibid.*, p. 134).

• Commenting on another text, John Chrysostom noted: "… for by our own merit we did not draw down the Divine influence" (*Nicene and Post-Nicene Fathers*, First Series, Vol. 11, p. 55).

4. Socio-Economic, Political, Psychological, and Scientific Insights

• For poll data indicating the tendency of Americans to compromise grace, see this Socio-Economic, Political, Psychological, and Scientific Insights section for the Second Lesson, Epiphany 1.

• For the psychological benefits of an emphasis on grace, see the last bullet point of this section for the First Lesson, Easter 2.

5. Gimmick

We have a great story today, the story of Paul's conversion to Christianity!

6. Possible Sermon Moves and/or Stories/Examples

• Rehearse the story, telling it dramatically.

• Too often we hear this text as a testimony to this great man of faith, Paul. We do so at the expense of appreciating what it is really about. Like life itself, this is not really a story of Paul and his faith. It (and life) is a story about what God does.

• Use John Calvin's remarks in the third bullet point of Theological Insights. Emphasize that this must be a story about God's mercy, because Paul was not a very nice person (arch-persecutor of the faith). Neither are we.

• Consider the last bullet point in Theological Insights (the comments of famed preacher of the early church, John Chrysostom). Martin Luther once made a similar point: "No matter how holy and righteous you are, beware of ever relying on the Lord by means of yourself or your righteousness" (*Luther's Works*, Vol. 10, p. 68).

• Observe why we do not like to hear this word. We think of ourselves as basically good. Follow the leads in the first bullet point of Socio-Economic, Political, Psychological, and Scientific Insights.

• Use the fourth and fifth bullet points of Theological Insights regarding John Calvin's assessment of the role of Ananias in the story. Stress how God can and does take us with all our faults and finds a way to use us!

• Note how He uses us, like He used Paul. Use the next-to-last bullet point in Theological Insights. Surrounded by the forgiving love of God, there is no way we cannot make a difference. Remind the congregation to consider that the next time they are asked to do something in the church or community and don't feel like they can. We can't miss being givers in light of all we receive from God.

• About this life of receiving, Martin Luther put it this way once in a sermon:

So one is not called a Christian because he does much, but because he receives something from Christ, draws from Him and lets Christ only give to him. If one no longer receives anything from Christ, he is no longer a Christian, so that the name Christian continues to be based only on receiving, and not on giving and doing. (*Complete Sermons*, Vol. 3, p. 329-330)

7. Wrap-Up
An appreciation that when it comes to the good things in life, when it comes to doing ministry, we don't do it, God does — an appreciation of His amazing grace, makes life all the sweeter. Close by noting leads referred to in the last bullet point of Socio-Economic, Political, Psychological, and Scientific Insights. Life is so much sweeter when we give God all the credit. Paul learned that and look what he did with the rest of his life. Thanks to God's amazing grace, we have that chance too.

Sermon Text and Title
"Christianity: A Very Worldly Religion"
Revelation 5:11-14

1. Theological Aim of the Sermon and Strategy
To proclaim that the unconditional love of God is evident in how Christ's atoning work (Justification by Grace Alone) inspires the praise of all creation. This leads to an appreciation of the goodness of creation and ecological concern (Social Ethics).

2. Exegesis (see Introduction to Selected Books of the Bible)
• Part of the author's vision of the glory of God and of the lamb.
• Reference is made to hearing the voice of angels and elders and living creatures (the Greek work *dzwoan* used here and in v. 14) surrounding God's throne. They are said to number in the thousands (v. 11). They sing of the worthiness of the lamb that was slaughtered, worthy of power and honor (v. 12).
• Every creature in heaven, on earth, and under the sea sings of blessing and honor to the lamb and the one seated on the throne (v. 13).
• Four living creatures/animals say "Amen," and the elders fall down and worship (v. 14).

3. Theological Insights (see Charts of the Major Theological Options)
• The text provides an eschatological vision that testifies to the significance of Christ's atoning work for affirming the goodness of creation.
• John Wesley notes that the text testifies to the praise God receives from all creatures (*Commentary on the Bible*, p. 599).
• He also called attention in the text to the angels worshiping the Son (vv. 11-12) as a way of showing that as we honor the Father, so also the Son (*Works*, Vol. 2, p. 353).
• The *Catechism of the Catholic Church* offers a solid statement of ecology and the care for creation:

> *Man's dominion over inanimate and other living beings granted by the creator is not absolute; it is limited by concern for the quality of life of his neighbor, including generations to come; it requires a religious aspect for the integrity of creation.* (2415)

4. Socio-Economic, Political, Psychological, and Scientific Insights
• Though Americans are only 4% of the world's population we account for 25% of the carbon dioxide pollution.
• The average American produces 29 pounds of garbage a week.
• Environmental destruction is also related to racism. People of color in America make up the majority of those living within 1.8 miles of the nation's hazardous waste dumps.
• Despite the preceding statistics, a 2009 Associate Press/NBC poll found that only 37% of Americans ever thought of the impact of their actions on the earth's health. A 2010 Gallup poll revealed that 48% of the American public think climate change is exaggerated.

5. Gimmick
The favorite family pet has died. Lament the feeling of loss. Then note the family child's questions about whether the dog will go to heaven.

6. Possible Sermon Moves and/or Stories/Examples
• Many animal lovers wish that animals were saved. Others, though, contend that only humans can have faith and so only they can be saved (Mark 16:16).
• Turn to the ecological crisis. Lament our waste and destruction of the earth and the risk of global warming. Cite the first two bullet points of Socio-Economic, Political, Psychological, and Scientific Insights.
• Others say the church has no business meddling in ecology, that our job is to preach Christ crucified (1 Corinthians 1:23), and that alone. Such attitudes are in line with most Americans. Use the last bullet point of Socio-Economic, Political,

Psychological, and Scientific Insights. Little wonder, since the network media don't have time for ecology and its agenda. Reality shows and sitcoms are much too preoccupied with finding individual happiness.
• What then are we to make of the dream that John had in the Second Lesson? He had a dream of what heaven is like and how God was being praised by all creatures. Of course the angels are singing. But in verse 13 it is said that every creature in heaven and on earth, and under the earth and in the seas are singing.
• Use the second and fourth bullet points of Exegesis to make the case that animals are present in heaven praising God!
• Refer to how we now have a biblical answer to the question posed by the child in the Gimmick. We have no certain promise that our pets or the wild animals we have encountered will be in heaven like we can be certain we will be there. But at least we know that dogs, cats, fish, and horses will be there. This calls attention to a dimension of Christian religion too often overlooked.
• Elsewhere in the Bible it is taught that Christ came to save the *world* (2 Corinthians 5:19; John 12:47). Christ came not just to save human beings but the whole world. That is why the animals in heaven praise Him too.
• This brings us back to ecology and the crisis we face. We have a God who cares about the earth and its resources. No way, then, that the church should be indifferent to the plight of the world.
• Turn to the creation stories in Genesis. God made humans out of the earth's dust (2:6). We are intimately related to the earth. A similar point is made in 1:26, 28, when God instructs Adam and Eve to have dominion over things of the earth. Some have taken this as authorization for capitalist economic development. But if we study the Hebrew text, where the Hebrew word *radah* is translated "have dominion" the correct translation of the Hebrew term is "rule." In ancient Hebrew to rule in the sense of this term refers to one who is "first among equals" (such as in Psalm 68:27 where the term is applied to the sense in which the Hebrew tribe of Benjamin is to lead others). This is our status as rulers of the earth. We are first among equals, not licensed to dominate and destroy the earth and all living things. We are only caretakers and guardians.
• Cite the last bullet point of Theological Insights to underline that Christian faith entails an ecological concern.
• Use of the things of the earth in the sacraments (water, bread, and wine) is a further indication of how the logic of Christian faith entails ecological sensitivity. Certainly a God like that cannot condone the ecological destructiveness of a nation like ours. Cite the third bullet point of Socio-Economic, Political, Psychological, and Scientific Insights.
• Urge the congregation not to hear the sermon as a demand to become ecologically sensitive. We do not serve a demanding God. We have a loving God who loves us so much as to die for the whole cosmos. Ask the congregation if they feel grateful to God for what He has done. If so, how can we not want to care for the things of the earth? How we dump our garbage and for whom we vote is not a matter of indifference to God.
• Thank God, though, that we have a Lord who forgives us all our wantonness and wastefulness.

7. Wrap-Up
The animals in heaven are singing along with the saints. Encourage the congregation to sing with them, saying "Amen" with our new ecological sensitivities.

Sermon Text and Title
"What Happens To You When You Die?"
John 21:1-19

1. Theological Aim of the Sermon and Strategy
To provide glimpses of the realities of our resurrection bodies (Eschatology).

2. Exegesis (see Introduction to Selected Books of the Bible)
• Post-resurrection appearances of Jesus, including His role in a miraculous catch of fish and His confrontation with Peter testing him to renounce his previous failures to confess Him.
• The appearance occurs in Galilee by the Sea of Tiberias (v. 1). Those present (Peter among them) are noted (v. 2). Simon directs the disciples with him to go fishing, but they caught nothing that night (v. 3).
• After daybreak Jesus appears, but the disciples did not recognize Him (v. 4). He dialogues with them and is told they had caught no fish (v. 5).
• Jesus instructs the disciples to cast their net on the boat's right side. They did so and were not able to haul the net in because of so many fish (v. 6). The disciple whom Jesus loved (also see 13:23; 19:26-27, either referring to John or to the community he was addressing) recognizes Jesus and tells Peter, who immediately clothes himself having been in the water. The other disciples present drag in the full net of fish (vv. 7-8).

- On shore, all see a charcoal fire with fish and bread on it (v. 9). Jesus directs some of the fish just caught be brought to it (v. 10).
- With 153 fish in the net, Peter brings them (v. 11). Jesus directs that they have breakfast. He gives them bread and fish, but it seems the disciples remain uncertain who He is (vv. 31, 12). It is reported that this is His third resurrection appearance to the disciples (v. 14).
- After breakfast, He asks Peter three times if he loves Him. Peter is reported to feel hurt (vv. 16-17). (This is reminiscent of Peter's triple denial of Jesus [18:17, 25-27]).
- Jesus says to Peter to feed Jesus' sheep (v. 17b).
- Jesus continues to tell Peter that while in his youth he fastened his own belt and went where he wished, but in growing older he would stretch out his arms and someone else would fasten a belt around him (v. 18). This was said to indicate the kind of death Peter would endure (under Nero in 64-68 AD) (v. 19).

3. Theological Insights (see Charts of the Major Theological Options)

- The reality of Jesus' resurrection and the message that it is for the faithful, despite our sin and unbelief (sin and Justification by Grace) receives testimony. In providing an account of Jesus' resurrection appearances the narrative offers insights about our resurrected reality (Eschatology).
- John Wesley saw the story as illustrating that "The love of Christ draws men through fire and water" (*Commentary on the Bible*, p. 470).
- John Calvin notes that the original failure to catch fish (v. 3) proves the truth of the miracle: "In the same manner, also, God often tries believers, that He may lead them the more highly to value His blessing" (*Calvin's Commentaries*, Vol. XVIII/1, p. 284).
- He also adds that "No man, therefore, will steadily persevere in the discharge of this office [the ministry], unless the love of Christ shall reign in his heart, in such a manner that, forgetful of himself and devoting himself entirely to Christ, he overcomes every obstacle" (*Ibid.*, p. 288).
- Augustine observes that all sin flows from the fountain of self-love (*Nicene and Post-Nicene Fathers*, First Series, Vol. 7, pp. 445-446).
- Leading twentieth-century Reformed theologian Karl Barth comments on Christ's resurrection appearances: "In this context self-manifestation means (1) that the execution and termination as well as the initiative lies entirely in His own hands and not in theirs [His followers]… Speaking further of these followers Barth adds: 'He controls them, but they do not control Him' " (*Church Dogmatics*, Vol. IV/2, p. 145).
- Martin Luther proceeds to elaborate on the awesomeness of what Christ has done for us in the resurrection:

Must not the heart presently start with alarm at its own boldness and say: Do you really think it is true that the great and majestic God, the maker of heaven and earth, has so regarded my misery and so mercifully looked upon me, deeply and manifoldly as I have sinned against Him…? How can such grace and such a treasure be grasped by the human heart, or in fact by any creature?
(*Complete Sermons*, Vol. 1/2, p. 330)

- Elsewhere Luther offers reflections on the resurrected bodies we shall have, of which Christ's resurrected body is the first fruit:

No matter how dishonorable or worthless it [the body] is at present, it will return in a form so honorable precious that its future honor and glory will surpass the present shame and dishonor many thousand times. Every creature will be amazed over it, all the angels will sing praises and smile admiringly at it, and God Himself will take delight in it.
(*Luther's Works*, Vol. 28, p. 187)

… it must follow that the resurrection is just as effective in us as it was for Him [Christ]… And faith must bring it about that this body's frail and mortal being is discarded and removed and a different, immortal being is put on, with a body that can no longer be touched by filth, sickness, mishap, misery, or death but is perfectly pure, healthy, strong, and beautiful, so that not even the point of a needle can injure it.
(*Ibid.*, p. 202)

4. Socio-Economic, Political, Psychological, and Scientific Insights

- A 2006 survey of those over sixty conducted by the AARP indicated that belief in eternal life was by no means certain among Americans. Two out of five men in that age range are uncertain. Since those expressing confidence indicated that such confidence had increased with age, it is a safe assumption that close to a majority of all Americans may have questions about what lies beyond death.

5. Gimmick
Tape a voice of a child asking, "What happens when you die?" The parent may respond that when you believe you go to heaven. But then the child asks, what happens to our body? Is it just the soul in heaven?

6. Possible Sermon Moves and/or Stories/Examples
• Recite the creedal affirmation of belief in the resurrection of the body. Repeat the phrase.
• Christians do not believe in free-floating souls in heaven. When we come back to life it will be with a body. What kind of a body? Our gospel gives us some hints.
• Recall that it is the story of one of Jesus' resurrection appearances. He appears to believers in Galilee by the Sea of Tiberias (v. 1). The Bible says that the disciples did not recognize Him at first (v. 4). After He dialogues with them, helps them catch a large number of fish, joins them at breakfast, and then they recognize Him!
• Ask what these events in Jesus life have to do with what happens to us in death. Note that Paul gives us cues in 1 Corinthians 15. He says that Christ is the first fruits of those who have died (vv. 20, 23). Christ as first fruit. In His body we get clues to what our resurrected body will be like.
• Cite the second quote by Martin Luther in the last bullet point of Theological Insights. Like Christ was perfectly pure and beautiful, no longer susceptible to injury, so our bodies will be that way when Christ comes again.
• Back to our story: Jesus had a body. But the disciples did not recognize Him at first. He wasn't completely changed. He was basically the same person He had been. They only recognized Him when He gives instruction on how to catch fish (vv. 6-7). Of course then they got the miraculously big catch of fish! After His resurrection there was nothing that could stop Him. He was not locked in by the boundaries of space and time.
• Our gospel gives us clues as to what our resurrected bodies are going to be like. After the resurrection, we will still have bodies, still look like ourselves (though maybe a little better). But like Jesus we will not be locked in by anything, not even our old hang-ups. We will be the perfect you and me.
• Note Paul's image in 1 Corinthians 15 of our earthly bodies like seeds for the resurrected body (vv. 42-44). Our bodies will be like seeds, giving rise to beautiful plants. Cite the first quotation by Martin Luther in the last bullet point of Theological Insights.
• The bodies we have now are the seeds that will flower to become the perfect you and me! In eternal life we will have bodies — lots better than flying around heaven just with souls or playing harps. Even in death you will be you and I will be me. Just the perfect versions.

7. Wrap-Up
Note how beautiful, almost majestic in its beauty, this vision of our eternal state is. It is enough to make us exclaim with Martin Luther. Use the quotation in next-to-last bullet point of Theological Insights.

Easter 4
April 21, 2013

Revised Common	Acts 9:36-43	Revelation 7:9–17	John 10:22-30
Roman Catholic	Acts 13:14, 33-43	Revelation 7:9, 14-17	John 10:27-30
Episcopal	Acts 13:15-16, 26-33 (34-39)	Revelation 7:9-17	John 10:22-30

Theme of the Day   God takes charge — historically this Sunday was historically a day for rejoicing.

Collect of the Day   The Good Shepherd Christ is petitioned that by His blood we might be made complete in all good and that we might do the Lord's will. Justification and Sanctification are emphasized.

Psalm of the Day   *Psalm 23*
• A Psalm expressing confidence in God the Shepherd's protection extols the comfort of Providence.
• God leads us in right paths (v. 3). Thus we need fear no evil (v. 4). Surrounded by goodness and mercy, the Psalmist pledges regular worship in the temple (v. 6). This is a Psalm about gratitude to God.

Sermon Text and Title
"The Surprises of Divine Originality"
Acts 9:36-43

1. Theological Aim of the Sermon and Strategy
To proclaim how God uses different means (the Spirit works differently in different contexts) to accomplish His means and the joy of these surprises. The role and status of women also gain attention in this context.

2. Exegesis (see Introduction to Selected Books of the Bible)
• Peter's resurrection of Dorcas (Aramaic name Tabitha) while in Joppa (a town west of Jerusalem).
• It seems that Dorcas, a disciple of Jesus, had been a woman devoted to good works (v. 36).
• Peter had been in Lydda (just ten miles southeast of Joppa) and is summoned to Joppa (vv. 37-38). Peter arrives where the grieving for Dorcas had begun (v. 39).
• The resurrection happens after Peter asks for privacy. Many in Joppa learn of it and come to believe (vv. 40-42). Peter stays in Joppa for a time with Simon a tanner (v. 43). Such an occupation forced workers to deal with ritually unclean animal carcasses. Peter's willingness to stay with Simon indicates that he had begun to disregard Jewish practices.

3. Theological Insights (see Charts of the Major Theological Options)
• The text witnesses to the many ways the Holy Spirit works and how grace is given. The implications of this divine originality for joyful Christian living (Sanctification) is suggested. See references to the Theology of the Cross in the first two bullet points of this section for the Second Lesson, Passion Sunday.
• John Calvin highlights that the title "disciple" here is applied to a woman and that it is not just a name proper to men (*Calvin's Commentaries*, Vol. XVIII/2, p. 397).
• Referring to how the miracle was accomplished he notes that "the operation of the Spirit is not always alike…" (*Calvin's Commentaries*, Vol. XVIII/2, p. 401).
• John Wesley speculates that for Dorcas being brought back to life was a surprise but more a matter of resignation than of joy. "But doubtless her remaining days were still more zealously spent in the service of her Savior and her God" (*Commentary on the Bible*, p. 480).
• John Wesley notes that "God moves His instruments, not when they please, but just when He sees it is needful" (*Commentary on the Bible*, p. 475).

4. Socio-Economic, Political, Psychological, and Scientific Insights
• On how surprise is good for our brains and makes us happy see the second bullet point of this section for First Lesson, Advent 2.
• On the unequal status of women, see the first bullet point of this section for the First Lesson, Advent 3. The "glass ceiling"

women encounter in ministry, even in those denominations ordaining women, is well known and hardly a surprise. One need only note how few women hold senior pastor positions in large congregations.

5. Gimmick
God has a way of surprising us and surprises are good things. It is like famed Russian writer Boris Pasternak put it: "Surprise is the greatest gift that life can grant us."

6. Possible Sermon Moves and/or Stories/Examples
• Our First Lesson from Acts is about God's surprising ways. It is hardly surprising to see God operate in novel, surprising ways. It's what Easter (which we continue to celebrate this Sunday, the Fourth Sunday of Easter) is all about. We have a God who made eternal life out of death.
• In our lesson we have the story of the tragic death of the faithful woman, Dorcas (not something she seemed to deserve), followed by her surprising resurrection, followed by Peter (devout Jew) breaking ritual purity by staying with a tanner (see and elaborate on the last bullet point of Exegesis).
• Another surprise (at least for those who think that the Bible does not permit women's leadership in the church) in verse 36 Dorcas is called a "disciple"! Note the second bullet point of Theological Insights.
• Surprise is what this text (like life in Christ) is all about. Elaborate on the newness and surprising character of the miracle Peter performed. He did it privately instead of in front of a big crowd (v. 40). Note John Wesley's comments about how the Spirit operates in different ways and with variety. Use the third bullet point of Theological Insights. God does not very often do things like we would expect.
• Don't kid yourself: Coming back to life was a surprise to Dorcas. Use John Wesley's comments in the last bullet point of Theological Insights. What a surprise that someone who is dead might prefer existence on the other side after all. That is a surprise God may have for all of us on the other side of the grave.
• Let's not forget the great surprise that Peter, that devout Jew, went to stay with a tanner. Reiterate the point made in the second bullet point. Talk about God's originality — doing a new thing. After centuries of stressing that the faithful maintain dietary and ritual purity, God had the faithful break down the barriers. God wants His faithful people open to new things, to a fresh way to serve. Ask the congregation if they are ready to accompany our Lord on that quest for novel directions in life.
• Note, though, that like Dorcas, like Peter, we don't have much choice in the matter of whether to accept what is novel. It just happens. Use the last bullet point of Theological Insights. Ultimately we are in God's hands; He's in charge.
• Comment on what a wonderful lifestyle results from this sense of feeling that God is in control. Such an openness to the new thing that God has in mind is a life of joy. Elaborate on the leads regarding the salubrious consequences for the brain of such a style of life noted in the first bullet point of Socio-Economic, Political, Psychological, and Scientific Insights. Openness to God's new ways is a nice, happy way to live.
• It is like British-American Jewish scholar Ashley Montago put it: "The moments of happiness we enjoy take us by surprise. It is not that we seize them, but they seize us." You are a lot happier when you see it as a surprise. With that way of looking at life, God is a little more real, because then you stop seeing the good things in life as something you deserve. You start feeling like what good you have must be from God.

7. Wrap-Up
It really is true. The good things in life are wonderful surprises and given God's propensity to seek to do new things, we need to be heads up for the divine originality, or we might miss it. Urge the congregation to be open to one of God's new ways this week.

Sermon Text and Title
"Hints of Heaven Are Here on Earth"
Revelation 7:9-17

1. Theological Aim of the Sermon and Strategy
To explore what heaven will be like and to proclaim that the eschatological vision of a God who cares for us can orient our lives in the present (Justification by Grace).

2. Exegesis (see Introduction to Selected Books of the Bible)
• A vision of the multitude of the redeemed, transpiring between the opening of the sixth and seventh seals (opened by the lamb [presumably Christ] in 6:1).

- The multitude from every nation stands before the lamb robed in white. They carry palm branches (symbolizing righteousness and victory) (v. 9).
- A praise Psalm is offered regarding salvation belonging to God and Christ (v. 10).
- Angels stood around the throne of God and also around elders and four living creatures. They worship God, singing a sevenfold ascription to God (vv. 11-12).
- In dialogue with an elder, John learns that those robed in white are those who have weathered persecution and been washed in Christ's sacrifice (vv. 13-14).
- Those who endured the persecution have a favored position, standing before the throne of God. They worship Him day and night, receiving shelter (v. 17). They will also hunger and thirst no more, enjoying comfort from the heat (Isaiah 49:10; Psalm 121:6) (v. 16).
- The lamb at the center of the throne will be the Shepherd of those who suffered. He will guide them, and God will wipe away their tears (v. 17).

3. Theological Insights (see Charts of the Major Theological Options)
- An eschatological vision testifying to the impact of Christ's atoning work (Satisfaction Theology) and to God's unconditional love (Justification by Grace).
- John Wesley points out that in glory none "shall… suffer or grieve any more…" (*Commentary on the Bible*, p. 600).
- John Calvin nicely describes the comfort those living may gain from this heavenly vision:

> … the entire company of believers, so long as they dwell on earth… would therefore have been desperately unhappy unless, with mind intent upon heaven, they had surmounted whatever is in this world… if, moreover, believers are troubled by the wickedness of three (greedy, arrogant) men… they will without difficulty bear up under such evils also. For before their eyes will be that day when the Lord will receive His faithful people into the peace of His kingdom, "will wipe away every tear from their eyes."
>
> (*Institutes*, III.X.6)

- Martin Luther offered similar reflections about how the glorious vision of the end helps us forget the trials and tears of daily life:

> This forgetting should gradually come upon us even in this life. For although at the present time, while worms and rottenness are before our eyes, we cannot be unmindful of them, nevertheless there will be a time God will wipe away every tear, as is stated in Revelation 7:17.
>
> (*Luther's Works*, Vol. 7, pp. 210-211)

- For more on Realized Eschatology (the impact of the eschatological vision on the present), see the second, third, and last four bullet points of this section for the Gospel, Advent 1.

4. Socio-Economic, Political, Psychological, and Scientific Insights
- See this section for the Second Lesson, Easter 3.

5. Gimmick
Begin by referring to heavenly delights or being in heaven. Ask the congregation if they have wondered what heaven is like. The book of Revelation gives us some clues.

6. Possible Sermon Moves and/or Stories/Examples
- Ask the congregation what they think heaven is like. It does not seem very exciting or fun place to be.
- The culprit is that we have been too immersed in the philosophy of ancient Greece (the ideas of Socrates and Plato) and not enough in the Bible.
- For the Greek Philosophers when something is perfect it stays the same (Plato, *Parmenides*, 129ff). In that case there would not be much to do in heaven.
- By contrast, ancient Hebraic thinking believes that the perfect can change. We see this is in the name used to describe God, Yahweh. His name translates both "I am who I am," but also "I will be who I will be." The Hebrew God can and does change (Genesis 6:6; Exodus 32:14; Judges 2:18). What is perfect can change!
- Return to the lesson. Use the fourth through sixth bullet points of Exegesis. The martyrs are said to be busy serving God! Specifically they serve Him by worshiping Him (vv. 15-16). The saints in heaven have something to do.
- Revelation makes clear that heaven is not a static and dull place. We will have something to do. We will be busy here on earth when He comes again — busy praising God and rejoicing, busy creating new good along with God. Recall that is God's nature as Yahweh, to keep on creating new good. He will not quit that habit in heaven or at the end of time.
- Our lesson reminds us that as we worship God now, serve Him during the week, we are doing the sort of thing done in

heaven! In that sense, as we worship and serve God we have a little of heaven on earth. We are doing the same thing as the faithful who died before us. In that sense we have fellowship with them.
• No more can we take worship or serving God for granted. For in those activities we are on threshold of heaven! There is much to rejoice about here in life. Consider the quote by John Calvin in the third bullet point of Theological Insights.
• Let us not be naïve. There are plenty of times when it is difficult, even painful to worship God or serve him. Martin Luther once noted that our text and its vision of the end can help us forget those trials on earth. Use the quote in next-to-last bullet point of this section.
• The quote by Luther reminds us our text's claim that God will wipe away every tear. The tears dry and are forgotten when we recall that what we do for the Lord on earth is a little hint of heaven.

7. Wrap-Up
Note what a glorious vision, what a wonderful view of life this is. Historically the Fourth Sunday of Easter has been a time of rejoicing. This vision of the end gives us much about which to rejoice.

Sermon Text and Title
"In the Hands of God"
John 10:22-30

1. Theological Aim of the Sermon and Strategy
To proclaim that our lives are in God's hands (Justification by Grace Alone).

2. Exegesis (see Introduction to Selected Books of the Bible)
• Jesus teaches His unity with the Father.
• At the festival of dedication (commemorating the rededication of the temple in 164 BC after its desecration by Antiochus Epiphanes in the Maccabean era), Jesus walks into the temple in the Portico of Solomon (a cloister on the east side of the buildings) (vv. 22-23).
• Jews gather around Him, asking Jesus to tell them plainly if He is the Messiah (v. 24). Jesus responds that He has told them and they did not believe and that the works He has done in His Father's name testify to Him (vv. 25-26).
• Jesus elaborates that His followers (His sheep [following up on His earlier image of the good shepherd in vv. 11-18]) hear Him and follow Him. He will give them eternal life. Apparently teaching "eternal security," He asserts that they are His forever (vv. 27-29).
• Finally Jesus asserts that He and the Father are one (v. 30).

3. Theological Insights (see Charts of the Major Theological Options)
• The account is a testimony to Jesus' messiahship (divinity) and to His mission of saving them (Justification by Grace Alone).
• Regarding the unity of Son and Father, early African theologian Calus Marius Victorinus compared their unity to the power to act (Father) and the action (the Son) (*Fathers of the Church*, Vol. 69, pp. 132, 159, 173-174, 224).
• John Wesley notes that those who are not Jesus' sheep will not follow Him because they "are proud, unholy, lovers of praise, lovers of the world, lovers of pleasure, not of God" (*Commentary on the Bible*, p. 464).
• John Calvin emphasized that faith does not really determine our response to Jesus:

> *So much the more unreasonable and absurd is it, that the authority of the gospel should depend on the belief of men; but believers ought rather to consider, that they are the more strongly bound to God, because while others remain in a state of blindness, they are drawn to Christ by the illumination of the Spirit.* (*Calvin's Commentaries*, Vol. XVII/2, p. 415)

In short, our salvation is certain, because it is *in the hand of* God; for our faith is weak, and we are too prone to waver (*Ibid.*, p. 416).
• In connection with the parable of the good shepherd, Martin Luther contended that sheep know their shepherd, for "sheep have the sharpest and most acute hearing of all animals" (*Complete Sermons*, Vol. 6, p. 83).
• The first Reformer spoke of the great comfort this parable offers: "It follows from this that we are not now, nor ever will be, forsaken, no matter how many temptations and sorrows we have here on earth" (*Complete Sermons*, Vol. 6, p. 74).

4. Socio-Economic, Political, Psychological, and Scientific Insights
• Cutting-edge neurobiology indicates that one who is scattered is not happy. The good monoamine that helps create happy

feelings, dopamine, is secreted especially when we are engaged in concentration (Stefan Klein, *The Science of Happiness*, pp. 218, 224).
• Neurobiological data also indicates that when we are engaged in an activity that leads us to forget ourselves, the executive part of our brain is immersed in pleasurable neurochemicals (Stefan Klein, *The Science of Happiness*, pp. 35-37, 56-57, 107).
• Likewise, concentration on what we must do to make our way in the world entails more exercise of the parietal lobe (the back part of our brain responsible for orienting us in time and space). When this part of the brain is not exercised, it does not stimulate the generation of more dopamine.

5. Gimmick
Everybody wanted to know whether Jesus was the Messiah. His works answer that question, He claimed (vv. 24-25).

6. Possible Sermon Moves and/or Stories/Examples
• What makes us sure about Jesus being the Messiah, being God? The miracles? His teaching? Ask the congregation. Then note that these are not what make Him the Messiah according to John's version of Jesus.
• Jesus refers to His works in His Father's name but He has not been believed by His critics (v. 25).
• John Wesley reflected on why Jesus was not believed by those present in this dialogue, why we do not believe in Jesus' messiahship. Use the third bullet point of Theological Insights. People who don't believe Jesus, those not His sheep, are lovers of the world and of pleasure. If you don't see Jesus' divinity, maybe it is because you are too worried about the things of the world.
• But what are the works of Jesus that clearly testify to His divinity? Jesus says His sheep know. They get salvation — eternal life — from Him and they'll never lose (vv. 28-29)!
• Emphasize the point that what makes Jesus divine is that He saves us. Not just that He saves us, but He makes it a sure thing! Use Luther's quote in the last bullet point of Theological Insights.
• It is as Abraham Lincoln said: "The shepherd drives the wolf from the sheep's throat, for which the sheep thanks the shepherd as his liberator, while the world denounces him for the same act."
• Jesus' divinity is apparent in the way in which He preserves us from evil and from falling away from Him. We can be absolutely certain of that precisely because He and the Father are one (v. 30).
• Use the insights of ancient African theologian Victorinus in the second bullet point of Theological Insights. Jesus takes the Father's potentiality to do good and puts it in action. Use the analogy of the potential of a great athlete (his years of training) distinguished from the actual execution. Thus the Michael Jordan we saw on the basketball court is different from but the same as the Michael Jordan known for his training for 8-12 hours a day in childhood and in the off-season.
• This all-powerful God is not about to abandon one in Him, is not too weak to hold on to anyone He is determined to save. To say that Jesus is God ensures that those He has chosen are saved regardless of what they do. Use the quotations by John Calvin in the fourth bullet point of Theological Insights. Faith is not what saves us. We who are saved belong to God, are in His hands.
• Celebrate the peace of mind and happiness that this insight brings. To experience oneself as in God's hands entails that we not need be concentrated on what we need to do (see third bullet point of Socio-Economic, Political, Psychological, and Scientific Insights). In fact, to be in God's hands, to have God in charge ensures we are not scattered but focused more on God than ourselves. Use the second and third bullet points of Socio-Economic, Political, Psychological, and Scientific Insights.

7. Wrap-Up
Jesus is God. His power and authority, the power of the Father, ensures that He is in charge, that all His sheep are in His hands. Tell the congregation to enjoy their location and that all their cares about the future are gone. The more they live that way, the more the natural dope in their brains will flow and make them happy. Yes, Jesus does indeed "have the whole world in His hands" (us too)!

Easter 5

April 28, 2013

Revised Common	Acts 11:1-18	Revelation 21:1-6	John 13:31-35
Roman Catholic	Acts 14:21-27	Revelation 21:1-6	John 13:31-35
Episcopal	Acts 13:44-52	Revelation 19:1, 4-9	John 13:31-35

Theme of the Day What God's love does to us.

Collect of the Day After noting that God teaches us the worthlessness of our acts with love, petitions are offered that the Lord's excellent gift of love be poured in our hearts and that being made alive by the Spirit we might know goodness and peace. Same emphases as the Easter 4 prayer.

Psalm of the Day *Psalm 148*

• Hymn calling on all created things (including animals, trees, and mountains) to praise God. There are obvious ecological implications in this Psalm.
• "Horn" in verse 14 refers to God's strength and power.
• The praise afforded by nature reminds us that it does not stand on its own and that it remains dependent on God and His guidance. Strong doctrine of Providence affirmed.

Sermon Text and Title
"God's Wonderful Goodness"
Acts 11:1-18

1. Theological Aim of the Sermon and Strategy
To proclaim God's wonderful goodness, how He takes ordinary flawed people and turns them into ministers/tools of salvation for others. Justification by Grace and the spontaneity of Sanctification are taught. Attention can be given to how since its inception the gospel has been an antidote to lack of openness to the other and the stranger (Social Ethics), though this is not the focus of the sermon proposed.

2. Exegesis (see Introduction to Selected Books of the Bible)
• Peter offers a defense of the practice of baptizing Gentiles. According to Luke, Peter was the first to convert a Gentile (ch. 10).
• The apostles and many of the faithful in Judea had heard that Gentiles had accepted God's word (v. 1). So when Peter went to Jerusalem conservative Jewish Christians criticized him (vv. 2-3).
• Peter responds, contending that while staying in Joppa (a town west of Jerusalem) he had a vision, seeing a large sheet coming down from heaven (vv. 4-5). He saw four-footed animals, reptiles, and birds, and heard a voice telling him to kill and eat the animals (vv. 6-7). Peter claims to have reneged, for he has never eaten anything unclean (v. 8).
• A second time the voice spoke, claiming that what God has made must not be deemed profane (v. 10). This happened a third time and all the elements of the vision returned to heaven (v. 10).
• At that moment, Peter reports, three men sent from the Mediterranean seaport town of Caesarea arrived at the house in which the vision occurred (v. 11). He reports that the Spirit told him to accompany them and not make a distinction between the Jews and them (apparently Gentiles) (v. 12a).
• Accompanied by six men, they go to Caesarea and enter a man's house who had seen an angel telling him to summon Simon who would give him a message that would save his household (vv. 12b-14).
• Peter proceeds to recount how when he began to speak to the man and his household the Holy Spirit fell on them as He had on the Jewish Christians (v. 15). Then he remembered the word of Christ regarding how the faithful would be baptized with the Holy Spirit (v. 16).
• Addressing the assembly of the apostles and the faithful, Peter asks how could he hinder God since the Gentiles had received the same gift that the Jewish Christians had received (v. 17). Hearing this, the apostles and other Jewish Christians proclaim that God has also given the repentance that leads to life to the Gentiles (v. 18).

3. Theological Insights (see Charts of the Major Theological Options)

• The text deals with the inclusivity of the gospel and, insofar as it is about the admission of the Gentiles, is an affirmation about Justification not being by works of the law and of the role of the Holy Spirit. Sanctification (how being justified transforms us into ministers of instruments of salvation) is also taught.

• John Wesley saw this text as a witness to the fact that the church may never exclude anyone (*Commentary on the Bible*, p. 481).

• John Calvin sees in this text a warning that the immoderate love of one's nation can hinder the acknowledgment of the work of God (*Calvin's Commentaries*, Vol. XVIII/2, p. 456).

• The Genevan Reformer speaks of the wonderful goodness of God in connection with the text:

> *This is assuredly wonderful goodness of God, who maketh men ministers of life, who have nothing by matter of death in themselves, and which are not only subject to death in themselves, but are also deadly to others.*
>
> (*Calvin's Commentaries*, Vol. XVIII/2, p. 460)

• Calvin further elaborates on the text's meaning, how it is all about grace:

> *So it shall come to pass, that the hope and assurance of salvation shall rest upon the free mercy of God alone, and that the forgiveness of sins shall, notwithstanding, be no cause of sluggish security... For it is a work proper to God alone to fashion and to beget men again, that they may begin to be new creatures.* (*Calvin's Commentaries*, Vol. XVIII/2, p. 464)

4. Socio-Economic, Political, Psychological, and Scientific Insights

• The words of Martin Luther seem to confirm recent scientific findings. He claimed that "therefore he who is imbued with the knowledge that God is love is happy" (*Luther's Works*, Vol. 30, p. 300). Neurobiological research indicates that belief in a loving God impacts the brain in such a way that it results in a positive sense of self and behavior leading to health and happiness (Andrew Newberg and Mark Waldman, *How God Changes Your Brain*).

• On American lack of openness to diversity, see the first two bullet points in this section for the First Lesson, Easter Sunday.

5. Gimmick

Dramatically recount the narrative in Exegesis.

6. Possible Sermon Moves and/or Stories/Examples

• This is a great story but ask the congregation what it has to do with us.

• Note that one angle is inclusivity and that the word of God is for everyone. The preacher could cite the data in leads in last bullet point of Socio-Economic, Political, Psychological, and Scientific Insights and the second bullet point of Theological Insights. America certainly needs to get over its lack of openness to diversity. Peter's ministry gives us a model for how Christian faith can move us away from narrow ethno-centric (racist) styles of being. (Consider John Calvin's comments in the third bullet point of Theological Insights.)

• Let's not forget that our story is about Peter's awakening to God's love for everyone, even Gentiles. Peter, the proud Jew who could be a thorn in the side for Paul's efforts to reach Gentiles (Galatians 2:11-14), the man who denied Jesus when arrest or punishment was threatened for acknowledging the Lord (Luke 22:58-62). Yet despite all Peter's flaws and checkered past, God overlooked those things and still used him for an important task! Just like he will use us, despite all the missteps in our lives.

• Use the John Calvin quotes in the fourth and fifth bullet points of Theological Insights. Forgiveness and salvation are a sure thing. It is all a testimony to the "wonderful goodness" of God.

• Goodness is such a nice, compelling term. God is not just good. He is goodness itself. Elaborate on goodness using selections from the following quotes by Ralph Waldo Emerson, a Tibetan Proverb, James Hamilton, and medieval mystic Meister Eckhart:

> *Wisdom has its root in goodness.*

> *Goodness speaks in a whisper, evil shouts.*

> *Goodness is love in action.*

> *Goodness is another name for compassion.*

• Goodness is all about love and compassion. To be on the receiving end of such wonderful love cannot help but change you and make you want to be different.

• Elaborate on the first bullet point of Socio-Economic, Political, Psychological, and Scientific Insights. With this sort of confidence and positive sense of self it is little wonder that we Peters can change and do great things for our Lord like Peter himself did.

7. Wrap-Up
State again that there is a wonderful goodness in God. How wonderful it is to be on the receiving end of such goodness, a goodness that changes us, gives joy, gives us like Peter the courage to change, to reach out to others not like us, and to bring some of God's goodness to others.

Sermon Text and Title
"A New Heaven and New Earth: Our Problems Are Fading Away!"
Revelation 21:1-6

1. Theological Aim of the Sermon and Strategy
To proclaim the Eschatological vision as a comfort to us and to the entire universe in dealing with problems in the present (Justification by Grace).

2. Exegesis (see Introduction to Selected Books of the Bible)
• The text portrays a vision of the new creation (predicted by Isaiah 65:17; 66:22) following the final judgment transpiring after the binding of Satan, reign of the martyrs, and a final conflict.
• The New Jerusalem coming from heaven is described as a mother (vv. 1-2). (Perhaps this is a reference to the church [Galatians 4:26].)
• Hymns of praising paragraphing Ezekiel 37:27 and Isaiah 25:8; 35:10 follow (vv. 3-4). They convey God's presence and the overcoming of all evil and mourning He brings.
• All things are made new (v. 5). As beginning and end, God gives the water of life (v. 6).

3. Theological Insights (see Charts of the Major Theological Options)
• A depiction of Future Eschatology, a vision providing comfort for the faithful in the present (Sanctification), for all evil is overcome (Justification by Grace and Classic View of Atonement).
• The early Church theologian Tertullian claims that our text demonstrates that all things were created by God out of nothing and that they shall come back to nothing when the first heaven and earth pass away (*Ante-Nicene Fathers*, Vol. 3, p. 496).
• John Wesley speculated that the new heaven and earth described in the text would manifest in a day when creatures would not have to kill other creatures in order to sustain themselves (*Works*, Vol. 6, pp. 294-295). But a more glorious change, he contended will come over human beings:

> *As there will be no more death, and no more pain or sickness preparatory thereto; as there will be no more sorrow or crying. Nay, but there will be a greater deliverance than all this; for there will be no more sin. And, to crown all, there will be a deep, an intimate, an uninterrupted union with God... a continual enjoyment of the three-one God, and of all creatures in Him!*
>
> (Ibid., p. 296)

• Modern Reformed theologian Karl Barth has claimed that faith is a crisis (*Epistle to the Romans*, pp. 32, 39-40, 91). The whole world as finite stands under judgment as finite and this awareness is itself a crisis (*Ibid.*, p. 77).

4. Socio-Economic, Political, Psychological, and Scientific Insights
• According to a 2006 Pew Research Center survey nearly 1 in 5 American Christians do not believe in Christ's second coming.

5. Gimmick
Read verses 3-4, stressing that God will wipe away every tear from our eyes.

6. Possible Sermon Moves and/or Stories/Examples
• Note how compelling it is that we have a God who wipes every tear from our eyes. A God like that makes life a lot nicer and easier to live. For this is a word of comfort about the whole universe.
• Read verse 1, noting that the new heaven and new earth take the place of the first heaven and earth that have passed away.

- Ask what these images have to do with us today. To get the relevance of this text we need to understand more about its background.
- Note how verse 4 and its reference to God swallowing up death forever seems to be a deliberate reference to Isaiah 25:8. (See third bullet point of Exegesis.)
- The book of Revelation frequently quotes Old Testament texts, especially the book of Daniel. Use the second bullet point of Revelation in Selected Books of the Bible.
- The links between the Old and New Testament that Revelation and our Second Lesson entail that we have to understand the links between the testaments in the context of the whole sweep of human history, from the creation of the universe to the day the book was written in the late first century to today. Thus we have in this text and in the book as a whole a testimony about God's plan for the *totality* of human history! In fact this is a universal, trans-historical event.
- This insight makes it even more awesome to consider that God will wipe away every tear (v. 4) and make all things new (v. 5). The comfort God gives entails that these are God's worldwide, universal aims! Consider the remarks of John Wesley in the third bullet point of Theological Insights.
- When we consider these great things God is doing, actually putting an end to all death, all conflict, the problems and anxieties and fears we encounter are not such a big deal after all. Our fears, problems, and anxieties are getting swallowed up, getting overwhelmed by God's comic, universal repair/re-creation job. If He is abolishing all death, all evil, all conflict, what chance does anxiety about a job, about a fight with a spouse, about lack of self-confidence have?
- The book of Revelation was written at a time when the Christians to whom it was written were suffering persecution from the Roman Empire. John's message (the message of his dreams) was that these persecutions are not the real crisis facing the world but that the real crisis is God's activity purging the world of all sin and evil, making it new! In fact the crisis faced by John's contemporaries has been transcended and overcome.
- Speaking of crises, note the famed twentieth-century theologian Karl Barth. In the spirit of former chief of staff for the Obama Administration Rahm Emmanual, who claimed "crises are something you don't want to waste," Barth contended that crises are good for faith. They are good in the sense that if you are not fully engaged in something it does not matter to you. This is why Barth thinks faith needs to be a crisis. (See last bullet point of Theological Insights.) If not, we begin to take it for granted.
- Barth helps us better understand this crisis too. The real crisis is not the persecution of first-century Christians. Certainly not global warming, economic turmoil, or even the little personal trials we face today. The real crisis is that the finite universe is under judgment; it must pass away. Consider again the last bullet point of Theological Insights. Also see Tertullian's comments in the second bullet point of that section.
- The book of Revelation, our lesson today, gives us a new perspective on the burdens of everyday life and on coping with the problems of our day which seem so pressing and heavy. They push us to interpret our lives in relation to God's all-encompassing care for and determination to redeem the universe — to cure it of all its ills. From that point of view we can understand our little trials as God tearing us away from ourselves, tearing us away from the latest trends, and our personal hang-ups so we can see the new thing God is creating. The real crisis is the turmoil created by the caring of the universe of all evil, not our little turmoils. That is the approach He uses to wipe away every tear from our eyes.

7. Wrap-Up
Lost in God's majesty. When you realize your place in the new heaven and the new earth, then all the problems start fading away. We have a God who makes all things new. What chance do our little problems have in face of such love? No, praise God, they all fade away!

Sermon Text and Title
"Love One Another"
John 13:31-35

1. Theological Aim of the Sermon and Strategy
To clarify the New Commandment to love one another (Sanctification), clarifying how such love is not something we do but a spontaneous response to God's overwhelming, intoxicating love (Justification by Grace).

2. Exegesis
See the last three bullet points of this section for the Gospel, Holy Thursday.

3. Theological Insights (see Charts of the Major Theological Options)
• See this section for the Gospel, Holy Thursday.
• On the New Commandment given by Jesus (vv. 34-35), Martin Luther offers several helpful comments:

> *Truly, if faith is there, he [the Christian] cannot hold back; he proves himself, breaks out into good works... Everything that he lives and does is directed to his neighbor's profit, in order to help him — not only in the attainment of this grace, but also in body, property, and honor.*
> (*Luther's Works*, Vol. 35, p. 361)

> *God is satisfied with my faith... Therefore He wants me to do my works to benefit my neighbor... He doesn't need my works at all... God is rich enough Himself without me and my works. He lets me live on earth, however, so that I may show the same kind of friendship to my neighbor that God has graciously shown to me.*
> (quoted in Paul Althaus, *The Theology of Martin Luther*, p. 133)

• The inevitability of these works of love, flow from the gospel, which intoxicates us:

> *Since these promises of God are holy, true, righteous, free, and peaceful words, full of goodness, the soul that clings to them with a firm faith will be so closely united with them and altogether absorbed by them that it not only will share in all their power but will be saturated and intoxicated by them.*
> (*Luther's Works*, Vol. 31, p. 349)

4. Socio-Economic, Political, Psychological, and Scientific Insights
• American life is infected by the malady of self-promotion. It is thought to be the only way to succeed in American life. For good examples just google "self-promotion as a key to success" to see the astounding number of sites devoted to this topic.
• On Americans' legalistic tendencies (inclination to portray salvation as a function of what we do), see this section for the Second Lesson, Epiphany 4.
• Neurobiological research indicates that the dopamine secreted in spiritual experience makes us more sociable. See Andrew Newberg and Mark R. Waldman, *Why We Believe What We Believe*, p. 267.

5. Gimmick
Read verse 34, the New Commandment to love one another as Christ has loved us.

6. Possible Sermon Moves and/or Stories/Examples
• Repeat verse 34. This teaching of Jesus goes against the grain of popular culture. Follow the leads in the first bullet point of Socio-Economic, Political, Psychological, and Scientific Insights.
• These attitudes saturate our environment, The media promotes them. *Jersey Shore* and *Sex in the City* have taught us to do whatever feels good. *Survivor* is all about self-promotion, putting yourself first at the expense of others — if necessary — in order to win.
• What social analyst Christopher Lasch wrote over thirty years ago is still true today. The "glad hand" (outward chumminess, aiming to sell oneself and one's personality to one's superiors as a commodity that is desirable and economically advantageous) has become the key to economic and social success (*The Culture of Narcissism*, pp. 122-123). As he put it:

> *Today men seek the kind of approval that applauds not their actions but their personal attributes. They wish to be not so much esteemed as admired. They crave not fame but the glamour and excitement of celebrity. They want to be envied rather than respected.*
> (*Ibid.*, pp. 116-117)

Loving other people isn't very glamorous in our context, doesn't make much sense.
• Then there are other problems with Jesus' comments. It seems like they could feed our legalistic tendencies to think we contribute to our salvation by what we do. See the second bullet point of Socio-Economic, Political, Psychological, and Scientific Insights.
• If we look at Jesus' words in verse 34, Jesus links the love He wants us to give each other to the love He gives us. Our love is related to the love He has for us! Let that sink in. Yes, we have a command to love but there is no love without God loving us too.
• Cite the two quotations by Martin Luther in the second bullet point of Theological Insights. When you have faith, you can't stop yourself. You feel this compelling need to do loving things!
• Invite the congregation to reflect on the loves in their lives, the people who really love them. It is not hard for us to love them back. Loving them just sort of happens. If human love motivates such loving response, imagine what God's love can do for us.
• This is a love that does not find loving a burden. As famed business coach Darren L. Johnson once put it: "If we need to be reminded to love one another, then we have already lost sight of the essence of our existence." In the nineteenth century,

Indian leader Sai Baba echoed a similar point, claiming that love for one another is "infectious and the greatest leaking energy."

• God's love is potent, so alluring, it's almost intoxicating. Use last bullet point in Theological Insights quotation by Luther. Christians are people who become drunk on Jesus. In His power, like a drunk is under the power of the booze, we wind up doing Jesus' bidding! Also consider the last bullet point of Socio-Economic, Political, Psychological, and Scientific Insights.

• Call it a New Commandment if you want: But all this talk about the love we are to do is really something a Christian who hangs around Jesus can't help but do.

• Two very practical comments by Mother Teresa about how to love one another are relevant and worth pondering: "We cannot do great things on earth, only small things with great love." "Jesus said love one another. He didn't say love the whole world."

7. Wrap-Up

Jesus' commandment to love is not so hard after all. Get drunk on Jesus, and you will not be able to help yourself.

Easter 6
May 5, 2013

Revised Common	Acts 16:9-15	Revelation 21:10, 22—22:5	John 14:23-29
Roman Catholic	Acts 15:1-2, 22-29	Revelation 21:10-14, 22-23	John 14:23-29
Episcopal	Acts 14:8-18	Revelation 21:22—22:5	John 14:23-29

Theme of the Day The Great things God's love does.

Collect of the Day The bountiful God who gathers people in His kingdom and promises them food from the tree of life is addressed. Petitions are then offered that we would be nourished by His word, and empowered by His Spirit to love one another and the word. Justification by Grace and a spontaneous Christian response are the focus of the prayer.

Psalm of the Day *Psalm 67*
• An Elohistic Psalm of thanksgiving for a good harvest attributed to David.
• Offers a petition that God would continue to be gracious, blessing the people and that His way and saving power be known among all nations (vv. 1-2). "Selah" at the end of verse 1 refers to a liturgical direction to add a musical interlude at that point.
• A prayer that all the Gentile nations might praise God, for He judges with equity (vv. 3-5).
• The good harvest is noted (v. 6) and petitions are offered that God would continue to bless Israel and that all the ends of the earth revere God (v. 7).

Sermon Text and Title
"Helpless Without God"
Acts 16:9-15

1. Theological Aim of the Sermon and Strategy
To make clear to the congregation our total dependence on God (Justification by Grace, with some attention to Providence).

2. Exegesis (see Introduction to Selected Books of the Bible)
• Paul's vision of the man of Macedonia, subsequent travels, and Lydia's conversion.
• Paul's vision beckons him to travel to Macedonia for help. He and his disciples (the author uses the pronoun "we" indicating for the first time that he was accompanying Paul) are convinced that this is a calling of God (vv. 9-10). They journey to Samothrace, an island on the way to Neopolis (a seaport of Philippi) and finally to Philippi in Macedonia (vv. 11-12). This was a first journey with the gospel to Europe.
• On Sabbath day they travel by the river outside Philippi to what was supposed to be a place of prayer. They meet a Gentile "worshiper of God" (one who believed in the God of the Jews but not a practicing Jew) named Lydia. Hearing the teaching of Paul and his followers, her heart was opened by God (vv. 13-14).
• She and her household are baptized. She urges Paul and his disciples to stay with her in her (Gentile) home (v. 15).

3. Theological Insights (see Charts of the Major Theological Options)
• The text witnesses to the role of grace in all good that transpires (Justification by Grace) and Providence.
• Famed twentieth-century theologian Karl Barth has contended that the Maedonian summoning of Paul (v. 9) is a word from "all those without." They are "waiting not only for the understanding and solidarity and participation, but for the helping action of the Christian community, for that which it alone in the whole world can do for them" (*Church Dogmatics*, Vol. IV/3 Second Half, p. 778):

> *Whether they are aware of it or not, their whole being and striving and existence utters the cry of the Macedonian... To be sure, they do not realize that they await and need what the community of Jesus Christ can do and is called to do for them if God acknowledges its activity... this is true of every man, since none can evade what God is and had done for him.*   (*Ibid.*)

- The famed preacher of the early church John Chrysostom points out in at least two ways in which God's grace reflects in this text. About the Gentile woman he points out that she does not ask to be judged a great, devout woman, but "speaks of no other token than that whereby she was saved" (*Nicene and Post-Nicene Fathers*, First Series, Vol. 11, p. 221). As for Paul and his companions, John writes: "For that they preach is not of men, but of the Holy Ghost" (*Ibid.*).

4. Socio-Economic, Political, Psychological, and Scientific Insights
- On Americans' legalistic tendencies (inclination to portray salvation as a function of what we do), see this section for the Second Lesson, Epiphany 4.
- On American lack of openness to diversity, see the first two bullet points in this section for the First Lesson, Easter Sunday.
- 2004 Fox News poll indicated 66% of Americans claimed to pray at least once a day.

5. Gimmick
Sometimes we don't know how badly we need God. Americans are guilty of this with our belief that you have to do things to please God and that we have to do something on our own in order to please Him. Use the first bullet point of Socio-Economic, Political, Psychological, and Scientific Insights.

6. Possible Sermon Moves and/or Stories/Examples
- The story in our First Lesson sets us straight. We are frankly helpless without God.
- Review the story and use the bullet point in Exegesis. Stress how Paul, this persecutor of Christians for their violation of Jewish customs (Acts 7:58; 8:1, 3; 9:1, 21), was willing to venture to Gentile territory to take the gospel to Europe! Also note how he winds up preaching to Lydia the Gentile woman (a believer in the Jewish God but not yet a Jew).
- Review Karl Barth's view of the story, as outlined in the second bullet point of Theological Insights. He correctly points out that the Macedonians summoning Paul indicate that they could not find God on their own. They knew they needed God but were helpless to find Him themselves. Americans sense this vague sense of needing God too. That is why we say we pray every day but most of us are not in church or synagogue on the Sabbath (see last bullet point of Socio-Economic, Political, Psychological, and Scientific Insights and the first bullet point of that section for the Second Lesson, below).
- Note how we may often experience this as active Christians. Somehow we may yearn for a closer walk with God, but just can't quite figure out how to proceed. We so want to get closer to God, but don't know how to do it. Like the father of the epileptic child said to Jesus, "I believe," we say, "help my unbelief" (Mark 9:24).
- Note also that even Paul did not decide to go the Macedonians/Greeks on his own. It took that vision from God to get him going. We really are helpless without God.
- Use the last bullet point in Theological Insights. Highlight how the devout Gentile woman had not found God on her own. She had not become convinced enough to convert to Judaism, even though she believed fervently in the Jewish God. Then she hears the word of God from Paul and all that changes. Like John Chrysostom noted, she does not appeal to her faith in interacting with Paul. She just passively had the Spirit open her heart!
- Like the characters in our story we really are hopeless without God. We are trapped by our sin and cannot do well on our own. We are always seeking our own well-being and pleasure, caught in that pattern so that we can never escape. (See the quotations in the last bullet point of Theological Insights for the First Lesson, Ash Wednesday. Certify the point further with citation of the second bullet point of Socio-Economic, Political, Psychological, and Scientific Insights.) Held in bondage by this insidious selfishness, there is no way we could get to God on our own. He has to do it for us, like he did for Paul, for the Macedonians, for the God-fearing woman.

7. Wrap-Up
Close with an admonition to the congregation to know their limits and their inability to get to God on their own. The relationship we have with God will be all the sweeter when we have that mindset — that what we have going with God is all His doing. Ask the congregation if although it is not the case that love is sweeter because it is a gift you come to count on, not something you have to keep earning in order to keep. (The fragility of many loves may be that many of us think the loves in our lives were earned, and so then love becomes a burden.) God's love is not a burdensome love that compels us to do something in order to have it. God's love is greater than that. Like its imperfect version human love, God's love does great things. It brings life out of death on a Cross, brings good out of nothing, and brings us peace of mind and faith even when we can't make those things happen on our own!

Sermon Text and Title
"To Stand in the Presence of God"
Revelation 21:10, 22—22:5

1. Theological Aim of the Sermon and Strategy
To call us away from all forms of idolatry to an appreciation that that life is only good in the presence of God, when He truly functions as our God, and that the incarnation has made that happen. Christology, Sanctification, and sin are themes considered.

2. Exegesis (see Introduction to Selected Books of the Bible)
• Vision of the New Jerusalem.
• In the Spirit, the writer is carried to a high mountain to see the holy city Jerusalem coming down from heaven (21:10).
• He sees no temple the in the city (the heavenly Jerusalem) and no need for sun and moon, for the glory of the Lord God and the lamb of God play that role (21:22-23).
• The nations will walk by this light and the world's kings have their glory subsumed by it (21:24). The gates of the city will never be closed (because there is perfect safety) (21:25). People bring to the city the glory and honor of the nations but nothing unclean may enter, for it is only those written in Christ's book of life (21:26-27).
• An angel shows the author the river of life flowing from the throne of God and the lamb (22:1). On either side of the river is the tree of life with twelve kinds of fruit (22:2).
• Nothing accursed will be found in the New Jerusalem. The throne of God and of the lamb and His servants will worship (22:3). They will see His face and His name will be on their foreheads (as a mark of protection, as per 7:3) (22:4).
• There will be no more night, nor will there be need for light and sun. For the Lord God is their light and His servants will reign forever (22:15).

3. Theological Insights (see Charts of the Major Theological Options)
• The eschatological vision provided by the text makes clear that true bliss is only to be found in lives oriented by God.
• Commenting on 21:27, Martin Luther writes:

> *This is where God's game begins, not that we may be destroyed, but that He may examine us and lead us to a knowledge of our foulness, yet not in such a way that we despair, but rather that we cry to Him, invoke His mercy, and learn that He shows His mercy wondrously.* (*Luther's Works*, Vol. 7, pp. 229-230)

• Luther also clarifies what a god is and how easy it is to lapse into idolatry:

> *A "god" is the term for that to which we are to look for all good and in which we are to find refuge in all need. Therefore, to have a god is nothing else than to trust and believe in that one with your whole heart. As I have often said, it is the trust and faith of the heart alone that make both God and an idol.* (*The Book of Concord* [Kolb and Wengert, eds.], p. 386)

• John Wesley notes that seeing God's face (22:4) is according to scripture "the most perfect happiness of the heavenly state" (*Commentary on the Bible*, p. 612).
• Karl Barth contended that the ongoing character of light in the vision is because "light has been the prototype and sight and declaration... of the knowledge of God" (*Church Dogmatics*, Vol. III/1, pp. 119, 121).

4. Socio-Economic, Political, Psychological, and Scientific Insights
• A 2011 Gallup poll indicated that 9 in 10 Americans say they believe in God. But a similar poll taken a year earlier indicated that less than 5 in 10 (43.1%) regularly attended worship services.
• On the neurobiological benefits of a life devoted to God, see the second bullet point of this section for the Second Lesson, Advent 1.

5. Gimmick
Read verses 10, 22-23. Repeat the point about not seeing a temple in the city and that in heaven there is no need for temples.

6. Possible Sermon Moves and/or Stories/Examples
• Ask what all this has to do with life for us on this side of Christ's second coming. The answer has to do with the fact that God has become incarnate in Jesus Christ.

- Christians believe in the incarnation and that God is found in earthly things: in Jesus' body. (Preachers believing in real presence view of the Lord's Supper can also add how their church believes that God is actually *in* the bread and the wine.) We even believe that God is present in our church buildings when we gather around the altar to worship Him. A God who became incarnate in Jesus still becomes incarnate in earthly things today.
- Historically one of the reasons church buildings have been considered special, even holy, is related to Christianity's incarnation emphasis, but also to its Jewish roots. (Note the ancient Hebrew belief that Yahweh was present in the temple [2 Chronicles 7:1; 1 Kings 9:3].) All the more striking, then, that in our lesson today we are told that there will be no temple in the heavenly Jerusalem.
- John's point seems to be here that we are to worship God spiritually. In our gospel today Jesus promises to send the Spirit (John 14:26). God is Spirit! He is not unduly attached to anything earthly.
- This seems like a contradiction, on one hand contending that God is linked to earthy things (as incarnate) and yet free of these things. But Christian faith involves a balancing act — the golden mean between extremes. Note how we Christians do that with the trinity — saying God is three but also one. Same with the idea that Christ is both divine and human, but still one.
- So it is with God's presence. We need the "golden mean." We need to find a way to affirm both the spirituality of God (defying identification with anything that is physical) and the incarnational nature of our Lord. We want to affirm God's presence in the church, His presence in the Bible and in preaching. We also want to affirm with the dream John had (in our lesson) that He is more than the visible means He uses, and He is a God who needs no sun or moon because His very presence lights up the heavens and the earth. Before such a God all our words, good deeds, church programs, church buildings, and ideas melt away into insignificance.
- There is nothing wrong with church worship, preaching, the sacraments, and good deeds done in the name of our Lord. They deserve veneration and respect. We must never forget that these are just means, noting that the God who lights up the heavens and the earth absolutely needs nothing.
- It is good that God became incarnate and still reveals Himself incarnationally. This is His way of making every realm of life His business, of taking away our excuse that He is not present in every sphere of our lives. This takes away our excuses for not worshiping, because an incarnate God is present in the ordinary things of life, including our singing and liturgy (see and introduce data in the first bullet point of Socio-Economic, Political, Psychological, and Scientific Insights).
- The problem is not with God's incarnational propensities but our sinful condition louses things up, our propensity to take creatures and make them our gods. Cite the quotation by Martin Luther in the third bullet point of Theological Insights. Elaborate on examples of how we make money, pleasure, power, our jobs, even our families and church programs our gods. Also consider the second bullet point in that section.
- The vision of the end times we read today calls us away from this sort of idolatry and reminds us not to let anything earthly (even church programs and buildings) get us way from spirituality — from faith, prayer, contemplation, and Bible Study.

7. Wrap-Up

Next time we feel drawn away from spirituality, too busy to pray, to contemplate God's mysteries, too caught up in the accumulation of wealth, influence, power, even church programs, remember John's vision in our lesson. The incarnate God is present in the most ordinary earthly things you are now encountering. God does not need those things; His glory and presence far outweigh the earthly activities in which we are engaged. Nothing that has been created (even church activities) can ultimately compete with the magnificent, loving God into whose presence we have come. Oh how good and glorious it is to be in the presence of God!

Sermon Text and Title
"Faith Is not Just Your Own Business and Neither Are Your Good Works"
John 14:23-29

1. Theological Aim of the Sermon and Strategy

To proclaim that faith is a work of God and not something we do (Justification by Grace along with Grace and Human Will as Theonomy) and that when God has His way with us, even the good works that follow the results of grace (Sanctification as Spontaneous).

2. Exegesis (see Introduction to Selected Books of the Bible)

- Part of Jesus' farewell discourse after the Last Supper addresses His teachings on believers' relation to the glorified Christ.

- In response to Judas' question of how Jesus reveals Himself to His followers and not to the world (v. 22), Jesus notes that those who love Him and keep His word will be loved by the Father (v. 23). But whoever does not love Him does not keep His words, and that word is from the Father (v. 24).
- Jesus claims to be saying these things while with the faithful (v. 25). The advocate (the Holy Spirit) whom the Father sends in Jesus' name will teach everything and remind them of all that He has said (v. 26).
- Jesus claims to leave peace with the faithful and not as the world gives. He exhorts them not to have troubled hearts (v. 27).
- Jesus admonishes the faithful for not rejoicing that He is going to the Father, who is greater than He is (v. 28). He claims to inform the disciples of this so that they may believe when it occurs (v. 27).

3. Theological Insights (see Charts of the Major Theological Options)
- The text testifies to the relation between Justification by Grace and Sanctification (as Spontaneous) as well as the work of the Holy Spirit in our faith (Grace and Human Will as Theonomy).
- John Calvin notes that "we are altogether alienated from God, and that we are infected and filled with hatred of Him, until He change our hearts" (*Calvin's Commentaries*, Vol. XVIII/1, p. 98).
- Calvin also notes that in verse 27 Jesus comforts His disciples from alarm they might feel with His upcoming departure. He promises them His actual presence through the Spirit (*Calvin's Commentaries*, Vol. XVIII/1, pp. 101-102).
- Jonathan Edwards observed that the peace Jesus leaves the faithful (v. 27) "fixes the aim of the soul to a certain end, so that the soul is no longer distracted and drawn by opposite ends to be sought… but the heart is fixed in the choice of one certain, sufficient, and unfailing good…" (*Works*, Vol. 2, p. 91). This peace he adds gives what most pursue — happiness and rest (*Ibid.*, p. 92).
- Regarding references to "peace," it should be remembered that Jesus and John were both Jews, so that the Greek term would still connote the Hebraic term *shalom*'s idea of "completeness," entailing that the blessing Jesus offers connotes a blessing on all aspects of life, a "harmonious equilibrium" among all parties (ie., justice and equality) not just the lack of conflict (Gerhard Von Rad, *Old Testament Theology*, Vol. 1, p. 130).
- Martin Luther does a nice job explaining how we do not love Christ, but lust for the flesh:

> *Thus all the world is adroit in avoiding toil… All aspire to advance in life and to attain high position. But when they obtain this and feel the labor and worry it involves, they soon grow weary and stop their efforts; for they sought only pleasure and ease.*
> (*Luther's Works*, Vol. 24, pp. 161-162)

> *… everyone is eager to get far ahead in life and to lord it over others.* (*Ibid.*, p. 162)

- But this sin does not interfere with the work of God in Luther's view. He writes: "I am holy because I can declare with unswerving faith and with an undaunted conscience…" (*Luther's Works*, Vol. 24, p. 170). Elaborating further on this point elsewhere he writes: "Everything depends, you see, on our being attached to Christ; there's no other way" (*Complete Sermons*, Vol. 6, p. 181).
- When this happens, a defiance of the world develops:

> *Thus there develops in man a confident defiance of everything upon earth, for he has God and all that is His. He does all that he is now required to do, and fears not.* (*Complete Sermons*, Vol. 2/1, p. 292)

- Regarding the love the faithful are to show (v. 23) Luther writes:

> *Since love does these things for those from whom no love had been received and who had deserved no love, and since we, aside from this, would still be in duty bound to love Him as our maker and God, even although we had not otherwise so greatly deserved it: how much more should we love Him, because He so greatly loved us and loved us first.*
> (*Complete Sermons*, Vol. 2/1, p. 311)

- Commenting on the Holy Spirit's role in our faith and its abolition of the law, the Reformer writes:

> *Thus all human works and laws vanish, yea, even the law of Moses; for such a being [the Holy Spirit] is superior to all law… We must not confine faith to ourselves, but must let it break forth in action.* (*Complete Sermons*, Vol. 2/1, p. 280)

- He adds how the Spirit is always with us, for we continue to feel our sin, fear of death, and the troubles of the world (*Complete Sermons*, Vol. 2/1, pp. 280-281):

> *The two must always be mingled in our feelings — the Holy Spirit and our sin and imperfection. Our case must be like that of a sick man who is in the hands of the physician; presently he will be better, Therefore let no one think: Such a one possesses the Holy Spirit, consequently he must be altogether strong, without infirmities, and do only precious works. No, not yet.*
> (*Ibid.*, p. 281)

• In another context commenting on the gifts of faith Luther spoke of Christians having been made so rich in their faith that we have a surplus of gifts that they spill over and lead us to give them away. Thus he claims that "a Christian lives not in himself but in Christ and the neighbor" (*Luther's Works*, Vol. 31, pp. 371, 365-366).

• Commenting on the assigned Psalm, John Calvin remarked:

> ... it is noticeable that yet he traces all the blessings they received to God's free favour; and from this we may learn, that so long as we are here, we owe our happiness, our success, and prosperity, entirely to the same cause.
>
> (*Calvin's Commentaries*, Vol. V/2, p. 2)

4. Socio-Economic, Political, Psychological, and Scientific Insights

• See this section for the Second Lesson. That the dopamine received from concentrating on God disposes us to socially commendable behavior, see the last bullet point of this section for the Gospel, Easter 5.

• On the selfish character of human love, see this section for the First lesson, Ash Wednesday.

• Google the latest statistics on deaths in our recent wars in the Near East and the latest unemployment statistics.

5. Gimmick

Faith saves! It can move mountains. Such rhetoric is typical in Christian circles but our Gospel Lesson shows how wrong we have been. Your faith is not your own.

6. Possible Sermon Moves and/or Stories/Examples

• According to John's gospel, the Last Supper had just transpired and Jesus was saying good-bye to His disciples. He wanted to offer them reassurance and continuing care. He promises them peace and His continuing presence through the advocate (the Holy Spirit) (vv. 26-27). (Consider John Calvin's remarks in third bullet point of Theological Insights.) Earlier in the farewell (prior to the beginning of our lesson), He had even promised that He would prepare a place for all of them to live (v. 3).

• In our context, with all the turmoil over our (seemingly) unending wars, continuing unemployment, inflation (pastor should emphasize any new pressing social issues), we are likely to wonder where God is in view of His promises. Could it be that Jesus' promises are but empty words? Then to make matters worse He seems to attach strings to the promises made in claiming that you need to love Him and keep His word (vv. 23-24).

• Preaching nearly 500 years ago Martin Luther offers some helpful, compassionate advice. Use his comments in the tenth bullet point of Theological Insights. We don't *have* to do anything to be saved.

• Luther's point about not confining faith to itself makes a profound point. It suggests that faith is not our own and that it's a work of God and His Holy Spirit!

• Too often we keep faith confined to ourselves, insisting it is *our* faith and we want to keep it that way. Since it is ours we feel like we have to do it right. But like a job without much satisfaction, then faith becomes a burden. And so we spend so much time fiddling with our faith, trying to get something out of it for ourselves, we never get around to using it for others.

• Weekly church-goers like us with these attitudes are likely to spend too much time sitting on our duffs week after week, just too burned out to do much more in the congregation and the community to ever get off our duffs.

• Martin Luther's advice (it is really Jesus' advice) is to give our faith a way, to stop acting like faith is a possession. Our faith, the acts of love faith wants to do, belong to God and the people of God. This is Jesus' point in speaking of those who love Him keeping His word (vv. 23-24). (Earlier in His farewell discourse [before our lesson began] Jesus had spoken of showing our love to Him by keeping His commandments [vv. 15, 21].)

• The famed ancient African theologian Augustine nicely illustrates this idea of a life spent giving away our faith and other gifts of God. He urged Christians to regard their possessions (including faith) as a traveler in an inn uses tables, cups, and couches in the inn. Guests do not own those items. Likewise faith (and the love God has given us) is not our own (*Nicene and Post Nicene Fathers*, First Series, Vol. 7, p. 229).

• Follow with Luther's comments in the next-to-last bullet point of Theological Insights. In Christ we cannot help but give away what God has given us. Also consider the first bullet point of Socio-Economic, Political, Psychological, and Scientific Insights. Like Augustine said, faith is not your own. Fact is, faith never was your own, Jesus seems to say in the Gospel Lesson that it a gift of the Holy Spirit (v. 26; 1 Corinthians 12:3). And likewise our good works too are fruits of the Holy Spirit (Galatians 5:22).

• There is a wonderful comfort in this awareness that neither faith nor the works done through us are our own but works of the Holy Spirit. It is sometimes hard to believe this, to accept the peace Jesus provides, in view of the ups and downs of life (vv. 27-28). Consider using data gained in the leads in the last bullet point of Socio-Economic, Political, Psychological, and

Scientific Insights. Take comfort then in Martin Luther's advice that as long as these doubts, sin, and the fear of death are around, we can be assured that the Holy Spirit is still around working on us. Use the eleventh bullet point of Theological Insights. The next time we feel low and wonder about our weak faith, no need to fear. The Holy Spirit is taking care of it for us. Faith is God's business and not our own.

7. Wrap-Up
Close by repeating how wonderful it is to know that faith and so its fruits are not just our business but belong to others. Sure, there are times when the insidious selfishness of sin (see sixth bullet point of Theological Insights) undercuts our generosity or crowds out the good we try to do. But the Holy Spirit keeps bugging us, reminding us that faith, good works, and even our lives are not our own business. What a wonderful word of comfort, joy, and peace Jesus has for us today — and every day.

Ascension of Our Lord
May 9, 2013

Revised Common	Acts 1:1-11	Ephesians 1:15-23	Luke 24:44-53
Roman Catholic	Acts 1:1-11	Ephesians 1:17-23	Luke 24:46-53
Episcopal	Acts 1:1-11	Ephesians 1:15-23	Luke 24:49-53

Theme of the Day The heavenly power and cosmic presence of Christ.

Collect of the Day Two alternatives are provided. In the first, petitions are offered that the faithful and their prayers for the world be received and that in the end everything be brought to the glory of God. In the second, we pray for faith to trust that He abides with us on earth to the end of time. Sanctification, Prayer, and Eschatology are the prevailing themes.

Psalm of the Day   *Psalm 47*
• A Korah Psalm celebrating God's enthronement as king of all nations.
• Summons to all the world to praise God (vv. 1-4). This universal theme is consistent with the theme of God's power manifested in the ascension.
• The Psalm is likely composed to accompany religious ceremonies connected with the Ark of the Covenant (vv. 5-9). God is proclaimed king over the nations.

or Psalm 93
• Hymn extolling God as king, composed perhaps for a festival.
• God is said to rule over the chaos (vv. 3-4). The powers of the chaos testify to Him, disposing the divine goodness.
• God is praised for His law and for the holiness of the temple (v. 5).

Sermon Text and Title
"The Ascension Lifts Us Out of Ourselves"
Acts 1:1-11

1. Theological Aim of the Sermon and Strategy
To proclaim the confidence and fresh perspective on life that the ascension of Jesus and Eschatological/cosmic perspective afford. The role of Eschatology in nurturing the experience of Justification by Grace is developed.

2. Exegesis (see Introduction to Selected Books of the Bible)
• The introduction to the book and the account of Jesus' ascension into heaven.
• Addressing Theophilus, the author begins by noting an earlier book (Luke) in which all Jesus did and taught from the beginning until the ascension is recorded (vv. 1-2).
• Forty days of Jesus' resurrection appearances are noted. He is said to have spoken of the kingdom of God ordering the apostles to remain in Jerusalem to wait for the Father's promise (vv. 3-4). As John the Baptist baptized with water, the apostles will be baptized with the Holy Spirit (v. 5).
• The apostles ask if their Lord will restore the kingdom to Israel (v. 6). Jesus replies that it is not for them to know the times or periods set by the Father (v. 7).
• They are told that they will receive power when the Holy Spirit comes upon them and will be Jesus' witnesses in Jerusalem, in all Judea, to the ends of the earth (v. 8).
• Then Jesus begins to ascend. Next, two men in white robes appear. These men (angels) inform them that Jesus will come again the same way that they had seen Him ascend into heaven (vv. 9-11).

3. Theological Insights (see Charts of the Major Theological Options)
• The ascension has implications for the nature of God, human nature, Realized Eschatology, and Justification by Grace.
• Karl Barth claims that the resurrection and ascension are two distinct but inseparable moments of the same event (*Church Dogmatics*, Vol. IV/2, p. 151). The ascension in his view is the joyous conclusion of the Easter history, showing that Jesus

is not to be sought in any kind of hiddenness, but in the hiddenness of God suggesting the revelation awaiting in the future (*Ibid.*, Vol. III/2, p. 454).

• John Calvin saw the text as a testimony to the kingdom of God and the things of heaven. He wrote:

> *Therefore, we may properly set the world, the flesh, and whatsoever is in man's nature against the kingdom of God, as contrary to it. For the natural man is wholly occupied about the things of this world, and he seeketh felicity here; in the mean season, we are as it were banished from God and He likewise from us; but Christ by the preaching of the gospel, doth lift us up unto the meditation of the life to come.* (*Calvin's Commentaries*, Vol. XVIII/2, p. 37)

• Calvin also noted that the cloud that overshadowed Jesus teaches "that our mind is not able to ascend so high as to take a full view of the glory of Christ; therefore let this cloud be a means to restrain our boldness..." (*Ibid.*, p. 50).

• Martin Luther preached on this text, seeing it as a time to preach on faith (in this case on an Article of Faith). About the perils of such preaching he wrote:

> *Now it is true, the preaching of faith is very lovely and winsome, but coupled also with subtle and potential risk, particularly for the fleshly heart. For preaching about faith is preaching about grace... When one now preaches about this goodness and grace of God, coarse and fleshly hearts object and willfully distort the grace of God, as Saint Jude says, in lasciviousness. But if one were to preach faith, and not grace, then people resort to their own works, and eventually they despair.* (*Complete Sermons*, Vol. 6, p. 113)

> *I would rather have people say that I preach too sweetly and that it hinders people from doing good works (even though me preaching does not do that), than that I failed to preach faith in Christ, and there was no help or consolation for timid, fearful consciences.* (*Ibid.*, p. 115)

• Luther applies Ephesians 4:8 to the ascension, contending that through it Christ has made captivity a captive. Death, hell, sin, and all that has ensnared us are now themselves captive (*Ibid.*, pp. 118-119):

> *Christ's power and might over sin are now given to those who believe in Him, who know that they, too, are masters over sin, while heretofore they were its slaves.* (*Ibid.*, p. 121)

• Luther adds that though sin tries to allure us, we can trample it under foot, "and instead desire to be gentle and humble, patient and friendly, kind and benevolent..." (*Ibid.*, p. 123).

4. Socio-Economic, Political, Psychological, and Scientific Insights

• Consider data indicating the captivity of the oppressed and how poverty cuts off options. See this section for the first bullet points of the First Lessons for Advent 1 and Advent 3.

• The American middle class is under siege. We have the highest income inequality since 1929. Adjusted for inflation the average male worker makes $800 a year less than his counterpart a generation ago.

• See the last bullet point of this section for the First Lesson, Advent 2, on the way in which a spiritual experience which get us contemplating things bigger than we are frees us from preoccupation with our own circumstances. The first bullet point of this section for the Second Lesson, Advent 1, indicates the neuro-chemical reasons why these experiences bring joy and happiness.

• Cutting-edge physics, the so-called String Theory, seems to further enhance the dynamics. It posits realities so different from our experience — additional dimension beyond height, width, depth — and many universes beyond our own (the multi-verse) (Brian Greene, *The Hidden Reality*, esp. pp. 83-88, 307ff).

5. Gimmick

The church has considered this day a glorious festival at least since the fourth century. At times there is despair and anxiety around us. Ask the congregation if they are not perhaps experiencing such despair or know others who are.

6. Possible Sermon Moves and/or Stories/Examples

• Describe Gary and Jermaine Alonzo, a married couple in the community (give them the age of the typical demographic of the congregation) and Jane Hanson a young single woman. The economy is wearing them down with little chance for making headway on salaries and all the job insecurity. Cite the second bullet point in Socio-Economic, Political, Psychological, and Scientific Insights. For wage inequality for the women in these examples, see the first bullet of this section for the First Lesson, Advent 3.

• Ask the congregation if they have not felt such despair and anxiety. Then the ascension story is for them.

• Review what the ascension is — Jesus' return to the Father in heaven. It sets the stage for His ongoing presence with us in the person of the Holy Spirit who was poured on us Sunday after next — on Pentecost. Then there is the promise that He will come again in the same way He left — His second coming.

- In the account of this miracle here in Acts we get more details on what happened than in the gospels of Luke or Mark, which also tell this story. What is especially significant for Gray and Jermaine and Jane (and us) is that we get a glimpse of the majesty of it all, of what the heavenly reality that awaits Jesus and us! We see the two men with white robes (presumably angels) in heaven (v. 10). Then we learn about His glorious return too (v. 11).
- There is something so grand, so majestic, about the thought of Jesus retuning to heaven! Use Karl Barth's reflection in the second bullet point of Theological Insights and the remarks by John Calvin in the third bullet point of Theological Insights for the Second Lesson. To see Christ exalted in the glories of the kingdom of God helps overcome our sense of unworthiness, because now we know that the great things lying ahead in heaven are for us!
- Overcome by glorious insights it is easy to forget yourself and your cares. Cite the quotation by John Calvin in the fourth bullet point of Theological Insights. Recognizing our limits in appreciating the glory of God does indeed restrain our boldness, sense of self-centeredness, and feeling that God and the world "owe us a living." Somehow our problems begin to melt away, overcome by an awareness of the awesomeness of God.
- Use the third bullet point in Theological Insights. John Calvin claims that the ascension story gets us focused on God's kingdom, on God's majesty, and away from the things of the world.
- Get the congregation to contemplate the awesomeness of God, His full power and glory, revealed this day in the ascension. Have them consider awesomeness of the planets and the stars in the evening sky. Introduce the idea of multi-universes taught by modern String Theory (see last bullet point of Socio-Economic, Political, Psychological, and Scientific Insights). Then add the idea of String Theory that there are other dimensions than height, width, and depth, that Jesus and God may dwell in them (see bullet point just noted). Invite the congregation to let these insights "blow their minds."
- Somehow worries about job insecurity and paying bills get lost in that sort of contemplation. There even seems to be biological reasons for that. Follow the leads in the third bullet point of Socio-Economic, Political, Psychological, and Scientific Insights. When you contemplate the things of eternity, when you catch a glimpse of the vision of Jesus, the things of everyday life don't occupy your brain as much and the back part of your brain that works hard when you concentrate on the things of the world goes dim.
- When such brain dynamics as just described transpire, your brain also gets doused with the brain chemical dopamine, a source of joy biologically.

7. Wrap-Up
No two ways about it. The ascension took Jesus away from the world physically. The ascension can do that to us too. Catching a glimpse of the glory of God revealed in this miracle (keep in mind that the awesome, majestic God transcending the universe walked on earth in the Man Jesus) lifts us out of ourselves. When that happens, the cares of everyday life won't matter so much and they don't have a chance to make much difference surrounded as they are by our Lord in all His majesty. Next time troubles hit, don't forget Jesus' ascension.

Sermon Text and Title
"The Triumph of God's Grace"
Ephesians 1:15-23

1. Theological Aim of the Sermon and Strategy
To testify to the ultimate triumph of God's loving grace over anything that might try to get in its way (Justification by Grace and sin are considered).

2. Exegesis (see Introduction to Selected Books of the Bible)
- Praise of the Ephesians and a thanksgiving for the blessings of God's cosmic plans.
- Paul praises the Ephesians for their faith and love toward the saints (v. 15).
- He prays that they may receive wisdom regarding the greatness of God's power for the faithful (vv. 17-19).
- God puts His power to work in Christ in raising Him and seating Him at the Lord's right hand (in the ascension) (v. 20).
- The ascension entails that all things are under Christ, including the church of which He is head. The church is then His body and He dwells in it (vv. 22-23; cf. Romans 12:5; 1 Corinthians 12:12-7).

3. Theological Insights (see Charts of the Major Theological Options)
- The text provides an opportunity to consider how sin (understood as despair and loneliness) Christology (since the ascension) is cosmic and how that impacts Christ's universal presence in and through the church.
- John Wesley notes that Jesus Christ is the fullness of the Father (*Commentary on the Bible*, p. 535).

- The ascension is a word that helps us appreciate grace even more. On this matter John Calvin wrote:

  Paul's object, therefore, was not only to impress the Ephesians with a deep sense of the value of divine grace, but also to give them exalted views of the glory of Christ's kingdom. That they might not be cast down by a view of their own unworthiness, he exhorts them to consider the power of God; as if he had said that their regeneration was no ordinary work of God, but was an astonishing exhibition of His power. (*Calvin's Commentaries*, Vol. XXI/1, p. 214)

- Calvin adds that Christ is a mirror of the glorious treasures of grace (*Ibid.*, p. 215).
- He also contends that the right hand of God (v. 20) fills heaven and earth (*Ibid.*, p. 216).
- Paul Tillich elaborated on this point, the meaning of the ascension: "The symbol then means that God's creativity is not separated from the new being in Christ…" (*Systematic Theology*, Vol. 2, p. 162).
- Martin Luther King Jr. further elaborated on this point:

  Whether we call it an unconscious process, an impersonal Brahman, or a personal being of matchless power and infinite love, there is a creative force in this universe that works to bring the disconnected aspects of reality into a harmonious whole. (*A Testament of Hope*, p. 20)

- The Westminster Confession of Faith explains how Christ's lordship in these ways is exercised over the church:

  By the indwelling of the Holy Spirit all believers being vitally united to Christ, who is the head, are thus united one to another in the church, which is his body. (*The Book of Confessions*, 6.054)

- Luther elaborates further on this union:

  Now just as God and man are one indivisible person in Christ, so Christ and we also become one inseparable body and flesh… Thus we, too, have been joined with Christ into one body and being, so that the good or the evil that happens to me happens also to Him. When I strike you or harm you, or when I show you honor I strike Christ, I do him harm, I show Him honor; for whatever happens to a Christian happens also to Christ Himself; He has a stake in it. (*Luther's Works*, Vol. 24, p. 149)

4. Socio-Economic, Political, Psychological, and Scientific Insights

- Nearly 3 in 10 of America's largest generation, the Millenniums, have no affiliation with the church or any other religious institution, as a 2010 Pew Research Center study found.
- A 2008 Baylor University poll indicated that nearly 1 in 2 Americans believed in a judgmental God (Paul Froese and Christopher Bader, *America's Four Gods*).
- See the last two bullet points of this section for the First Lesson.

5. Gimmick
Read verses 20-22a.

6. Possible Sermon Moves and/or Stories/Examples

- God's power is at work in both the resurrection and in today's miracle, the ascension. Everything has been put under Christ. Everything!
- Use the second and third bullet points of Theological Insights. In the ascension we see God in all His glory! This is a glory overflowing with love. John Calvin says that Paul's point in invoking Easter and Jesus' ascension is to make sure we not be cast down by our own unworthiness, for God is working to change them, that even death will be the way to life.
- Nice sentiments, but a lot of Americans, nearly half of us do not believe these words. See the second bullet point of Socio-Economic, Political, Psychological, and Scientific Insights. Americans caught up in this vision of God are inevitably unhappy, ever fretful that their own lives don't measure up, and will in the end get the punishment they deserve for shortcomings. All of us will die someday, have lost loved ones, and have had disappointments. They all count as punishments for a life not lived well when you have a judgmental god.
- Even those of us not caught up in the idea of an angry God, without assurance that grace ultimately triumphs, life is full of despair. Famed French intellectual Blaise Pascal described such an outlook on life so poignantly:

  I see the terrifying spaces of the universe hemming me in, and I find myself attached to one corner of this vast experience without knowing why I have been put in this place rather than that, or why the brief span of life allotted to me should be assigned to one moment rather than another of all the eternity that went before me and will come after me. I see only infinity on every side hemming me in like an atom or like the shadow of a fleeting instant. All I know is that I must soon die, but what I know least about is this very death which I cannot evade. (*Pensées*, p. 158)

- We have no meaning in life as long as eternity and infinity are not friendly toward us. Nothing in our past but meaningless business, nothing right now but blind chance, nothing up ahead but annihilation.

- Another French intellectual Albert Camus described the life of despair just as forcefully. He says despair is accepting your condition even when you can't stand it (*The Rebel*, p. 14). Famed German-American theologian Paul Tillich put it:

> *The pain of despair is the agony of being responsible for the loss of the meaning of one's existence and of being unable to recover it. One is shut up in one's self and in the conflict with one's self.* (*Systematic Theology*, Vol. 2, p. 75)

- The ascension story helps take away this despair. Because in the ascension, Jesus the Man and the God of love returned to the Father. The one who died for us is also the word of God who created the cosmos (John 1)! God's love or grace is the glue that holds the universe, the created order, together. Our lesson says that all things are under His feet (v. 22).
- Cite Martin Luther King's point in the seventh bullet point of Theological Insights. The creative force of the universe is one of love.
- A writer named Eric Collier offers a thoughtful elaboration on this point: "God's power, glory, and majesty makes me feel like I don't deserve to be in the same room with Him. His love, mercy, and compassion lets me know I don't belong anywhere else." Yes, God is awesome. So is His Son now in heaven. We do not deserve His love and grace. Where else is there a safe place to go, what with all the death and despair that is around?
- Yes, death and meaninglessness still surround us. Ultimately they cannot win. Christ's ascension assures us. The Dutch heroine of the Holocaust, Corrie ten Boom, powerfully described the outcome of the ascension. It provides a word of hope while we despair over God's rule in the world, despair over the growing apparent irrelevance, despair over the direction of our own lives: "No matter how deep our darkness — He is deeper still." No matter how low we go, Christ is there. The ascension entails that in the church, in the world, we are never alone. Where God is, there is Jesus and His guiding, unifying love!

7. Wrap-Up
Christ is in heaven! His ascension means that this loving, grace-filled presence of God is everywhere, higher than the heights, deeper than the depths, more inside than the heart, and yet enveloping all that is beyond us. Death, meaninglessness, despair, and a sense that we cannot recover from them or fight them are gone. They do not have a chance in face of the cosmic character of grace. Next time they strike remember the ascension. It will reinforce for you that the cosmos has meaning and is filled with God's love (because Jesus is right there at God's side).

Sermon Text and Title
"Jesus Takes Us With Him"
Luke 24:44-53

1. Theological Aim of the Sermon and Strategy
To proclaim how the ascension affirms, how He continually brings us into the presence of God (Justification by Grace).

2. Exegesis (see Introduction to Selected Books of the Bible)
- The conclusion of Jesus' commissioning of the disciples during His final resurrection appearance (vv. 44-49), followed by the account of His ascension (vv. 50-53). Only in Acts is reference to the latter also made.
- Jesus says the words He uttered to the disciples (that the Messiah should suffer [v. 26]) demonstrate that the Law of Moses, the prophets, and Psalms have been fulfilled (v. 44).
- Jesus opens the minds of the disciples to understand that His suffering and resurrection fulfill these Old Testament texts (vv. 45-46).
- This word is to be proclaimed with the word of repentance and forgiveness of sins (v. 47). As witnesses, the disciples are to receive what the Father promises (power from on high) and remain in Jerusalem until this is received (vv. 47-48).
- Jesus leads the disciples to the east of Jerusalem to Bethany, blessed them and then ascends to heaven (vv. 50-51).
- The disciples respond with worship, to return to Jerusalem with joy, and are continually in the temple blessing God (vv. 52-53).

3. Theological Insights (see Charts of the Major Theological Options)
- An examination of the relationship between the ascension and the joy it brings to the faithful (Justification by Grace). The implications of the ascension for the godhead are also examined.
- Martin Luther commented in an Ascension Day sermon on the significance of the ascension:

> *We must, therefore, conceive of His ascension and lordship as something active, energetic and continuous, and must not imagine that He sits above while we hold the reins of government down here. Nay, He ascended up thither for the reason that He can*

best do His work and exercise dominion. Had He remained upon earth in visible form, before the people, He could not have wrought so effectually, for all the people could not have been with Him and heard Him. Therefore, He inaugurated an expedient which made it possible for Him to be in touch with all and reign in all, to preach to all and be heard by all, and to be with all.
(*Complete Sermons*, Vol. 2/1, pp. 190-191)

- In an exposition, the Reformer commented on the significance of Jesus Christ's return to the godhead:

For in Christ a part of our flesh and blood, that is, our human nature sits in heaven above at the right hand of God... It is an unspeakably great glory and honor for humankind to have been raised so high by Him, not merely to heaven among the holy angels and archangels... but to the level of direct equality with God Himself. (*Luther's Works*, Vol. 13, p. 243)

- In a different sermon Luther was elaborating on Jesus' claim that the word of repentance and forgiveness is to be proclaimed (v. 47):

Because Christ wants this proclamation of repentance to go out among all peoples, there is no person on earth in His mind who is to be excused or excepted, but must confess and acknowledge they are sinners... For the cornerstone of this building, of how to become a Christian, must in every case be to confess our sins, for otherwise you can neither rejoice in your forgiveness nor be comforted. (*Complete Sermons*, Vol. 6, p. 36)

- Elaborating on the need for this awareness of sin he proclaimed:

So a Christian is at the same time sinner and saint. As persons we are sinful by nature and in our own name are sinners. But Christ marks us with another name, forgiveness of sins. (*Ibid.*, p. 39)

- This repentance is not our own doing, but a work of God's word, Luther insists (*Ibid.*, Vol. 1/2, p. 340).
- Such repentance must be life-long the Reformer claimed in another sermon on this text:

For a Christian is not instantaneously or suddenly cleansed perfectly, but the reformation and change continue as long as he lives... For even though all wickedness be overcome, we have not yet overcome the fear of death.
(*Ibid.*, Vol. 1/2, p. 315; cf. *Ibid.*, pp. 340, 347)

- The Reformer notes that we do not want to believe that we are sinners (*Ibid.*, p. 339).
- He compares forgiveness to the sun, which keeps shining in the darkness, and so keeps shining on us though we try to darken it by our falling away from it (*Ibid.*, pp. 347-348).
- Knowing God's great love, Luther adds, makes us willingly do His will (*Ibid.*, p. 316). About such forgiving love he writes:

But now forgiveness is so great and powerful, that God not only forgives the former sins you have committed; but looks through His fingers and forgives the sins you will yet commit. (*Ibid.*, p. 317)

4. Socio-Economic, Political, Psychological, and Scientific Insights
- Fully 1 in 4 Americans feel that God is distant, according to a 2006 Pew Survey. There is no reason to believe that these numbers have improved in recent years.
- Statistics from the Center for Disease Control indicate that 1 in 20 Americans are depressed. See the last two bullet points of this section for the Second Lesson, Lent 2, on how many Americans are depressed or lack self-worth. But other studies suggest that the pendulum has swung too far and that we have too much self-esteem/confidence and that that is eroding our national character (David Brooks, "The Modesty Manifesto," *The New York Times* [March 10, 2011]).

5. Gimmick
What are we to make as twenty-first-century people of Jesus' ascension into heaven? How can this quaint miracle story make a difference in our everyday lives?

6. Possible Sermon Moves and/or Stories/Examples
- Explain our situation. We are not a very happy group of people in the early twenty-first century. Use the second bullet point of Socio-Economic, Political, Psychological, and Scientific Insights for the First Lesson.
- Besides all the pressures, we don't like ourselves much and are discontent (or bluff the emptiness with too much bravado about self-esteem). Use the second bullet point of Socio-Economic, Political, Psychological, and Scientific Insights for this lesson.
- Note the texts cited in the last bullet point of Theological Insights for the First Lesson. Our bondage to self, compulsively driven to doing things that please us and to heck with everyone else we feel so empty and unhappy. We human beings are a mess! See the third and fourth bullet points of Theological Insights but awareness of Jesus' ascension can help.

- Use Martin Luther's comments in the second bullet point of Theological Insights.
- Christ's ascension to heaven makes it possible for Him to administer to everyone from His heavenly perspective. That's good news! We would have more limited access to Him, those of us trapped in the mad quest for self-gratification, those of us who despise ourselves, were He still with us in the Man Jesus. No, we all need access to Him.
- Then Luther says forgiveness is "active, energetic, and continuous." Ask the congregation what this means. It entails that Jesus is consistently ascending, and when we remember who He is a lot of the problems we face in life can be addressed.
- Recall, Jesus is both God and human — the perfect human being that God intended us to be. In a sense He represents us. No, we share His humanity. The great African theologian of the early church Athanasius claims that as Christ's humanity was exalted on Easter and in His ascension, so the bodies we share with Him are exalted too. The ascension, he says, is about Jesus appearing before God for us (*Nicene and Post-Nicene Fathers*, Second Series, Vol. 4, p. 330)!
- Use the third bullet point of Theological Insights. Martin Luther points out like Athanasius that because we share Christ's human nature, we are raised with Him to heaven in the ascension, to sit right by the Father. We really are somebody! All the insecurities, the uncertainty, the bondage to empty selfish striving are overcome. When Jesus goes to be with the Father, He takes us along, to level off equality with God!
- Talk about self-respect. Make no mistake about it: We don't deserve it. Our self-worth is Jesus' doing. We don't deserve it. We just went along for the ride, and so our sense of self-worth must include gratitude. Consider the last bullet point in Theological Insights.

7. Wrap-Up

Martin Luther, recall, claimed that Christ's ascension and lordship is active, energetic, and continuous. Not just once and done. Tell the congregation to keep in mind the next time they feel low, devoid of self-worth, or a little too filled with themselves that the ascension is taking care of all those problems. Again and again as we feel those feelings, Christ comes to raise us up to God, though we don't deserve it. Again and again He brings us to the Father's throne as an equal like He is, affirming us, but always with the reminder that He (Jesus) does the flying and soaring, and we are just along for the ride. How good it is that when in need, when needing to escape, Jesus takes us with Him, ever ready to have us ascend to the heights with Him! So wonderful is the ascension that we will want to celebrate it again and again.

Easter 7
May 12, 2013

Revised Common	Acts 16:16-34	Revelation 22:12–14, 16-17, 20-21	John 17:20-26
Roman Catholic	Acts 7:55-60	Revelation 22:12-14, 16-17, 20	John 17:20-26
Episcopal	Acts 16:16-34	Revelation 22:12-14, 16-17, 20	John 17:20-26

Theme of the Day   Living by God's awesome vision.

Collect of the Day   We pray that God would form the minds of His faithful people into His one will, so that we would love what He commands and desire He promises, ever fixed on Christ. Sanctification and the unity of the faithful are emphasized.

Psalm of the Day   *Psalm 97*
- A hymn celebrating God's kingship. For its genre, see the first bullet point of the Psalm for Transfiguration regarding enthronement Psalms.
- The earth is summoned to rejoice that the Lord is king (v. 1).
- Various manifestations of the Lord (clouds and thick darkness, righteousness and justice the foundation of His throne [v. 2], fire and lightning [vv. 3-4], melting mountains [v. 5], and the heavens [v. 6]) are identified).
- Idolators will realize their folly (v. 7).
- Judah hears and rejoices in God's judgments (v. 8). He is exalted over all gods (v. 9).
- Examples of God's justice are offered (vv. 10-11).
- A renewed call to worship the Lord is decreed (v. 12).

Sermon Text and Title
"Forgiven!"
Acts 16:16-34

1. Theological Aim of the Sermon and Strategy
To proclaim our forgiveness despite our sin (Justification by Grace).

2. Exegesis (see Introduction to Selected Books of the Bible)
- Paul's casting out spirits from the slave girl in Philippi, the subsequent arrest of Paul and Silas, an opportunity for escape, and the conversion of their jailer.
- Luke reports (using the first person plural) the encounter with a female slave who had a spirit of divination, which brought her owners much money by fortune telling (v. 16). She followed Paul, crying out that he and his disciples were slaves of the most high God proclaiming the way of salvation (v. 17). After days of this Paul becomes annoyed and casts out the spirit from her in Christ's name (v. 18).
- Her owners are concerned about the loss of money from her fortune telling and so seize Paul and Silas bringing them before authorities, claiming they had been disturbing the peace and are Jews advocating customs contrary to Roman law (vv. 19-21). The crowd joins them in this attack (v. 22a).
- Magistrates have Paul and Silas stripped and flogged, throwing them in jail and placing them in stocks (vv. 22b-24).
- At midnight while Paul and Silas were worshiping God and the prisoners were listening to them, suddenly there was an earthquake that loosened chains and opened the doors in the prison (vv. 25-26).
- When the jailer awoke to see the prison doors open, he prepares to kill himself assuming the prisoners have escaped (v. 27). Paul tries to stop him, claiming none had escaped (v. 28).
- The jailer falls down before Paul and Silas, bringing them outside and asking them what he must do to be saved (vv. 29-30). Informed that he need only believe in the Lord Jesus, he brings them into his house, gives them food, and he and his household rejoice because he had become a believer (vv. 31-34).

3. Theological Insights (see Charts of the Major Theological Options)
- The text testifies to the healing character of grace, given without condition despite sin. It is all about Justification by Grace.

- John Wesley notes how this text testifies to the countercultural character of the Christian message: "But this is a property of gospel truth: It has something in it peculiarly intolerable to the world" (*Commentary on the Bible*, p. 485).
- Along similar lines, the great preacher of the early church John Chrysostom notes that the message of this text is that God "more desires to forgive thee thy sins (than thou to be forgiven)" (*Nicene and Post-Nicene Fathers*, First Series, Vol. 11, p. 227).
- Commenting on the lesson, John Calvin offers a penetrating observation about our sin illustrated in the crowd's reactions (v. 22a):

> *Foolishness and inconstancy are indeed common vices among all people, and almost continual, but the wonderful force of Satan doth therein betray itself, in that those who are in other matters modest and quiet, are for a matter of no importance in a heart, and become companions of most vile persons, when the truth must be resisted.*
> (*Calvin's Commentaries*, Vol. XIX/1, p. 114)

- Commenting on the jailer falling down before Paul and Silas in gratitude (v. 29), John Calvin comments: "Hereby it appeareth what a good thing it is for men to be thrown down from their pride that they may learn to submit themselves to God" (*Calvin's Commentaries*, Vol. XIX/1, p. 120).
- He also added comments on what Christian life looks like, as illustrated in the lesson:

> *Therefore, let us know that faith is not a vain or dead imagination, but a lively sealing [sense] of the grace of God, which bringeth perfect joy by reason of the certainty of salvation.* (*Calvin's Commentaries*, Vol. XIX/1, p. 123)

- Commenting on the assigned Psalm, Calvin's insights are relevant to theme of forgiveness:

> *He evidently denies that we can have any righteousness, till God subjects us to the yoke of His word, by the gentle but powerful influences of His Spirit.* (*Calvin's Commentaries*, Vol. VI/1, p. 61)

4. Socio-Economic, Political, Psychological, and Scientific Insights
- See this section for the Second Lesson, Epiphany 4, for data indicating how Americans tend to minimize original sin.
- For neurobiological research on how a loving, forgiving God is good for health and happiness, see the first bullet point of this section for the First Lesson, Easter 5.
- Lack of forgiveness or anger seems to be a very unhealthy, unhappy way to live (Andrew Newberg and Mark Waldman, *Why We Believe What We Believe*, pp. 188-189).

5. Gimmick
Our story has a lot of good things along with some bad. It is truly a celebration of Easter (on this last Sunday of Easter). This is a word of new life despite our sin. Heads up: What the story offers is good for us (both physically and spiritually).

6. Possible Sermon Moves and/or Stories/Examples
- Note the emphasis on the text as about forgiveness. Use the comments by famed early church preacher John Chrysostom in the third bullet point of Theological Insights. God wants to forgive us more than we want to have it. How true!
- We don't need all that forgiveness we say. We are Americans, fundamentally good, decent people and besides that we are American Christians — church goers.
- Use and interpret the statistics referred to in the first bullet point of Socio-Economic, Political, Psychological, and Scientific Insights. To stress forgiveness truly is countercultural. John Wesley is right — see the second bullet point of Theological Insights.
- Our lesson is full of sin. We see it in the slave owner happy to exploit others. We see it in his anger when Paul healed this female slave (vv. 18-19), mad that Paul had cured his slave, which would cost him the fees he charged for her to tell fortunes. We see it in the crowd who is stirred up by the owner and in the magistrates who punished Paul and Silas (vv. 22-24). We see it in the jailer who was on the verge of committing suicide when it looked like all the prisoners escaped after the earthquake (vv. 25-27).
- We would never do those things you say. Use the fourth bullet point of Theological Insights — Calvin's comments about how like the crowd we are often foolish and inconsistent. It is true. The latest trend, the latest fashion, catches our passion until someone or something else entertains us more. It is like the famed French intellectual of the eighteenth century Blaise Pascal once said:

> *When men are reproached for pursuing so eagerly something that could never satisfy them, their proper answer, if they really thought about it, ought to be that they simply want a violent and vigorous occupation to take their minds off themselves, and that is why they choose some attractive object to entice them in ardent pursuit.* (*Pensées*, p. 69)

- How about the magistrates and their abuse of power? Ask the congregation if they do not do that whenever they have some clout on the job or in their families. Do not we all look for ways to make the institutions in which we work try to serve our ends? Famed American Christian Reinhold Niebuhr made a profound point: "Even when the individual is prompted to give himself in devotion to a cause or community, the will-to-power remains" (*Reinhold Niebuhr*, p. 51).
- Even in the seemingly innocent jailer we see sin. How like him we would end and curse the good things God has given us in the moments of crises in life. It is as noted French existentialist Albert Camus once wrote: "All healthy men have thought of their own suicide." One of the reasons the jailer may have fallen down before Paul and Silas in gratitude for not running away (v. 29) was to confess his sin. Use Calvin's comments in the fourth bullet point of Theological Insights.
- The jailer was forgiven and brought into fellowship with the faithful and made part of the church. Just as the woman was healed, our story is all about forgiveness (the message of Easter). That's the word for us — forgiveness.
- Forgiveness: What a wonderful reality. It is like songwriter Peter Allen once put it: "Forgiveness is a funny thing, it warms the hearts and cools the sting."
- Former United Nations Secretary General Dag Hammarskjold talked about forgiveness profoundly too: "Forgiveness is the answer to the child's dream of a miracle by which what is broken is made whole again, what is soiled is made clean again." We who were broken have been made whole again, made whole and made clean by the one (God) who made us.
- How good and healthy it is to be made clean. Follow the leads in the last two bullet points of Socio-Economic, Political, Psychological, and Scientific Insights. Living with forgiveness, with a forgiving God, leads to health and happiness.

7. Wrap-Up
Ask the congregation if it is not wonderful to be forgiven. Also remind them it is only for sinners. How good to come clean with our shortcomings, to get off our false pedestals and away from the strict God, and to enjoy all the joy that comes from being wrapped up in the arms of Jesus and a loving God.

Sermon Text and Title
"Life Between Times"
Revelation 22:12-14, 16-17, 20-21

1. Theological Aim of the Sermon and Strategy
To exhort and proclaim the good news and blessings of a life lived with the glorious expectation of Christ's return and glorious presence in view. Sanctification and Eschatology are the core themes.

2. Exegesis (see Introduction to Selected Books of the Bible)
- Portions of the epilogue of the book communicates words attributed to Jesus.
- The risen, ascended Jesus claims to be coming soon with a reward to repay according to everyone's work. He claims to be Alpha and Omega, the first and the last (vv. 12-13, 20).
- Those who wash their robes in order to have a right to the tree of life may enter the city (the New Jerusalem) (v. 14).
- The speaker expressly identifies Himself as Jesus. He claims to have His angel with His testimony to the churches. He is the root and descendent of David (v. 16). The Spirit and the bride (the church) say, "Come." Anyone thirsty should come (v. 17).
- A concluding blessing that the grace of the Lord be with all the saints (v. 21).

3. Theological Insights (see Charts of the Major Theological Options)
- The eschatological vision of the text leads to an examination of Christian life between the times.
- Karl Barth has claimed that the text testifies to a present that looks back to Jesus and expects His final revelation. All this time is the time of the Man Jesus:

> *Can the Christianity and the church that really derive from and are grounded in the resurrection of Jesus Christ ever be anything better than the place where, from out of and beyond all the required representations of Jesus Christ, the kingdom, the covenant, reconciliation and its fruit, men can only cry and call out: "Lord, have mercy upon us! Even so, come, Lord Jesus?" Is not perhaps the surest test of genuine Christianity and church life whether the men united in it exist wholly in this expectation and therefore not at all in a supposed present possession of the glorious presence of their Lord?*
>
> (*Church Dogmatics*, Vol. IV/3, p. 322)

- About living between times, Jürgen Moltmann writes:

> *"Christianity" has its essence and its goal not in itself and not in its own existence, but lives from something and exists for something that reaches far beyond itself... If we would fathom its essence then we must enquire into that* future *on which it sets its* hopes *and expectations.*
> (*Theology of Hope*, p. 325)

> *The horizon of expectation within which a Christian doctrine of conduct must be developed is the eschatological horizon of expectation of the kingdom of God, of His righteousness and His peace with a new creation, of His freedom and His humanity for all men.*
> (*Ibid.*, p. 334)

Moltmann also quotes nineteenth-century German writer Johann von Goethe to make the case that in a sense the eschatological moment is always present:

> *Why go chasing distant fancies?*
> *Lo, the good is ever near!*
> *Only learn to grasp your chances!*
> *Happiness is always here.*
> (*Theology of Hope*, p. 27)

• For another helpful quote by Moltmann, see the last bullet point of this section for the Second Lesson, Advent 1.

4. Socio-Economic, Political, Psychological, and Scientific Insights
• For neurobiological data on the benefits of living lives open to the future, see the first bullet point of this section for the Second Lesson, Advent 1.
• The scientific community is exploring the possibility that religion may have offered evolutionary advantages to Homo sapiens, regarding the trust and cooperation religion nurtures among adherents (Nicholas Wade, *The Faith Instinct*).

5. Gimmick
Use the second bullet point in Theological Insights. Make the point that on the Last Sunday of Easter we are reminded that we live in the time of Jesus, the time between His resurrection and His second coming!

6. Possible Sermon Moves and/or Stories/Examples
• So what? What difference does it make to know that we live in the time between times?
• Living between the times, dedicated to Jesus, seeing the present as His time, is to live life with expectancy. This is a life that gets us "out of the box," out of the ordinary hum-drum way of living. Nobody gets bored when they live between the times of Jesus. Everything is urgent. Any minute He could come. In the best sense, this is life lived on the edge.
• Use remarks by Rudolf Bultmann and Martin Luther King Jr. in the sixth and seventh bullet points of Theological Insights for the Gospel, Advent 1.
• It is like the inventor of the electric starter Charles Kettering said: "My interest is in the future because I am going to spend the rest of my life there."
• Use the two quotations by Theologian of Hope Jürgen Moltmann in the third bullet point of Theological Insights and follow the lead in the last bullet point of that section. A life lived with the end in view can take risks and allows you to challenge what is in order to work for a future that foreshadows the hopes of the coming kingdom, world of peace, and freedom.
• A life like this is full of joy and a lot of fun. Consider the quotation by Johann von Goethe in the fourth bullet point of Theological Insights. To live with Christ's future in view is to live with an awareness of Christ's presence that the good is ever near and that happiness is always here.
• Use the lead in the first bullet point of Socio-Economic, Political, Psychological, and Scientific Insights. Someone with a future orientation, always looking for new possibilities, lives a life of more pleasure and happiness than someone stuck in the present or the past.
• To live between the times in the time of the Man Jesus is to live with joy, to live with the future in view, but also to live with Jesus and His past. With a lifestyle like this you are never alone, always with Jesus, always with His heritage as well as with His future in view.
• With present, future, and past all held together Christians can live like early twentieth-century American Journalist William Allen White said: "I am not afraid of tomorrow, for I have seen yesterday and I live today."

7. Wrap-Up
For Christians living between the times, yesterday and today are good, filled with Jesus, and the end looks even better. What a blessing that Jesus has elected us to live in this time.

Printed in the USA
CPSIA information can be obtained
at www.ICGtesting.com
LVHW070925250224
772754LV00014B/527